Resilience in Children, Families, and Communities

Linking Context to Practice and Policy

Resilience in Children, Families, and Communities
Linking Context to Practice and Policy

Edited by

Ray DeV. Peters
Queen's University
Kingston, Ontario

Bonnie Leadbeater
University of Victoria
Victoria, British Columbia

and

Robert J. McMahon
University of Washington
Seattle, Washington

Kluwer Academic / Plenum Publishers
New York, Boston, Dordrecht, London, Moscow

Library of Congress Cataloging-in-Publication Data

Banff International Conference on Behavioural Science (32nd : 2000 : Banff, Alta.)
    Resilience in children, families, and communities : linking context to practice and
policy/edited by Ray DeV. Peters, Bonnie Leadbeater, and Robert J. McMahon.
        p.   cm.
    "The work presented ... 32nd annual Banff International Conference on Behavioural
Science held in Banff, Alberta, Canada in March 2000. The conference addressed the
topic of resilience in children from cities and communities ... "—Pref.
    Includes bibliographical references and index.

    1. Child welfare—Congresses.   2. Social work with children—Congresses.
3. Family social work—Congresses.   4. Resilience (Personality trait)
5. Children—Government policy—Congresses.   6. Social policy—Congresses.
I. Peters, Ray DeV., 1942-II. Leadbeater, Bonnie J. Ross, 1950-III. McMahon,
Robert J. (Robert Joseph), 1953-IV. Title.

HQ789.B376 2000
362.7—dc22

                                                                    2004048556

ISBN 978-1-4419-3463-5   e-ISBN 978-0-387-23824-1

© 2010 by Kluwer Academic/Plenum Publishers, New York
233 Spring Street, New York, New York 10013

http://www.kluweronline.com

10 9 8 7 6 5 4 3 2 1

A C.I.P record for this book is available from the Library of Congress

This volume honors the research, resilience
and wonderful humor of Emmy E. Werner

Contributors

Nancy H. Apfel, Yale University, New Haven, Connecticut

Michael W. Arthur, University of Washington, Seattle, Washington

Dan Dodgen, Substance Abuse and Mental Health Services Administration Rockville, Maryland

Renita R. Glaser, University of Washington, Seattle, Washington

Deborah Gorman-Smith, University of Illinois, Chicago, Illinois

J. David Hawkins, Univeristy of Washington, Seattle, Washington

David Henry, University of Illinois, Chicago, Illinois

Marianne Key-Carniak, Oakland University, Rochester, Michigan

Bonnie Leadbetter, University of Victoria, Victoria, British Columbia, Canada

Ann S. Masten, University of Minnesota, Minneapolis, Minnesota

Kenneth I. Maton, University of Maryland Baltimore County, Baltimore, Maryland

Francesca Pernice-Duca, Michigan State University, East Lansing, Michigan

Ray DeV. Peters, Queen's University, Kingston, Ontario, Canada

Jennifer R. Riley, University of Minnesota, Minneapolis, Minnesota

Cynthia J. Schellenbach, Oakland University, Rochester, Michigan

Katreena Scott, OISE/University of Toronto, Toronto, Ontario, Canada

Victoria Seitz, Yale University, New Haven, Connecticut

Andrea Solarz, Consultant, Arlington, Virginia

Laura-Lynn Stewart, OISE/University of Toronto, Toronto, Ontario, Canada

Kathleen Strader, Healthy Families America Midwest Regional Resource Center, Pontiac, Michigan

Patrick Tolan, Univeristy of Illinois, Chicago, Illinois

Richard E. Tremblay, University of Montréal, Montréal, Quebec, Canada

Emmy E. Werner, University of California, Davis, California

David Wolfe, University of Western Ontario, London, Ontario, Canada

Preface

This volume honors the work of Emmy Werner, one of the leading researchers in defining the field of resilience in human development. Her research has examined resilience within the social context of adversity in a longitudinal study of a large sample of Kauai children from birth through age 40 disadvantaged by poverty and minority status. This landmark study has had a strong impact on resiliency research since it began in 1955 and it is a pleasure to dedicate this volume to Emmy and her long and productive career in resilience research.

The work presented in this volume was first discussed at the 32nd Annual Banff International Conference on Behavioural Science held in Banff, Alberta, Canada in March, 2000. That conference addressed the topic of resilience in children from cities and communities, and the chapters in this volume expand the discussions at that conference.

Within the past 10 years, there has been growing interest in the psychological construct of resilience. Spurred by the research of Emmy Werner, Norman Garmezy, and Michael Rutter in the early 1970's in which many children in high-risk environments were found to show normal development, scholarly interest in resilience expanded rapidly through the 1990's.

Resilience refers to "a dynamic process encompassing positive adaptation within the context of significant adversity. Implicit within this notion are two critical conditions: (1) exposure to significant threat or severe adversity; and (2) the achievement of positive adaptation despite major insults on the developmental process" (Luthar, Cicchetti, & Becker, 2000, p. 543; see Roberts & Masten, Chapter 2; Werner, Chapter 1).

The early research on childhood resilience was rooted in the fields of developmental psychopathology, abnormal psychology and mental health, and focused primarily on identifying protective factors in children showing adaptive functioning under a host of adverse conditions

including schizophrenic parents, socioeconomic disadvantage, maltreatment, urban poverty, community violence and catastrophic life
events. Also, the early research efforts focused primarily on identifying the personal characteristics of resilient children that differentiated
them from children who evidenced less adaptive functioning in similar
adverse environments. Subsequent research, however, indicated that resilience in children also may be strongly related to factors external to the
child, including parent and family influences as well as characteristics
of their wider social environments such as their local neighborhoods
and schools (Werner, Chapter 1).

Most recently, research on resilience has expanded on several
fronts. There is increased interest in research which moves beyond
merely identifying protective factors to an attempt to understand why
and how protective factors influence adaptive development; i.e., the
processes and underlying mechanisms of resilience.

A second development has been to expand the concept of resilience
from characteristics of individuals, to characteristics of groups of individuals, particularly families, peer groups and neighborhoods. This notion goes beyond the above-mentioned recognition that families, groups
and neighborhoods provide important sources of protection for individual children. Rather, it applies the concept of resilience to families
and other social groups by, for example, studying resilience in families. What factors and processes differentiate well adapting families
from those who show poor adaptive functioning under comparably high
levels of stress, adversity or risk?

A final expansion of resilience research is concerned with applying
the findings of previous work to the development and evaluation of
intervention strategies and social policies that are designed to promote
and strengthen resilience in children, in families and in broader social
groups. This is the main topic of the present volume.

We have assembled a group of resilience researchers from across
North America who discuss both conceptual and practical challenges
arising from attempts to apply the theoretical construct of resilience,
along with existing empirical resilience findings, to the formulation of
intervention strategies and social policies.

The volume is organized into three sections. Section I focuses on defining the scope and limits of resilience, Section II focuses on programs
directed at supporting resilience in families, and Section III focuses on
programs that are directed at neighborhoods and communities.

Section I consists of four chapters describing various approaches to
the definition and study of resilience, and the challenges of extending
empirical findings to intervention programs, emphasizing the importance of context in resilience-enhancing interventions. In Chapter One,

an introduction to the volume, Werner describes the history of resilience research and outlines future challenges to the field. In Chapter Two, Roberts and Masten set the conceptual framework for the volume by discussing the importance of context in resilience research and important challenges in attempting to link a contextual resilience framework to intervention efforts. Following this is a chapter by Tremblay, in which he questions the relevance of the concept of resilience in light of findings from empirical studies on the development of physical aggression in very young children. He discusses the implications of those findings for social learning theories of social development, describes the long-term results of the Montreal Prevention Experiment and argues for the importance of intervening very early with young boys who are at high risk for later conduct problems. In Chapter Four, Leadbeater, Dodgen and Solarz discuss the concept of resilience in terms of the paradigm shift that has occurred in research, practice and policy on a range of social problems. They describe how a resilience framework fosters attention on specific risk and protective factors rather than general population factors, emphasizes competence rather than deficiency, focuses on long-term adaptation rather than immediate outcomes, and emphasizes an ecological view of human adaptation rather than limiting analyses to individual characteristics. The chapter concludes with a discussion of the important role public policy needs to play in supporting this paradigm shift.

Section II begins the discussion of resilience-based intervention programs. The three chapters in this section describe resilience enhancement programs for high-risk women, children and youth. In Chapter Five, Seitz and Apfel describe a comprehensive competence enhancement program for pregnant teenagers, and also the results of an 18-year longitudinal follow-up study of short-term and long-term benefits to teen mothers and their children. In Chapter Six, Scott, Stewart and Wolfe present an analysis of teen dating violence in high-risk adolescents, in this case youth who have histories of abuse. They describe the procedures and outcome results of a program that has been operating for over 10 years to prevent abuse and promote positive teen dating relationships. They present an analysis of factors that appear to differentiate resilient from non-resilient youth in these relationships. In Chapter Seven, Schellenbach, Strader, Pernice-Duca, and Key-Carniak apply a developmental-ecological framework to a strengths-based resilience model, utilizing individual, family and community levels of analyses of resilience factors in adolescent mothers. The chapter concludes with a description of a community-based prevention program for adolescent mothers and their children, discussing the implication of this work for social policy and system change.

9

Section III consists of four chapters, all of which describe the expansion of resilience concepts and practice to include neighborhoods and communities. In Chapter Eight, Maton expands the ecological approach to resilience intervention to include broader cultural and societal factors. He describes a framework to guide intervention efforts for enhancing children's resilience at each level of ecological influence. In their chapter on promoting resilience in inner city children, families and neighborhoods, Gorman-Smith, Tolan, and Henry describe a developmental-ecological framework, apply this ecological framework to an analysis of inner-city children, families and neighborhoods, and discuss the implications of this analysis for understanding resilience and intervention efforts in this particular high-risk context. In Chapter Ten, Peters examines the value of high-risk vs. universal interventions for resilience enhancement. He then continues the discussion of neighborhood resilience as an important part of the conceptual basis for a multi-site intervention project for young children and their families living in eight disadvantaged neighborhoods throughout the Canadian province of Ontario. In Chapter Eleven, Arthur, Glaser, and Hawkins expand the focus on resilient communities by reporting the results from a large-scale study concerning factors that are associated with the degree to which communities adopt science-based prevention and promotion interventions for high-risk adolescents.

This volume constitutes a leading-edge analysis and description of the current status of the concept of resilience in human development; expands the concept to families, communities, and society; presents a variety of well-developed interventions for children and youth from the prenatal period to early adulthood; and outlines the implications of this work for public policy.

The Banff Conferences on Behavioural Science

This volume is one of a continuing series of publications sponsored by the Banff International Conferences on Behavioural Science. We are pleased to join Kluwer Academic/Plenum Press in bringing this volume to an audience of practitioners, investigators, and students. The publications arise from conferences held each spring since 1969 in Banff, Alberta, Canada, with papers representing the product of deliberations on themes and key issues. The conferences bring together outstanding behavioral scientists and professionals in a forum where they can present and discuss data related to emergent issues and topics. As a continuing event, the Banff International Conferences have served as an expressive 'early indicator' of the developing nature and composition of the behavioral sciences and scientific applications to human problems and issues.

Because distance, schedules, and restricted audience preclude wide attendance at the conferences, the resulting publications have equal status with the conferences proper. Presenters at the 32nd Banff Conference wrote a chapter specifically for the present volume, separate from his or her presentation and discussion at the conference itself. Consequently, this volume is not a set of conference proceedings. Rather, it is an integrated volume of chapters contributed by leading researchers and practitioners who have had the unique opportunity of spending several days together presenting and discussing ideas prior to preparing their chapters.

Our 'conference of colleagues' format provides for formal and informal interactions among all participants through invited addresses, workshops, poster presentations, and conversation hours. When combined with sightseeing expeditions, cross country and downhill skiing, and other recreational activities in the spectacular Canadian Rockies, the conferences have generated great enthusiasm and satisfaction among participants. The Banff Centre, our venue for the Conferences for more than 30 years, has contributed immeasurably to the success of these meetings through its very comfortable accommodation, dining, and conference facilities. The following documents conference themes over the past 36 years.

1969	I	Ideal Mental Health Services
1970	II	Services and Programs for Exceptional Children and Youth
1971	III	Implementing Behavioural Programs for Schools and Clinics
1972	IV	Behaviour Change: Methodology, Concepts, and Practice
1973	V	Evaluation of Behavioural Programs in Community, Residential, and School Settings
1974	VI	Behaviour Modificaiton and Families and Behavioural Approaches to Parenting
1975	VII	The Behavioural Management of Anxiety, Depression, and Pain
1976	VIII	Behavioural Self-Management Strategies, Techniques, and Outcomes
1977	IX	Behavioural Systems for the Developmentally Disabled A. School and Family Environments B. Institutional, Clinical, and Community Environments
1978	X	Behavioural Medicine: Changing Health Lifestyles
1979	XI	Violent Behaviour: Social Learning Approaches to Prediction, Management, and Treatment
1980	XII	Adherence, Compliance, and Generalization in Behavioural Medicine
1981	XIII	Essentials of Behavioural Treatments for Families
1982	XIV	Advances in Clinical Behaviour Therapy
1983	XV	Childhood Disorders: Behavioural-Developmental Approaches
1984	XVI	Education in '1984': Celebrating the 80th Birthday of B. F. Skinner
1985	XVII	Social Learning and Systems Approaches to Marriage and the Family
1986	XVIII	Health Enhancement, Disease Prevention, and Early Intervention: Biobehavioural Perspectives
1987	XIX	Early Intervention in the Coming Decade

1988	XX	Behaviour Disorders of Adolescence: Research, Intervention, and Policy in Clinical and School Settings
1989	XXI	Psychology, Sport, and Health Promotion
1990	XXII	Aggression and Violence Throughout the Lifespan
1991	XXIII	Addictive Behaviours Across the Lifespan: Prevention, Treatment, and Policy Issues
1992	XXIV	State of the Art in Cognitive/Behaviour Therapy
1993	XXV	Anxiety and Depression in Adults and Children
1994	XXVI	Prevention and Early Intervention: Child Disorders, Substance Abuse, and Delinquency
1995	XXVII	Child Abuse: New Directions in Prevention and Treatment Across the Lifespan
1996	XXVIII	Best Practice: Developing and Promoting Empirically Validated Interventions
1997	XXIX	Stress: Vulnerability and Resilience
1998	XXX	Children of Disordered Parents
1999	XXXI	Suicide: Prediction, Prevention, and Intervention
2000	XXXII	Resilience: Children, Families, and Communities
2001	XXXIII	Emotional Self-Regulation: Development, Successes, and Failures
2002	XXXIV	Adolescent Substance Abuse: Innovative Approaches to Prevention and Treatment
2003	XXXV	Early Childhood Development: From Research to Policy and Practice
2004	XXXVI	Terrifying Experiences: Resilience and Vulnerability to Psychological Trauma

We would like to acknowledge the expert guidance and support that we received from Siiri Lelumees and Anna Tobias at Kluwer Academic/Plenum Press. It has been a pleasure working with them. Also we would like to thank Meghan Provost and Gail Irving for the excellent assistance in preparing the manuscript. Special thanks to our colleague on the Planning Committee, Dr. Ken Craig. While preparing this volume, Ray Peters was on the faculty at Queen's University, Bonnie Leadbeater at the University of Victoria, and Bob McMahon at the University of Washington.

Ray DeV. Peters
Bonnie Leadbeater
Robert J. McMahon

Contents

PART I

The Conceptual and Empirical Framework for Linking Resilience to Intervention and Policy

CHAPTER 1

Resilience Research

Past, Present, and Future

E<small>MMY</small> E. W<small>ERNER</small>

The contributions in this volume bring back fond memories of the 32nd International Conference on Behavioural Science held in Banff, Canada in March 2000 at which I received an unusual award: a sweater for the most hapless skier among the participants. I must confess, I actually can't ski at all, but the two path diagrams that I presented at the close of that meeting looked as if I darted back and forth in deep snow, surrounded by tree stumps and goal posts, yearning to reach a place of rest. My intent had been to illustrate the complex chain of protective factors, linked across time, that enabled most of the females and males in our 40-year longitudinal study on the island of Kauai to overcome the adversities they had encountered in their formative years. My husband, who thought they represented my erratic driving record, suggested I put them discreetly in the Appendix of our most recent book, *Journeys from Childhood to Midlife: Risk, Resilience, and Recovery* (Werner & Smith, 2001).

In the mid-1950's when our study began, behavioral scientists had tended toward a more simplistic account of the impact of biological and psychosocial risk factors on the development of children by reconstructing the history of individuals who had failed in school, become delinquents or criminals, or suffered from serious mental health problems. This *retrospective* approach had created the impression that a poor developmental outcome is inevitable if a child is exposed to perinatal trauma, poverty, parental psychopathology, or chronic family discord, since it examined only the lives of the "casualties," not the lives of the successful "survivors."

During the last two decades of the twentieth century, our perspective changed (Garmezy & Rutter, 1983). *Prospective* longitudinal studies in North America and Europe have now followed individuals from childhood to adulthood and have fairly consistently shown that even among children exposed to multiple stressors, only a minority develop serious emotional disturbance or persistent behavior problems. Today, many behavioral scientists who study children who grow up in high-risk conditions have shifted their focus from negative developmental outcomes to the study of individuals who have made a successful adaptation to life. Hence there is now a growing body of research—as illustrated in this volume—that deals with the phenomenon of *resilience*—the dynamic process that leads to *positive* adaptation within the context of significant adversity (Luthar, 2003; Luthar, Cicchetti, & Becker, 2000).

A lively debate has begun over conceptual and methodological issues centering on whether resilience is a state or trait, whether successful coping in the face of adversity is domain-specific, and on the challenge of linking the construct of resilience to effective models of intervention (see Roberts & Masten, Chapter 2; Rutter, 2000; Tremblay, Chapter 3). Methodological issues that have confronted researchers who study the buffering process of *protective* factors in the lives of such individuals include: (1) the selection of age-appropriate measures of adaptation; (2) the need to use multiple criteria to determine successful outcome; (3) the need for low-risk comparison groups; and (4) the need to observe individuals at multiple measurement points in time.

Just as risk factors and childhood stressors may co-occur within a particular population in a particular developmental period, protective factors are also likely to occur together to some degree (Gore & Eckenrode, 1994). Protective factors not only contribute to individual differences in response to adversity at any given point in time, but the presence of certain protective factors also determines the likelihood of emergence of others at some later point in time. The task of delineating such interconnections should become an important agenda in intervention programs, like the ones described in Sections II and III in this book.

Our current understanding of the roots of resilience comes from about a dozen longitudinal studies in North America and Europe. They include Asian-American, African-American and Caucasian children who have been exposed to a variety of psychosocial risk factors, such as chronic poverty, parental mental illness and substance abuse, divorce, chronic family discord, and child abuse. Most of these studies have focused on school-age children; investigations that began in infancy and preschool are still quite rare, and so are studies that have followed high-risk children into adulthood. (For a detailed review of their methodology and findings, see Werner, 2000).

Despite the heterogeneity of these studies, one can discern a common core of individual dispositions and sources of support that contribute to resilience in individual development and that have been replicated independently in two or more longitudinal studies in different contexts. These protective buffers appear to make a more significant impact on the life course of children who grew up in adversity than do specific risk factors or stressful life events, and transcend ethnic, social class and geographic boundaries.

Good health; an easygoing, engaging temperament; intellectual and scholastic competence; an internal locus of control; a positive self-concept; the ability to plan ahead; and a strong religious faith or sense of coherence were among the protective factors that made it possible for many children and young people to overcome adversity in their lives. So were the role model of a competent mother who was sensitive to the needs of her child; affectionate bonds with alternate caregivers—such as grandparents, older siblings, teachers, and elder mentors—and an external support system in the neighborhood, church, youth groups or school that rewarded competence.

Among the handful of prospective studies that have first reported these findings is the Kauai Longitudinal Study, which has monitored the impact of a variety of biological and psychosocial risk factors, stressful life events, and protective factors on a multi-racial cohort of children, born in 1955 on the Hawaiian island of Kauai, the westernmost county of the USA. Our investigation documented the course of all pregnancies and their outcomes in the entire island community and assessed the effects of multiple risk factors, such as poverty, perinatal trauma, parental psychopathology, and adverse child-rearing conditions on the development and adaptation of some 500 individuals at ages 1, 2, 10, 18, 32, and 40 years (Werner, 2002).

Many of the protective factors that contributed to resilience among those exposed to multiple risk factors were also beneficial to those who lived in more favorable environments, but they did have a stronger predictive power for positive developmental outcomes among individuals especially challenged by childhood adversity (see Peters, Chapter 10).

Since we collected data at multiple time periods on the children, their families, and the community in which they lived, we were able to trace, in a number of path models, patterns of temporal relationships that illustrate the complexity of the phenomenon of resilience. They show the direct and indirect links between protective factors within the individual and outside sources of support in the formative years of life and how these variables, in turn, relate to positive developmental outcomes in adulthood (Werner & Smith, 1989, 1992, 2001).

When we examined these links, we noted that individuals who made a successful adaptation in adulthood in the context of significant adversity had relied on sources of support within their family and community that increased their competencies and efficacy, decreased the number of stressful life events they subsequently encountered and opened up new opportunities for them. The lessons we learned from an examination of the process that linked these protective buffers over time were twofold: first, the extraordinary importance of the early childhood years in laying the foundation for resilience, and second, the possibilities for recovery at later stages in development that were available to most individuals who seized a variety of opportunities offered to them in their community.

Individual dispositions and competencies were strongly related to the number of stressful life events encountered and reported by the men and women in this cohort. Children who had displayed a greater amount of autonomy and social maturity at age 2 reported fewer stressful life events by age 10. Individuals with higher scholastic competence at age 10 reported fewer stressful life events in adolescence. Men and women who displayed a higher degree of self-efficacy and planfulness in their teens reported fewer stressful life events in their thirties and forties— even though they had grown up in poverty and under adverse rearing conditions.

Many of the individuals who managed to successfully "beat the odds" sought out people and opportunities that led to positive turnarounds in their lives. They selected or constructed environments that, in turn, reinforced their active, outgoing dispositions and rewarded their competencies. In many ways, they made their own environments, picked their own niches (Scarr, 1992).

We noted, however, that protective factors **within** the individual (an "engaging" temperament, scholastic competence, an internal locus of control, and self-esteem) tended to make a greater impact on the quality of adult adaptation for females than for males who successfully coped with adversity in their lives. In contrast, **outside** sources of support in the family and community tended to make a greater difference in the lives of the men who "beat the odds." These gender differences need to be systematically explored in intervention programs designed to enhance competence and self-efficacy and to provide emotional support.

Several turning points led to shifts in life trajectories during the third and fourth decade of life among the men and women in our cohort. They also have been noted in other longitudinal studies that have followed children and adolescents into adulthood in the United States and Great Britain (Rutter, 1996). These positive changes took place after they left high school, mostly without the benefit of planned intervention by professional "experts."

Among the most potent forces for positive changes for high-risk youth who had a record of delinquency and/or mental health problems in adolescence, and for teenage mothers, were continuing education at community colleges; educational and vocational skills acquired during voluntary service in the Armed Forces; marriage to a stable partner; conversion to a religion that required active participation in a "community of faith"; recovery from a life-threatening illness or accident that required a lengthy hospitalization; and occasionally, psychotherapy.

We also noted that the "troubled" teenagers who made use of opportunities that opened up for them in their twenties and thirties, and whose life trajectories subsequently took a positive turn, differed in significant ways from those who did not. They were more active and sociable, had been rated as more affectionate and less anxious by parents and teachers in middle childhood, possessed better problem-solving and reading skills, and had been exposed to more positive interactions with their primary caregivers in infancy and early childhood than youths whose coping problems persisted into mid-life.

In sum: Throughout our study, there were large individual differences among "high-risk" individuals in their responses to adversity as well as to the opening up of opportunities. The very fact of individual variation in coping skills among the men and women who live in adverse conditions suggests that educational, rehabilitation, or therapeutic programs designed to improve their lives will have variable effects, depending on the dispositions and competencies of the participants. This is an issue that needs to be carefully addressed in the intervention programs described in the following chapters.

Many "second generation" studies of prevention and intervention now under way in North America represent efforts to learn from deliberate attempts to alter the course of development of so-called "high-risk" children and youth in a positive direction (Luthar, 2003; Masten & Coatsworth, 1998). In the United States, unfortunately, these efforts, though commendable, tend to take place in a social policy vacuum, for unlike the countries of the European Union, the federal government has not yet made any major commitments to universal policies that benefit children and families.

Even Head Start, the only nationwide program for young children and families who live in poverty in the USA and among the First Nations of Canada, reaches only a minority of those who are eligible. We really still do not know how selection effects (who gets in, who gets left out among those who are eligible) ultimately influence the reported outcomes for this program. I make this point not to discourage any of the "competence enhancement" programs and "strength building policies" that have been promulgated by the professional experts in this book, but simply to make a plea for humility when it comes to advocating these programs and for careful evaluation of their effectiveness.

Sandra Scarr (1992) has alerted us to the fact that it is not easy to intervene deliberately in children's lives to change their development unless their environments are outside the normal species range. We know how to rescue children from extremely bad circumstances and to return them to normal developmental pathways—but only within the limits of their heritable dispositions, such as intelligence, temperament (activity, sociability) and psychobiologic reactivity (cardiac and immunologic responses under stress).

In her book entitled *Within Our Reach: Breaking the Cycle of Disadvantage,* Lisbeth Schorr (1988) has isolated a set of common characteristics of programs that have successfully prevented poor outcomes for children who grew up in high-risk families. Such programs typically offer a broad spectrum of health, education and family support services; cross professional boundaries; and view the child in the context of the family, and the family in the context of the community. These programs provide children with sustained access to competent and caring adults who teach them problem-solving skills, enhance their communication skills and self-esteem, and provide positive role models for them.

Hopefully, many of the intervention programs described in this volume share the same characteristics and, most importantly, actively generate support by the community in which they have been introduced when funds provided by outside agencies for research purposes are no longer available. If that happens, they have passed a crucial test of their effectiveness and relevance!

Only recently has research on resilience begun to focus on the adult years. The study of resilience across the lifespan is still relatively uncharted territory. We urgently need to explore the "reserve capacity" of older people; i.e., their potential for change and continued growth in later life (Staudinger, Marsiske, & Baltes, 1993). We also need to consider the effectiveness of intervention programs for adults in settings such as churches, hospitals, community colleges and the military which opened up opportunities for many individuals in our study who had a troubled childhood and youth, but who turned their lives around in their twenties, thirties and forties.

Future research on resilience needs to focus more explicitly on gender differences in response to adversity. Ours has been one of the few longitudinal studies of risk and resilience that included sizeable numbers of men *and* women. We have consistently noted that a higher proportion of females than males managed to cope effectively with adversity in childhood and adulthood. They also relied more frequently on informal sources of support and managed to recover from a "troubled" adolescence more often than males who grew up in adverse conditions. These findings need to be replicated in different contexts and need to be taken into account when designing intervention programs at different stages in the life cycle.

In the future, developmental researchers interested in the phenomenon of resilience need to make greater use of designs that explore gene-environment correlations and interactions (Rutter & Silberg, 2002). There is ample evidence of the important role genetic factors play in the susceptibility of individuals to psychopathology, such as alcoholism, antisocial behavior, autism, and the major psychoses. Several studies, including our own, have suggested that adverse environments— including serious pre- and perinatal stress—have the most negative impact on individuals who are genetically vulnerable—for example the offspring of alcoholic and schizophrenic mothers (Werner & Smith, 2001).

It stands to reason that gene-environment interaction also plays a significant role in relation to the phenomenon of resilience. We need more evidence from twin, adoptee, and family studies about the mediating effect of genetic influences that lead to positive adaptation in the context of adversity. Existing longitudinal studies of twins in the USA (for example the Minnesota and the Virginia Twin Studies) and in Europe (especially in the Scandinavian countries) could address this issue with their large data bases (see Rutter, 2000, for a discussion of these studies).

Future research on risk and resilience also needs to acquire a cross-cultural perspective that focuses on the children of the developing world who enter North America in ever increasing numbers as immigrants and refugees from the horrors of war in Asia, Africa, and Latin America. Like many Native American children, they have been exposed to many biological and psychosocial risk factors that increase their vulnerability far beyond that of their peers born and raised in more affluent and stable conditions. They also have to manage the difficult transition from the context of "traditional" rural societies to the "modern" industrialized world of urban North America. We need to know more about individual dispositions and sources of support in the family and community that enable these children and their families to transcend cultural boundaries and operate effectively in a variety of high-risk contexts.

Last, but not least, we need more long-term evaluation studies of intervention programs that represent deliberate attempts to alter the course of development of high-risk children and youth in a positive direction. Did they succeed in reducing the overall level of risk in the individuals who participated? Did they open up new opportunities for them and experiences that foster self-esteem and self-efficacy? Did these positive changes last *beyond* the period of intervention and *carry forward* into other contexts? Were the programs cost-effective and, most of all, did they reach the most vulnerable children and youth in a given community?

As of now, there are very few intervention programs in North America for one of the largest groups of "high-risk" children and youth, the children of alcoholics. A report on U.S. children, based on the 1992 National Longitudinal Alcohol Epidemiologic Survey estimates that one out of four children (some 28 million) lived in households where one or both parents had been abused or dependent on alcohol at some time before their children reached age 18. This extraordinary number (that exceeds the number of children living in poverty in the United States) defines one of today's major public health problems. In the future, there needs to be an expansion of intervention programs for these youngsters, since they are especially vulnerable to the negative impact of adverse family environments because of their genetic susceptibility to substance abuse (see McMahon & Peters, 2002, for a discussion of programs for children of disordered parents).

In sum: Because the processes leading to resilience are much more complex than we thought previously and are greatly influenced by context, it is not likely that we will discover a "magic bullet," a single coherent intervention program that will succeed every time with every youngster who grows up in adverse circumstances. Knowing this does not mean we need to despair. But it does mean, as Rutter admonishes us, "That caution should be taken in jumping too readily onto the bandwagon of whatever happens to be the prevailing enthusiasm of the moment" (Rutter, 2002, p. 15; see also the discussion by Tremblay, Chapter 3).

I have spent most of my professional life observing and documenting the extraordinary capacity of ordinary human beings to overcome great odds. Occasionally, I have found it helpful to re-read one of my favorite *Grooks*, an aphorism written by the Danish physicist and poet Piet Hein. It's called THE ROAD TO WISDOM

> The Road to Wisdom?—Well, it's plain and simple to express:
> Err and err and err again
> But less and less and less.

I hope this book will be a helpful guide along the road!

REFERENCES

Garmezy, N., & Rutter, M. (Eds.). (1983). *Stress, coping and development in children*. New York: McGraw Hill.

Gore, S., & Eckenrode, J. (1994). Context and process in research on risk and resilience. In R. J. Haggerty, L. R. Sherrod, N. Garmezy, & M. Rutter (Eds.), *Stress, risk, and resilience in children and adolescents* (pp. 19–63). New York: Cambridge University Press.

Hein, P. (1966). *Grooks*. Garden City, NY: Doubleday.

Luthar, S. (Ed.) (2003). *Resilience and vulnerability: Adaptation in the context of childhood adversities*. New York: Cambridge University Press.

Luthar, S., Cicchetti, D., & Becker, B. (2000). The construct of resilience: A critical evaluation and guidelines for future work. *Child Development, 71*, 543–562.

Masten, A. S., & Coatsworth, J. D. (1998). Resilience in individual development: The development of competence in favorable and unfavorable environments: Lessons from research on successful children. *American Psychologist, 53*, 205–220.

McMahon, R. J., & Peters, R. DeV. (Eds.). (2002). *The effects of parental dysfunction on children*. New York: Kluwer Academic/Plenum Press.

Rutter, M. (1996). Transitions and turning points in developmental psychopathology as applied to the age span between childhood and mid-adulthood. *International Journal of Behavioral Development, 19*, 603–626.

Rutter, M. (2000). Resilience reconsidered: Conceptual considerations, empirical findings, and policy implications. In J. P. Shonkoff & S. J. Meisels (Eds.), *Handbook of early childhood intervention* (2nd ed., pp. 651–682). New York: Cambridge University Press.

Rutter, M. (2002). Nature, nurture, and development: From evangelism through science toward policy and practice. *Child Development, 73*, 1–21.

Rutter, M., & Silberg, J. (2002). Gene-environment interplay in relation to emotional and behavioral disturbance. *Annual Review in Psychology, 53*, 463–490.

Scarr, S. (1992). Developmental theories for the 1990s: Development and individual differences. *Child Development, 63*, 1–19.

Schorr, L. (1988). *Within our reach: Breaking the cycle of disadvantage*. New York: Anchor Press.

Staudinger, U. M., Mariske, M., & Bates, P. B. (1993). Resilience and levels of reserve capacity in later adulthood: Perspectives from life span theory. *Development and Psychopathology, 5*, 541–556.

Werner, E. E. (2000). Protective factors and individual resilience. In J. P. Shonkoff & S. J. Meisels (Eds.), *Handbook of early childhood intervention* (2nd ed., pp. 115–132). New York: Cambridge University Press.

Werner, E. E. (2002). Looking for trouble in paradise: Some lessons learned from the Kauai Longitudinal Study. In E. Phelps, F. F. Furstenberg, & A. Colby (Eds.), *Looking at lives: American longitudinal studies of the twentieth century* (pp. 297–314). New York: Russell Sage.

Werner, E. E., & Smith, R. S. (1989). *Vulnerable but invincible: A longitudinal study of resilient children and youth*. New York: Adams, Bannister, Cox (originally published by McGraw Hill, 1982).

Werner, E. E., & Smith, R. S. (1992). *Overcoming the odds: High risk children from birth to adulthood*. Ithaca, NY: Cornell University Press.

Werner, E. E., & Smith, R. S. (2001). *Journeys from childhood to midlife: Risk, resilience, and recovery*. Ithaca, NY: Cornell University Press.

CHAPTER 2

Resilience in Context

JENNIFER R. RILEY & ANN S. MASTEN

Over the course of their development, humans show an amazing capacity for adaptation. *Resilience* refers to patterns of positive adaptation in the context of past or present adversity, which is one class of adaptive phenomena observed in human lives. Resilience is explicitly inferential, in that two conditions are required to describe resilience in an individual's life: (a) that significant adversity or threat to adaptation or development has occurred and (b) that functioning or development is okay, either because adequate adaptation was sustained over a period of adversity or because recovery to adequate functioning has been observed.

The concept of resilience is contextual in multiple ways. Judgments about adversity or risk refer directly to the events, or context, of a person's life. Resilience is always judged in the context of risk or adversity exposure and isolated adverse experiences have a different significance for development than the same experience occurring in the midst of many other negative experiences. Moreover, judgments about how well a person is doing in life require an evaluative context. We judge how people are doing in the context of expectations for human development, including developmental milestones universally observed around the same ages (such as learning to talk or walk) as well as cultural expectations more and less unique to a particular sociocultural milieu (such as learning religious rituals or behaving appropriately in school). History provides another context, in that the expectations parents or societies have for children change over time and historical epochs. In addition, developmental scientists often evaluate resilience on the basis of competence or achievements in *age-salient developmental tasks,* which encompass the major psychosocial expectations for children in a given time and culture (Masten & Coatsworth, 1998).

Adversity refers to experiences or events with the potential to disrupt normative functioning enough to cause negative outcomes. Examples of adverse experiences or events include growing up in a violent family, sexual abuse, or experiencing a tornado. Adversities represent one type of risk factor. More generally, the term *risk factor* refers to any characteristic of a group that predicts negative outcomes. In other words, a risk factor indicates that there is an elevated probability of an outcome viewed as undesirable. Risk factors for child development include a wide range of individual and contextual predictors of various negative outcomes, including housing status (e.g., homeless, dangerous neighborhood), perinatal status (e.g., low birth weight, prematurity), genetic history (e.g., child in a family loaded with bipolar disorder), socioeconomic status (e.g., growing up in poverty; child of a single, unemployed mother who has not finished high school), parenting quality (e.g., harsh parenting, neglect), etc. Such risk factors predict worse outcomes on major indicators of child well-being and development, and the broadest risk factors often predict poor outcomes on multiple indicators, such as academic achievement, physical health, emotional health, and behavior. Risk factors also tend to aggregate in the lives of children, leading many investigators to focus on cumulative risk (Masten, Best, & Garmezy, 1990; Sameroff, Gutman, & Peck, 2003).

Resilience is inferred when risk or adversity is high enough to pose a significant threat to healthy development or functioning and yet positive outcomes are nonetheless observed. For example, homeless children and other children growing up in poverty generally have a high level of cumulative risk and such children have elevated probabilities of educational, behavioral, and physical health problems (Luthar, 1999; Masten, 1992; Masten & Sesma, 1999). Complex processes may account for these risks. Academic achievement, for example, may be compromised by mobility; lack of attendance; poor health related to poor health care, lead exposure, or poor nutrition; worse schools and teachers in lower income neighborhoods; home environments not conducive to homework; negative peer influences; traumatic exposure to violence that generates post-traumatic stress symptoms or chronic anxiety; and other possibilities. If a homeless child performs better in school than one would expect among children in the same context, one has observed a pattern of adaptive success suggesting resilience.

Judgments regarding adaptive outcomes are influenced to some degree by the severity of the hazard and the time frame for judging adaptation. In circumstances of massive trauma such as war or natural disasters, survival itself may be the primary criterion for resilience in the short term. Over the long term, as more normative conditions are restored, one would begin to look for positive psychosocial functioning in developmental tasks appropriate to a person of that age in that cultural milieu and time. Thus, over time, expectations would normalize to those expected for most children of that place and time.

RESILIENCE IN THE CONTEXT
OF PROCESSES AND SYSTEMS

The concept of resilience is best understood from the perspective of developmental processes and interacting person-environmental systems. An individual is a living system, with the dual task of self-regulation and organization on the one hand (maintaining coherence as a living and developing organism) and adapting to the world in which the individual lives and grows on the other hand (Masten & Coatsworth, 1995). The individual as a living system lives in continual interaction with many other social and physical systems described theoretically in the work of Bronfenbrenner (1979), Lerner (Ford & Lerner, 1992), Thelen (Thelen & Smith, 1998) and others. Accordingly, resilience has been conceptualized in terms of dynamic developmental processes (Cicchetti, 2003; Egeland, Carlson, & Sroufe, 1993; Yates, Egeland, & Sroufe, 2003). Development of an individual arises from many interactions within the organism (e.g., genetic, cellular, hormonal, neural, cardiovascular, and other systems) and between the organism and the systems in which the life of an individual is embedded, including interactions with family members, peers, schools, community organizations, the media, etc. Moreover, these systems are interconnected. Physical stress in the form of illness may impact irritability in an individual, which may in turn affect social skills or attention in school; reciprocally, violent or toxic school environments can contribute to the stresses that result in personal illness. Some systems such as family and peer networks coexist while others such as culture provide more of an over-arching milieu encompassing more immediate influences.

Placing the concept of resilience in context lends toward more fruitful study as it moves discussion away from observations *that* resilience has occurred to the study of *how* resilience occurs. For example, parenting quality and cognitive abilities are often identified in studies of resilience (Masten & Powell, 2003). Among children experiencing adversity, those who have better outcomes than expected often have a supportive caregiver and/or cognitive abilities as resources. If one were to stop the investigation there, one would accumulate little more than a laundry list of protective factors. It has been essential for progress on understanding resilience phenomena to study the processes by which such factors prevent expected negative outcomes or promote positive outcomes (Luthar, 2003).

Contextual levels provide a means for understanding and organizing resilience research. In an early review of resilience studies, Garmezy (1985) described three general sources of protective factors observed in studies of children who flourished in spite of adversity: child characteristics, family attributes, and aspects of the greater social environment. Others have conceptualized protective factors as existing at the individual, social, and societal levels (Olsson, Bond, Burns, Vella-Brodrick, & Sawyer, 2003). In terms of Bronfenbrenner's embedded systems framework, protective factors could be examined within the functioning of the individual; at the microsystem level of family, peer groups, or classrooms; systems at the community level, such as schools, recreation and park programs, or religious organizations; and, macrosystems at even higher levels, such as the media, national policy, and state or federal government agencies. Similarly, markers of positive outcomes may manifest themselves in different arenas at different system levels and resilient adaptation may be achieved through internal processes such as self-regulation or external processes such as high quality supportive relationships.

Recognizing that resilience processes may take place at the level of the individual, family, organization, town, society, etc., has several implications. First, it indicates that the protective processes through which resilience occurs may take place at any level or in the dynamic interactions between levels. Towns may put together shelters, food shelves, or similar organizations that provide resources to families in need or enact policies that subsidize low-income housing to avert episodes of homelessness among poor families. Many existing systems such as reaching the police or medical assistance by dialing 911 facilitate positive outcomes in the aftermath of injury or crime or even serve to prevent traumatic experiences, as when a child calls for help under threat of family violence. Second, this notion implies that the family, organization, or society itself may demonstrate resilient functioning. Communities that experience tragedy may survive emotionally by conducting memorial services and using other means to process grief. Families experiencing grave economic threat may recover or avoid financial ruin by consolidating efforts and capitalizing upon community resources (Patterson, 2002). These different levels are interconnected and embedded within each other, creating adaptational systems within adaptational systems. Children attending schools with many resources likely do better in life than children attending schools with few resources, and all of these children will likely have greater successes if they live in a wealthy, resourceful nation rather than one ravaged by the effects of war.

Reviews of the literature on resilience in the adaptation of children have highlighted the importance of basic adaptive processes for resilience, such as those involved in ordinary parenting, learning, and self-regulation (Masten, 2001). From this perspective, resilience does not occur because someone was fortunate enough to possess a unique or special characteristic. While unique characteristics such as special talents in sports or creative arts may provide protection to some individuals in the midst of adversity, more common and basic systems appear to account for most of the robust findings in the resilience literature. Among the widely reported protective factors for children, the roles of caregivers and cognitive abilities stand out above the rest (Masten, 2001). These fundamental adaptive systems are evident in the child or the child's context at birth and continue to develop over the life course. Relationships with caregivers in the form of parents, grandparents, notable teachers, or mentors involve the attachment system and often play a key role in helping children succeed in the face of adversity. Basic cognitive systems that may influence resilience encompass various aspects of internal resources such as problem solving, attention, and the capacity for learning that are shaped and honed over development by experience interacting with brain development (Curtis & Nelson, 2003; Masten & Coatsworth, 1998).

Resilience processes may take many forms (Masten, 1999). Protective features may be constantly present and provide a buffer against adversity before it occurs. Growing up in a family that provides one with a "secure base" is widely believed to protect children from a host of life threats by providing a sense of felt security and confidence that adults can be counted on to help children (Yates et al., 2003). Similarly, an easy-going personality may afford general buffering from adversities. Protective features may also occur only in response to the adversity, triggered in much the way an airbag inflates upon impact or the immune system responds to an infectious agent. As noted earlier, 911 emergency services exemplify this type of protection, as do other social services triggered by emergencies (e.g., a crisis nursery). Parents and other adults undoubtedly have the capacity to alter their behavior radically in response to impending threat and create a psychological or physical shield against threats to their children or carry out daring rescue missions. In addition, protective features may directly impact the organism, or influence adaptation indirectly by enhancing the quality or availability of helpful resources or protective systems. For example, children in poverty may be helped directly with academic assistance programs or indirectly by programs that teach their parents better stress management skills.

Finally, because resilience is embedded within contexts such as family and society as well as developmental history, it is dependent upon and cannot be separated from these larger contexts. Thus, resilience is not an attribute that an organism either has or does not have. Rather, resilience refers to a pattern of adaptation that may or may not be present from one time to another and from one domain to another (Luthar, Cicchetti, & Becker, 2000; Masten et al., 1990; Wyman, 2003). In longitudinal studies, children show resilient adaptation at some times and then maladaptation at others (Egeland et al., 1993). The same child may experience adversity at different time points and demonstrate positive outcomes in one instance and negative outcomes in another. This literature also suggests that positive adaptation increases the likelihood of later positive adaptation (Sroufe & Rutter, 1984). Some children may appear to show resilience more often than others, but this resilient adaptation is inextricably tied to the multiple contexts in their developmental history and life experiences (Sroufe, 1997).

RESILIENCE AND "BLAMING THE VICTIM" ISSUES

The complexity and contextual nature of resilience also has implications for understanding maladaptation or the absence of resilience. One of the most damaging consequences of viewing resilience as an individual trait is the idea that a child is somehow deficient or lacking in the "right stuff" if they do not manage to succeed in the face of adversity (Luthar et al., 2000; Yates & Masten, in press). To *blame the victim* in this way demonstrates a fundamental misunderstanding of resilience. First, by definition, resilience requires that a child has experienced significant adversity or risk. Children who experience adversity, particularly in cases of severe or prolonged adversity, might be *expected* to show negative outcomes. Second, because adaptation is embedded within the context of developmental history and multiple systems of interactions, including families, schools, and neighborhoods, resilience has a great deal to do with processes *outside* of the individual child or involving relationships with other people. Often, children who develop problems in the context of disadvantage and adversity have very few resources. For these children, development is not protected by the normal systems of human adaptation that operate to keep development "on track."

Resilience depends upon complex interactions of individuals and their contexts, as well as the nature of the child, unfolding events, and the families, peer groups, schools, communities, cultures, and societies in which the interactions are embedded. Many protections for children stem from people, institutions, and actions in the environment of the child, rather than from the child himself or herself. Children do not make it on their own in situations of adversity; and when they don't make it, it is often because basic protections for human development are lacking. This does not mean, however, that "blame" should be shifted to families and societies, although clearly adults have more responsibility as well as greater access to resources than children for protecting a child's development. Healthy development requires that the functioning of adults charged with protecting and socializing children also be supported by many systems, and it depends to a considerable degree on their own life circumstances. Exhausted or mentally ill parents with no social supports may not be able to muster the energy or external resources to provide basic protections for their children. Extremely impoverished communities or those devastated by war, famine, or disease may also not be able to provide the kind of basic supports essential to facilitate positive child-rearing.

POSITIVE CONTEXTS FOR RESILIENCE IN CHILDREN

At the core of an individual's developmental history is the infant-caregiver relationship (Yates et al., 2003). In this kind of relationship, children learn how to relate to others, regulate their emotions, and develop a sense of self. Early relationships with caregivers provide a foundation for the attachment system, one of the basic systems promoting positive adaptation. If children experience a secure attachment relationship in infancy and this pattern continues, they are likely to have an important protective system in place and operating when adversity occurs. They appear to learn positive ways of interacting with others and a healthy sense of self-efficacy in problem solving. Thus, as children with a responsive caregiver encounter risks later in life they have a double-dose of protective factors: a good caregiver and a track record of prosocial and cognitive-based skills. Yet, since all contextual levels may be affected by risk, a parent's ability to function effectively and provide a protective context for his or her child may be impaired by adversity, such as job stress, divorce or death. Because development is cumulative, interruptions in good parenting are not likely to erase the benefits of a strong early foundation, both because the child is more likely to have the expectations, trust, and motivation to connect with other caring adults, and because the child is more likely to have a solid base of skills for competent functioning that scaffolds future adaptation. If parenting is adversely affected, a child with a positive attachment history may still show resilient adaptation. It is also possible that a child who has a rocky beginning in terms of early relationships can develop a more positive attachment system through later positive relationships (Egeland et al., 1993).

A key tenet of developmental psychopathology is that similar processes govern positive and negative adaptation (Sroufe & Rutter, 1984). Thus, a negative attachment relationship during infancy may undermine the development of otherwise protective features. Instead of learning prosocial skills and ways of interacting with others that involve warmth and intimacy, a child may learn that interactions are cold and rebuffing. Instead of gaining a sense of mastery, a child may feel ineffective in influencing the world around him or her. Instead of providing protective features, the caregiver may become a source of adversity. Adversity arising from attachment figures poses particular threats to development because of the potential for undermining fundamental protective systems. Thus, it is not surprising that maltreatment by caregivers carries great risk for children (Cicchetti & Lynch, 1995).

The role of the attachment system in resilience also illustrates how protective processes sometimes viewed as individual attributes, such as good self-regulation, develop in contexts that may or may not include adversity. If an infant is malnourished during its first few years, his/her body will not develop as strongly as properly nourished children. Relative to other children, this child is at greater risk for illness. Medical care may help this child overcome illnesses and improve the immune system, but it may not completely undo the damage already done while basic biological systems were developing. Similarly, if an infant receives sporadic, inconsistent care because he/she has a parent with a severe and persistent mental illness, lives in an orphanage, or experiences the repeated trauma of sexual abuse during the years when the early systems of emotion regulation and mastery motivation or self concept are forming, there may be enduring consequences for how these systems work (Gunnar, 2001; Shonkoff & Meisels, 2000). Later experience with loving, consistent caregivers or mentors may help this child learn to form positive relationships and improve these systems, but there may well be residual issues related to early adversity. Similarly, maltreatment can cause permanent brain damage (for example, due to head trauma) no matter how good the medical and emotional care provided subsequently.

The attachment system illustrates the importance of context for resilience, but children may be adversely affected by other contextual systems as well. As studies examining cumulative risk have shown, experiencing multiple risk factors across multiple domains and levels stacks the odds against children doing well (Masten, 2001). Further, if a higher-order system fails, the adverse effects may trickle down and have large, although indirect, effects on children. When a country is consumed by war, basic governmental resources may become unavailable, affecting the supply of protection, food, and clean water. Massive trauma or disasters are defined by large-scale collapse of adaptive systems at the community level or beyond, as occurs with natural and man-made disasters (Masten & Hubbard, 2003; Wright, Masten, Northwood, & Hubbard, 1997). Inner-city violence and poverty also may overwhelm adaptive capacities at the community level (see Gorman-Smith et al., this volume).

IMPLICATIONS OF CONTEXTUAL PERSPECTIVES ON RESILIENCE FOR PREVENTION AND INTERVENTION

Theoretical and empirical advances in understanding resilience have provided a framework for conceptualizing prevention and intervention (Cicchetti, Rappaport, Sandler, & Weissberg, 2000; Coie et al., 1993; Cowen, 2000; Luthar & Cicchetti, 2000; Masten & Garmezy, 1985; Masten & Powell, 2003; Sandler et al., 2003; Weissberg, Kumpfer, & Seligman, 2003; Wyman, 2003; Wyman, Sandler, Wolchik, & Nelson, 2000; Yoshikawa, 1994). Consideration of multiple levels of context provides a variety of arenas to target in designing ways to intervene in reducing risk, increasing resources or access to resources, and mobilizing or enhancing protective systems (Masten & Powell, 2003; Olsson et al., 2003). Targeting multiple levels of influence simultaneously may be important for maximizing resilient outcomes (Masten, 1999; Maton, this volume; Wyman et al., 2000; Weissberg et al. 2003; Yoshikawa, 1994). Support systems such as parents, teachers, and community programs may be aided. Given the importance of developmental history, the early infant-caregiver relationship is an excellent target for intervention (Yates et al., 2003).

In addition, the concept of resilience allows for the risk and protective factors within resilient adaptation to be completely different from each other. This notion provides greater flexibility and opportunity for successful intervention. It may not be possible to eliminate poverty for large numbers of children, but it is possible to promote healthy development among poor children through effective nutrition, housing, healthcare, and preschool programs. When the risk factor is an event that has already taken place, such as criminal activity resulting in incarceration of a mother, there is still opportunity to foster more positive outcomes; for example, by facilitating a network of positive relationships with caring adults in the child's life. Further, it may be unrealistic if not impossible to effectively change certain risk factors, but other adaptational systems may be used. For example, if parent participation in a parenting program seems unlikely for certain families, resources can still be directed toward community-based mentoring programs, thus still tapping relationship systems.

CONCLUSION

Resilience cannot be identified, understood, or facilitated without consideration of context at many levels and in multiple ways. This conclusion is increasingly evident in the history of research on resilience in development, but it also follows directly from the basic tenets of developmental psychopathology and developmental systems theory. This is not a coincidence; these broad theoretical perspectives share historical roots with the study of resilience (Cicchetti & Garmezy, 1993; Luthar, 2003; Masten, 1989). Identifying resilience involves judgments about adaptation that are inherently contextual, both in terms of an individual's life and in terms of expectations for development. Intervening effectively to promote positive adaptation necessitates a deep appreciation of context in order to strategically plan what to do, at what level, and when. Underestimating the importance of context can result in misplaced blame, ineffective interventions, findings that fail to replicate, and theory that does not generate useful ideas. Future progress in understanding naturally occurring resilience or designing more effective interventions for children at risk for problems requires closer attention to context in all its manifestations, including how the individual child interacts with multiple levels of context on the road to resilience.

Early pioneers in the field of resilience studies were keenly aware of the contextual nature of resilience (see Masten et al., 1990). Norman Garmezy, Lois Murphy, Michael Rutter, and Emmy Werner, among others, launched the first generation of scholarship on resilience in development with an intellectual depth and appreciation for the complexity of individual lives, contexts, and the course of development through time that has guided a generation of scholars. Werner's extraordinary scholarship and enduring contributions to the field are evident in her influence on contemporary scholars of resilience, as they continue to wrestle with the issues and complexities she identified decades ago. Her work stands as a beacon for the abiding hope shared by generations of scholars that understanding resilience processes will teach us how to promote and protect healthy child development.

ACKNOWLEDGMENTS

Preparation of this chapter was facilitated by a Graduate Research Fellowship from the National Science Foundation awarded to the first author. The second author's work on resilience has been supported by grants from the National Institute of Mental Health, the National Science Foundation, the William T. Grant Foundation, and the University of Minnesota.

REFERENCES

Bronfenbrenner, U. (1979). *The ecology of human development: Experiments by nature and design.* Cambridge, MA: Harvard University Press.

Cicchetti, D. (2003). Forward. In S. S. Luthar (Ed.), *Resilience and vulnerability: Adaptation in the context of childhood adversities* (pp. xix–xxvii). New York: Cambridge University Press.

Cicchetti, D., & Garmezy, N. (Eds.). (1993). *Development and Psychopathology, special issue: Milestones in the development of resilience* (Vol. 5). New York: Cambridge University Press.

Cicchetti, D., & Lynch, M. (1995). Failures in the expectable environment and their impact on individual development: The case of child maltreatment. In D. Cicchetti & D. J. Cohen (Eds.), *Developmental psychopathology: Vol. 2. Risk, disorder, and adaptation* (pp. 32–71). New York: Wiley.

Cicchetti, D., Rappaport, J., Sandler, I., & Weissberg, R. P. (Eds.). (2000). *The promotion of wellness in children and adolescents.* Washington, DC: CWLA Press.

Coie, J. D., Watt, N. F., West, S. G., Hawkins, J. D., Asarnow, J. R., Markman, H. J., Ramey, S. L., Shure, M. B., & Long, B. (1993). The science of prevention: A conceptual framework and some directions for a national research program. *American Psychologist, 48,* 1013–1022.

Cowen, E. L. (2000). Psychological wellness: Some hopes for the future. In D. Cicchetti, J. Rappaport, I. Sandler, & R. P. Weissberg (Eds.), *The promotion of wellness in children and adolescents* (pp. 477–503). Washington, DC: CWLA Press.

Curtis, W. J., & Nelson, C. A. (2003). Toward building a better brain: Neurobehavioral outcomes, mechanisms, and processes of environmental enrichment. In S. S. Luthar (Ed.), *Resilience and vulnerability: Adaptation in the context of childhood adversities* (pp. 463–488). New York: Cambridge University Press.

Egeland, B., Carlson, E., & Sroufe, L. A. (1993). Resilience as process. *Development and Psychopathology, 5,* 517–528.

Ford, D. H., & Lerner, R. M. (1992). *Developmental systems theory: An integrative approach.* Newbury Park, CA: Sage.

Garmezy, N. (1985). Stress-resistant children: The search for protective factors. In J. E. Stevenson (Ed.), *Recent research in developmental pathopathology: Journal of Child Psychology and Psychiatry Book Supplement #4* (pp. 213–233). Oxford: Pergamon Press.

Gunnar, M. R. (2001). Effects of early deprivation: Findings from orphanage-reared infants and children. In C. A. Nelson & M. Luciana (Eds.), *Handbook of developmental cognitive neuroscience* (pp. 617–629). Cambridge, MA: MIT Press.

Luthar, S. S. (1999). *Poverty and children's adjustment.* Thousand Oaks, CA: Sage.

Luthar, S. S. (Ed.). (2003). *Resilience and vulnerability: Adaptation in the context of childhood adversities.* New York: Cambridge University Press.

Luthar, S. S., & Cicchetti, D. (2000). The construct of resilience: Implications for interventions and social policies. *Development and Psychopathology, 12,* 857–885.

Luthar, S. S., Cicchetti, D., & Becker, B. (2000). The construct of resilience: A critical evaluation and guidelines for future work. *Child Development, 71,* 543–562.

Masten, A. S. (1989). Resilience in development: Implications of the study of successful adaptation for developmental psychopathology. In D. Cicchetti (Ed.), *Rochester Symposium on Developmental Psychopathology: Vol. 1. The emergence of a discipline* (pp. 261–294). Rochester, NY: University of Rochester Press.

Masten, A. S. (1992). Homeless children in the United States: Mark of a nation at risk. *Current Directions in Psychological Science, 1,* 41–44.

Masten, A. S. (1999). Resilience comes of age: Reflections on the past and outlook for the next generation of research. In M. D. Glantz, J. Johnson, & L. Huffman (Eds.), *Resilience and development: Positive life adaptations* (pp. 289–296). New York: Plenum Press.

Masten, A. S. (2001). Ordinary magic: Resilience processes in development. *American Psychologist, 56,* 227–238.

Masten, A. S. & Coatsworth, J. D. (1995). Competence, resilience, and psychopathology. In D. Cicchetti & D. J. Cohen (Eds.), *Developmental psychopathology: Vol. 2. Risk, disorder, and adaptation* (pp. 715–752). New York: Wiley.

Masten, A. S., & Coatsworth, J. D. (1998). The development of competence in favorable and unfavorable environments: Lessons from successful children. *American Psychologist, 53,* 205–220.

Masten, A. S., & Garmezy, N. (1985). Risk, vulnerability, and protective factors in developmental psychopathology. In B. B. Lahey & A. E. Kazdin (Eds.), *Advances in clinical child psychology* (Vol. 8, pp. 1–52). New York: Plenum Press.

Masten, A. S., & Hubbard, J. J. (2003). *Global threats to child development: A resilience framework for humanitarian intervention.* Unpublished manuscript, University of Minnesota.

Masten, A. S., & Powell, J. L. (2003). A resilience framework for research, policy, and practice. In S. S. Luthar (Ed.), *Resilience and vulnerability: Adaptation in the context of childhood adversities* (pp. 1–25). New York: Cambridge University Press.

Masten, A. S., & Sesma, A. (1999). Risk and resilience among children homeless in Minneapolis. *CURA Reporter, 29*(1), 1–6.

Masten, A. S., Best, K. M., & Garmezy, N. (1990). Resilience and development: Contributions from the study of children who overcome adversity. *Development and Psychopathology, 2,* 425–444.

Olsson, C. A., Bond, L., Burns, J. M., Vella-Brodrick, D. A., & Sawyer, S. M. (2003). Adolescent resilience: A concept analysis. *Journal of Adolescence, 26,* 1–11.

Patterson, J. M. (2002). Understanding family resilience. *Journal of Clinical Psychology, 58,* 233–246.

Sameroff, A., Gutman, L. M., & Peck, S. C. (2003). Adaptation among youth facing multiple risks. In S. S. Luthar (Ed.), *Resilience and vulnerability: Adaptation in the context of childhood adversities* (pp. 364–391). New York: Cambridge University Press.

Sandler, I., Wolchik, S., Davis, C., Haine, R., & Ayers, T. (2003). Correlational and experimental study of resilience in children of divorce and parentally bereaved children. In S. S. Luthar (Ed.), *Resilience and vulnerability: Adaptation in the context of childhood adversities* (pp. 213–240). New York: Cambridge University Press.

Shonkoff, J. P., & Meisels, S. J. (Eds.) (2000). *Handbook of early childhood intervention* (2nd ed.). New York: Cambridge University Press.

Sroufe, L. A. (1997). Psychopathology as an outcome of development. *Development and Psychopathology, 9*, 251–268.

Sroufe, L. A., & Rutter, M. (1984). The domain of developmental psychopathology. *Child Development, 55*, 17–29.

Thelen, E., & Smith, L. B. (1998). Dynamic systems theory. In R. Lerner (Vol. Ed.) & W. Damon (Series Ed.), *Handbook of child psychology, Vol 1. Theoretical models of human development* (pp. 563–634). New York: Wiley.

Weissberg, R. P., Kumpfer, K. L., & Seligman, M. E. P. (2003). Prevention that works for children and youth: An introduction. *American Psychologist, 58*, 425–432.

Wright, M. O., Masten, A. S., Northwood, A., & Hubbard, J. J. (1997). Long-term effects of massive trauma: Developmental and psychobiological perspectives. In D. Cicchetti & S. L. Toth (Eds.), *Rochester Symposium on Developmental Psychopathology, Vol. 8, The effects of trauma on the developmental proces* (pp.181–225). Rochester, NY: University of Rochester Press.

Wyman, P. A. (2003). Emerging perspectives on context specificity of children's adaptation and resilience: Evidence from a decade of research with urban children in adversity. In S. S. Luthar (Ed.), *Resilience and vulnerability: Adaptation in the context of childhood adversities* (pp. 293–317). New York: Cambridge University Press.

Wyman, P. A., Sandler, I., Wolchik, S., & Nelson, K. (2000). Resilience as cumulative competence promotion and stress protection: Theory and intervention. In D. Cicchetti, J. Rapport, I. Sandler, & R. P. Weissberg (Eds.), *The promotion of wellness in children and adolescents* (pp. 133–184). Washington, DC: Child Welfare League of America Press.

Yates, T. M., & Masten, A. S. (2004). Fostering the future: Resilience theory and the practice of positive psychology. In P. A. Linley & S. Joseph (Eds.), *Positive psychology in practice* (pp. 521–539). Hoboken, NJ: Wiley.

Yates, T. M., Egeland, B., & Sroufe, L. A. (2003). Rethinking resilience: A development process perspective. In S. S. Luthar (Ed.), *Resilience and vulnerability: Adaptation in the context of childhood adversities* (pp. 234–256). New York: Cambridge University Press.

Yoshikawa, H. (1994). Prevention as cumulative protection: Effects of early family support and education on chronic delinquency and its risks. *Psychological Bulletin, 115*, 28–54.

CHAPTER 3

Disruptive Behaviors

Should We Foster or Prevent Resiliency?

RICHARD E. TREMBLAY

"Unless you give infants everything they want, they cry and get angry, they even beat their own parents ... Thus an evil man is rather like a sturdy boy" (Hobbes, 1641/1998, p. 11)

As I start this chapter, we have been struck by three important epidemics. The first was the outbreak of the Severe Acute Respiratory Syndrome (SARS) in the winter of 2003. The second is the "show your belly button fashion" (SBBF) that I started to notice last May when the weather was finally getting warmer and women could walk on the streets of Montreal without a fur coat. The third is the use of the word "resiliency" by the media gurus and all those who are afraid of SARS but dying to show-off their belly buttons.

The confusion concerning a word adopted by academic psychologists to describe their scientific progress is not new. At the last 20th century International Congress of Psychology, held in Stockholm in 2000, I had a discussion with David Magnusson on the advancement of knowledge in developmental psychology. David made important contributions through his pioneering longitudinal studies (e.g., Magnusson, Dunér, & Zetterblom, 1975; Magnusson, Klinteberg, & Stattin, 1992), his theoretical development of person-context interaction (Magnusson, 1988; Magnusson & Stattin, 1998), and his methodological innovations (Magnusson & Bergman, 1990). He was also chairman of one of the prestigious Nobel prize committees. At one point in our conversation, he suggested that most of what appeared to be "new" in psychology was mainly putting new words on old facts. We need words to think and communicate, but words are simplifications of reality, and when words used by scientists become buzz words, they can confuse more than clarify. SARS and belly buttons appear to be concrete, objective observations, but what is "resilience"?

My main area of research has been the development of disruptive behavior from childhood to adulthood, and I have focused more specifically on physical aggression. When I started to study the development of disruptive behavior, without being clearly conscious of the fact, I was somewhat following a social learning approach (e.g., Bandura, 1973). With a group of colleagues, I initiated a longitudinal study to understand how some kindergarten children from poor inner-city areas became "delinquents" while others did not. To use the term that became a buzz word in the late 1980s, I was looking for the factors that could explain the "onset" of delinquency (Tremblay, Pihl, Vitaro, & Dobkin, 1994). I probably had in mind that some were "resilient" with regard to the bad influence of peers or to the surge of testosterone during adolescence (e.g., Schaal, Tremblay, Soussignan, & Susman, 1996; Tremblay, Mâsse, Vitaro, & Dobkin, 1995; Vitaro, Tremblay, Kerr, Pagani-Kurtz, & Bukowski, 1997). It was certainly part of my thinking that parents could be both protective and risk factors, since a large part of the study was meant to assess the quality of the parent-child interactions throughout the elementary school years (e.g., Lavigueur, Saucier, & Tremblay, 1995; Lavigueur, Tremblay, & Saucier, 1995).

But I clearly had no idea of the conclusions I would come to 15 years later. In fact, when we started to see that things were not what we expected they would be, my reaction was far from open-minded. I still remember a meeting, probably in the fall of 1988, when my colleague Marc Leblanc, a criminologist who had never studied humans younger than 12 years of age, described the results of the analyses he had done of the self-reported delinquency questionnaire we had given to the 1,037 boys we had been following since their kindergarten year. We were asking them if they had *ever* exhibited any of 27 "delinquent" behaviors, and if they answered "yes," at what age that particular behavior had occurred for the first time. The boys' self-reports were indicating relatively high rates of "delinquency" in that sample from schools in low socioeconomic areas. We had started to ask these questions concerning "delinquent" acts at 10 years of age because we were hoping to catch them before they initiated (onset) their delinquent activities. There is in fact a law in Canada that a child cannot be deemed a "delinquent" before 12 years old! We of course expected that some would break that law, but since they were only 10 years old, I was worried that they did not really understand the questions, or that they simply were having fun making us believe that they were doing the bad things that they were seeing their older brothers and neighbors doing. In other words,

I had the impression that we were not getting reliable reports of their true behavior.

With the 10-year-olds, we were using a questionnaire that had been designed to study delinquent behavior in adolescents, and I was saying to my criminologist colleague, who appeared to be coming from another planet, that he should not take these answers too seriously. It worried me even more when he showed us the results concerning the age at which the boys were saying they had started to commit these "delinquent" acts (the "age of onset" concept). The colleague who came from the world of adolescent and adult criminals was telling us that some 10-year-old boys were reporting that they had started, at age 4 and 5, to use weapons in fights, to steal goods worth more than $100, as well as to steal following breaking and entering. I distinctly remember my outrage. How could he be so naïve and believe that he was getting reliable answers? Not only were we using with 10-year-olds an instrument created for adolescents, but we were asking them to recall when they had started to do these things that we expected would start later. How could 10-year-olds remember what they were doing at 4? There were few boys who were reporting onset of these "serious" "delinquent" behaviors at age 4, but this was proof that, at least some of them did not understand the questions we were asking them, and thus they were still much too young for that self-reported delinquency instrument. I strongly appealed to him not to report these data, especially the ones on age of onset, since it would discredit the whole study. Well, at least a few reviewers and an editor of a serious scientific journal had a less sanguine reaction than I had, and the results were eventually published (Leblanc et al., 1991). But, as with most of our great scholarly publications, it did not get much attention (eight citations up to October 2003), and thus my fear of the longitudinal study being discredited was, in hindsight, exaggerated. I certainly could not foresee at that time that 10 years later we would be publishing results that would be much more outrageous.

THE CONCEPT OF "RESILIENCE"

The word "resilience" has spread in the world of psychology and psychiatry like an epidemic. We do not know exactly what it is, but it is a nice word, it appears to refer to something concrete that we would all like to have, and the epidemic process appears to be working, as people who have been in contact with it use the "resilience" word. The best sign that the "resiliency" epidemic knows no frontier is that France has been severely hit, although there is relatively little contact between French psychologists and Anglo-Saxon psychologists. As I write these words in September 2003, a large proportion of the inhabitants of France seem to be attributing their ups and downs in life to their "resilience," or lack of (Tisseron, 2003). Books on "resilience" are instantaneous best sellers. Every television and radio program dealing with human behavior uses the concept to explain all that goes well or goes wrong. Every health-minded French citizen wants to know how he can increase his "resilience"; and every psychologist, psychiatrist, counselor, nutritionist, chiropractor, massage therapist, physiotherapist, osteopath, acupuncturist, and so on, is selling the magic formula.

I agreed to write this chapter because I wanted to reflect on this fad, and thought that I could possibly help in understanding what we are talking about. However, I must admit that as I write these words I have not closely followed the debates concerning the concept of "resilience," and I am far from being certain what people mean when they are using the word. I read that Werner and Smith (1982, p. 36) used Webster's New Collegiate Dictionary definition of resilience: 1. The capability of a strained body to recover its size and shape after deformation caused especially by compressive stress. 2. An ability to recover from or adjust easily to misfortune or change. According to Murray (2003), participants at the 2003 American Psychological Association Annual Meeting were being asked to take home the message that "Resilience is not something we are born with—it's a set of learned behaviors, and it takes strategizing to build."

Intuitively, the concept appears to apply relatively well to some physical illnesses, and some mental illnesses. An illness appears at a certain point in time (onset), after the person has been attacked, for example, by a virus or a psychologically traumatic event. Some individuals will become ill and others will not. Those who do not become ill can be considered resilient. Among those who become ill, some will not recover their healthy state, while others will. The "resiliency" label also appears to be applied to the latter. One can try to build resiliency with regard to some viruses and some trauma, for example, by taking vitamins and following the APA Practice Directorate's public education campaign "Road to Resilience"! These efforts to increase resiliency can be considered preventive interventions. However, it seems very likely that humans are born with individual differences in resilience regarding attacks from viruses and traumatic events.

This developmental perspective concerning physical illnesses and some mental illnesses (e.g., depression) seems to work well. It is very obvious that health generally declines with age. Overall, children and adolescents are much healthier than adults, and young adults are much healthier than older adults. Thus, except for illnesses that we are born with, illnesses "onset" at a certain age. However, some humans are less ill than others throughout their lives, and some appear to simply die of old age, after a healthy life. Although they live in the same environment as others who become miserably sick and die young, their bodies resist the invasions of bacteria, microbes, and viruses. Some smoke like chimneys and die without a trace of cancer, others drink like sponges and celebrate their 100th anniversary standing straight and tall while listening to the crowd sing "God Save the Queen." These fortunate people have been labeled "resilient" after the fact. In spite of the adversity that they had to endure, or that they brought upon themselves, they did not lose their health, or if they did, it was momentary, and they bounced back. Like a resilient piece of rubber, they bounced back to their original healthy state after having been hit by an agent that creates an illness. How well does this perspective apply to disruptive behaviors?

THE DEVELOPMENT OF DISRUPTIVE BEHAVIORS

Disruptive behavior generally refers to three sub-groups of behaviors: physical aggression, hyperactivity (intense motor activity) and oppositional behavior. I believe that most of the work on these three topics, until recently, was based on the idea that children start to exhibit these behaviors (onset) as they grow older. For example, the classic work of Bandura, Ross, and Ross (1961; see also Bandura, 1973) on aggression indicated that children learn to physically aggress others by imitation. The more they witness physical aggression, the more likely they are to learn to use it. This is why television would apparently be such a powerful cause of the physical aggression we see in our schools and our neighborhoods. It appears clear that physical aggression on television has substantially increased since television was made available to the public more than half a century ago, and each new generation of youth from industrialized countries has apparently been learning to physically aggress more than the previous one with the increase of physical aggression on television (Eron, 1982; Huesmann & Eron, 1986; Johnson, Cohen, Smailes, Kasen, & Brook, 2002). Obviously there are many who do not use much physical aggression, and those would be children who were either not exposed to violent television or who for some reason were resilient with regard to the social learning mechanisms of aggression through television viewing. Since children would also learn to physically aggress from aggressive parents, peers, and neighbors, those who were exposed to these social learning factors and did not learn to physically aggress would also be considered resilient.

The work on oppositional behavior indicates a similar developmental pattern. According to at least three decades of observational work on children's aversive behaviors, they learn to be oppositional because their parents use inappropriate parenting behaviors (Patterson, 1982; Patterson, Reid, & Dishion, 1992). One would also expect that oppositional behavior is learned through social learning, and that peer influence and television play an important role, but I can't recall any empirical work done along these lines. On the other hand, although hyperactivity is strongly correlated to physical aggression and opposition (Farrington, Loeber, & Van Kammen, 1990; Lahey, McBurnett, & Loeber, 2000; Nagin & Tremblay, 1999), I have not seen any theory linking hyperactivity to television content or peer imitation. Because prescriptions for Ritalin tend to reach a peak for 9- to 10-year-old children (Romano, Baillargeon, Wu, Robaey, & Tremblay, 2002), one could hypothesize that, like aggression and opposition, hyperactivity is something you catch not long after you enter school. However, there have been suggestions that hyperactivity precedes antisocial behaviors such as aggression, and would even be one of the causes of antisocial behavior (e.g., Farrington et al., 1990; Moffitt, 1993).

Thus, if the development of physical aggression, opposition, and hyperactivity was like an illness that starts at a given point in time following an exposure to specific causal factors, the "resiliency" model would posit that some who are exposed get it, while others who are also exposed do not get it. I would argue that we should talk of "resilience" only if most of those who are exposed get it. The resilient ones would be a minority. On the other hand, if it is only a minority of those who are exposed who get it, then the "in" word should be "vulnerable."

Unfortunately, the development of physical aggression does not appear to follow the traditional model of an illness. I believe that we now have enough evidence to confirm that physical aggression, opposition, and hyperactivity are behaviors that appear during infancy in all normally developing children. Clearly, there is much inter-individual variability in the frequency of these behaviors, but infants do not appear to need to be exposed to violence on television, nor to be physically abused by their parents to initiate (onset) hitting, kicking, pushing, pulling, and biting others when angry or when they want to have something. These behaviors start at the end of the first year after birth, and humans appear to be at their peak in frequency of physical aggression between 24 and 42 months after birth (see Tremblay, 2003; and Figure 3-1). The same process appears to apply to opposition and hyperactivity. Children do not need to learn to say no nor learn to throw tantrums (e.g., Goodenough,

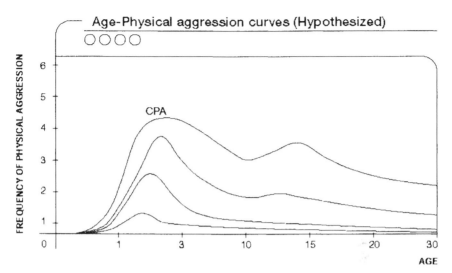

Figure 3-1   Age-physical aggression curves (Hypothesized) (CPA: Chronic physical aggression).

1931; Potegal, 2000). Data from a longitudinal study in Belgium indicates that the developmental trajectories in temper tantrums are very similar to the physical aggression trajectories (Sand, 1966; Tremblay & Nagin, in press). Children also do not need to learn to run. As soon as they start to stand firmly on their feet, they propel themselves on fast forward, using their legs and feet to keep going without stumbling, which they often do. If humans are at their peak in frequency of physical aggression and opposition during toddlerhood, they are also at their peak in frequency of running. This reminds me of an Italian colleague who once came to my house and after having observed squirrels in the garden said in amazement that these animals never walk. Indeed, young children are like squirrels, they run. And parents, rather than teaching them to run say many times a day "Don't run, don't run." At the 2002 meeting of the International Society for Research on Aggression, Shaw, Lacourse, and Nagin (2002) presented trajectories of hyperactivity during early childhood that matched almost perfectly the trajectories of physical aggression during that period.

In summary, disruptive behaviors such as physical aggression, opposition, and hyperactivity are at their peak in frequency during the toddler years. The expression "the terrible twos" probably stuck because it summarizes a phenomenon that all those who have spent some time with young children recognize. From the developmental trajectory work on these behaviors, which started only a few years ago (see

Nagin & Tremblay, 1999), it does not appear that there is any substantial increase in frequency later on in development for any statistically significant group of children (e.g., Broidy et al., 2003; Coté, Tremblay, Nagin, Zoccolillo, & Vitaro, 2002; Shaw, Gilliom, Ingoldsby, & Nagin, 2003). Thus, onset occurs in early childhood long before exposure to violent television, deviant peers, and demanding school performance. And if onset is universal, there are no "resilient" children (in the sense of children who would not exhibit onset of physical aggression, opposition, and hyperactivity) except possibly children who are physically sick to the point that they don't have the energy to do what normal children do.

THE SOCIALIZATION PERSPECTIVE

I have come to the conclusion that what we call disruptive problems are in fact resilience problems, but in the opposite meaning to the one given by "modern" psychology and psychiatry. In fact, after following the development of children for 20 years, I am simply saying what Thomas Hobbes (1641/1998) stated very clearly almost 400 years ago in his insightful treaty on social life and how humans become citizens: "an evil man is rather like a sturdy boy." Disruptive school children, adolescents, and adults are resilient children, they have resisted the socialization process, they remain in their original form. In fact they all eventually become less physically aggressive, less oppositional, and less active, but compared to others they behave more like children, they have remained, more than others, in their "primitive" state. If in the physical illness domain a resilient individual is one whose physiology resists longer to the wear and tear of biological life, in the domain of disruptive behavior the resilient individual is one who is resistant longer to the socialization pressures.

The socialization challenge lies in keeping the energy of the toddler years while channelling them so that they fit in the social fabric. Some children are born with a biological makeup that will easily bend to the pressure of the environment. Yes, they hit, and kick, and run, and say no, but they quickly learn to inhibit these behaviors when they realize that when you hit you may be hit back, when you run you fall and hurt your knees, and when you say no you get a frowning face rather than a smiling face. Other children are born much more "resilient", that is, harder to mold into the social fabric. To use the analogy that Steve Porges uses, they are born with a turbo motor (e.g., Porges, Doussard-Roosevelt, Portales, & Greenspan, 1996; Suomi, in press). When they want something they will cry until they get it, they will run until they catch you, and they will hit you if you don't comply. From day one they are those on the high-level trajectories of physical aggression, hyperactivity, and opposition. They need a very strong environment to get hold of themselves and learn that they must take into account those they are interacting with. Helping these children learn to "self-regulate" and not disrupt their social environment will be more of a challenge. Fortunately in most cases, and unfortunately in other cases, nature has evolved in such a way that children with turbo motors are more likely to have parents with turbo motors (e.g., Caspi et al., 2002; Dionne, Tremblay, Boivin, Laplante, & Pérusse, 2003; Lahey, Piacentini, McBurnett, & Stone, 1988; Rowe & Farrington, 1997). In the fortunate cases, these parents have learned to self-regulate and they will have both the energy and the skills to create an environment which will be appropriate for learning to self-regulate. In the unfortunate cases, the parents have not learned to self-regulate, and the environment they offer the child is so chaotic that the child will, like his parents, be "resilient" with regard to their erratic socialization pressures.

However, although trajectories appear to be set early (see Figure 3-1), we must realize that these trajectories are terrible simplifications of everyday behavior. The best analogy is the Dow-Jones index that investors look at everyday. If we had a daily index of a child's frequency of oppositional behavior or physical aggression, we would see that from day to day it goes up and down, as if it was completely unpredictable. You start seeing some kind of logic only when you step back and look at trends over months and years. The trajectories of disruptive behaviors must be seen in this perspective. Children on the high trajectory of physical aggression are not getting up every morning and hitting everyone they meet during the day, and those on the low trajectory are not spending their days saying yes to all that is asked of them and never pushing others around. We are all born with a motor made to survive in the jungle, and to adapt somewhat to the social environment we are in. Successful socialization provides a veneer over the jungle fabric. I am always amazed to see that this veneer is sufficient to generate a relatively peaceful environment on the street, in public transportation, at the job. But we are all made of that resilient fabric which will unleash the tiger in us if we feel that we are in danger, or if we are prevented from getting something we strongly desire. This is why, if we listen to all the news that can be heard in one day, we will hear daily that someone who has always been a peaceful citizen, a good employee, and a supporting spouse killed his wife and children, or his boss and fellow employees. This is also the reason why prevention by early intervention will have long-term impacts, but will not eradicate the risk of the appearance of disruptive behaviors. We need societies that are constantly aware of the importance of situational prevention. The social fabric needs constant lubrication, otherwise the veneer of some becomes scratched and the resilient fabric plays its role.

HELPING THE "RESILIENT" CHILDREN

If all adults are at risk of being at some point in time "robust children," as Hobbes would say, we can imagine how difficult it is to "behave" for children who did not learn, or rather learned less well when they were young, how to behave in a socially accepted way. Can we help these "resilient" children once they are in the school system? My usual answer to this question is why wait until they get to school? We know that the factors that handicap the socialization process are already being put in place during pregnancy. We know that there are interventions that start during pregnancy and that show long-term impacts (Olds et al., 1998). We know that some interventions during the preschool years have also shown long-term impacts (e.g., Campbell, Pungello, Miller-Johnson, Burchinal, & Ramey, 2001; Campbell, Ramey, Pungello, Sparling, & Miller-Johnson, 2002; Schweinhart, Barnes, & Weikart, 1993). Why wait until they are in school? I guess the answer should be that we are not waiting, that we are providing programs during pregnancy and the preschool years, but that these programs are not reaching all the children that need them, or that these programs are not sufficient for the most "resilient" children. Thus, support programs are needed during the elementary school years.

The Montreal Longitudinal Experimental Study was designed to test to what extent a multimodal intervention for disruptive boys in kindergartens of low socioeconomic area schools would have a long-term impact. When the intervention was planned in the early 1980s, parent training and social skills training were perceived as the alternative to the traditional psychodynamic approach to treating disruptive children (e.g., Meichenbaum, 1977; Michelson, Sugai, Wood, & Kazdin, 1983; Patterson, Reid, Jones, & Conger, 1975). Most experiments targeted either parenting skills or children's social-cognitive skills (e.g., Lochman, Nelson, & Sims, 1981; Patterson et al., 1975). The interventions were also generally aimed at children older than 10 years of age and had a relatively short duration, usually less than 1 year, and often less than 6 months. To increase the chances of having a positive impact on the resilient fabric we decided to target younger children, as well as parents, to include well-adjusted peers, and to maintain the intervention for 2 years.

The parent-training component was based on a model developed at the Oregon Social Learning Center (Patterson, 1982; Patterson et al.,

1975). The procedure involved (a) giving parents a reading program, (b) training parents to monitor their children's behavior, (c) training parents to give positive reinforcement for prosocial behavior, (d) training parents to punish effectively without being abusive, (e) training parents to manage family crises, and (f) helping parents to generalize what they had learned. Having the professional who worked with a family meet the boy's teacher to discuss his adjustment and means of helping him complemented this component. Teachers, however, were generally not able to spend much time discussing teaching strategies for one child, and resources to implement a structured teacher-training program were not available.

Work with parents and teachers was carried out by two university-trained childcare workers, one psychologist, and one social worker, all working full-time. The professionals were trained for 10 months before the start of the program and received regular supervision for the duration of the experiment. Each of these professionals had a caseload of 12 families. The team was coordinated by a fifth professional who worked on the project part-time. Work with the parents was planned to last for 2 school years with one session every 2 or 3 weeks. The professionals, however, were free to decide that a given family needed more or fewer sessions at any given time. The maximum number of sessions given to any family was 46 and the mean number of sessions over the 2 years was 17.4, including families that refused to continue.

The social skills training component was implemented in the schools. One or two disruptive boys were included in groups of three to five peers who were identified by teachers as highly prosocial. The same group of professionals who conducted the parent training offered the social skills training during lunchtime. To create a team approach, different professionals were responsible for the parent and child training with each family. The two professionals responsible for a given family met regularly to discuss treatment strategy. The multidisciplinary team of professionals also met weekly to study a few cases. This helped maintain a consistent treatment approach. For the social skills training component of our intervention, two types of training were given to the disruptive boys within the small group of prosocial peers in school. During the first year, a prosocial skills program was devised, based on other programs (Cartledge & Milburn, 1980; Michelson et al., 1983; Schneider & Byrne, 1987). Nine sessions were given on themes such as "How to make contact," "How to help," "How to ask ⟨⟨why⟩⟩," and "How to invite someone in a group." Coaching, peer modeling, role playing, and reinforcement contingencies were used during these sessions. The program was aimed at self-control during the second year. Using material from previous studies (Camp, Bloom, Hebert, & Van Doorminck, 1977;

Goldstein, Sprafkin, Gershaw, & Klein, 1980; Kettlewell & Kausch, 1983; Meichenbaum, 1977), 10 sessions were developed on themes such as "Look and listen," "Following rules," "What to do when I am angry," "What to do when they do not want me to play with them," and "How to react to teasing." Coaching, peer modeling, self-instructions, behavioral rehearsal, and reinforcement contingencies were also used during these sessions.

From the 1,037 boys assessed in kindergarten, those above the 70th percentile on the kindergarten teacher-rated disruptive behavior scale were randomly allocated to a treatment or control group. At the end of the 2-year intervention and up to the second year after the intervention, no significant differences were observed between the treated and the control groups. Because of these disappointing results, it is likely that the follow-up of the preventive experiment would not have continued had it not been part of a longitudinal study. Most preventive delinquency interventions have follow-up periods of less than 1 year (Tremblay & Craig, 1995; Tremblay, LeMarquand, & Vitaro, 1999).

Three years after the end of the intervention, when most of the boys were in their last year of elementary school, the annual assessments revealed statistically significant positive effects. The boys from the treatment group reported less delinquent behavior, they were rated by their teachers and their peers as being less disruptive, more of them were still in an age-appropriate classroom, and they tended to have less disruptive friends than the control group boys (McCord, Tremblay, Vitaro, & Desmarais-Gervais, 1994; Tremblay et al., 1991, 1992; Vitaro & Tremblay, 1994).

Assessments of the boys up to 17 years of age revealed that the intervention had long-term beneficial influences on the boys' development, but these depended on age, domain, and data source. With respect to global school adjustment, measured by being in an age-appropriate regular classroom, the intervention appeared to have a positive impact before the transition to high school and in the latter part of high school (Tremblay, Vitaro, Nagin, Pagani, & Séguin, 2003). The boys who remained in an age-appropriate regular classroom during elementary school were in a very different social and intellectual environment compared to those who were held back or placed in special classes or schools. The quality of that environment may have had beneficial effects upon other aspects of their development (e.g., self-esteem, attitudes toward school, antisocial behavior). This was confirmed by the school dropout data observed when the boys were 17 years of age: the school dropout rate for the control group was twice as high (21.6%) as the one for the treated group (10.5%) (Vitaro, Brendgen, & Tremblay, 1999).

Antisocial behavior was assessed both with self-reports and court records. The latter did not reveal any significant differences between the groups. One would have hoped that an intensive early intervention with disruptive boys would have reduced the number of boys who were officially treated by the courts as juvenile offenders. Clearly, such a procedure is costly both in terms of social resources and human suffering for the boys and their families. Thus, from the perspective of official delinquency, this type of intervention with these at-risk boys does not appear to have achieved its aim. However, from the perspective of self-reported antisocial behavior, the intervention reduced the number of antisocial behaviors from ages 13 to 17 (Lacourse et al., 2002; Vitaro, Brendgen, & Tremblay, 2001). Path analysis showed that reduction in disruptiveness and increase in parental supervision by age 11, as well as association with nondeviant peers by age 12, were part of a chain of events that was found to mediate the effect of the program on the initial level of antisocial behavior at 13 years. The analysis also showed that the program had an indirect effect through these variables on the growth of delinquency from 13 to 16 years of age.

With developmental trajectory analyses we showed that disruptive kindergarten boys who did not participate in the preventive intervention were at higher risk of following a high-level antisocial trajectory, and less likely to be on a low-level antisocial trajectory (Lacourse et al., 2002). We also tested whether the 2-year (between 7 and 9 years of age) preventive intervention targeting the disruptive kindergarten boys and their families would deflect them to a low-level antisocial behavior trajectory during adolescence. Results did confirm this hypothesis especially for physical aggression. Boys from the intervention group, compared to those from the control group, were more likely to follow the lowest-level trajectory and less likely to follow high-level trajectories. We also did not observe any differences in the probability of following specific physical aggression trajectories between the boys from the intervention group and those who were not among the most disruptive in kindergarten.

I believe this is the first demonstration of an intervention with disruptive elementary school children showing such a significant impact on the developmental course of physical aggression during adolescence. In fact, I have seen no evidence in the literature of any intervention with a long-term follow-up that showed a significant reduction in levels of physical aggression. These results are impressive because the intervention could have had a significant impact by simply deflecting some of the high-risk boys from a medium-level trajectory to a low trajectory. However, the results show that the disruptive boys who participated in the intervention were deflected from high-level trajectories to lower-level trajectories. Interestingly, we did not observe a significant impact of the intervention on the developmental trajectories of theft. Thus, the parent training and social skills training which was attempting to reduce disruptive behaviors such as physical aggression, opposition, and hyperactivity did not change an antisocial behavior which is considered "covert" rather than "overt" (Loeber & Schmaling, 1985). Taking away things from others is a behavior that starts as early as physically aggressing others (Tremblay, Japel, et al., 1999; Tremblay, 2004). In early childhood behavior is rarely covert, but as children become more cognitively sophisticated and learn to delay gratification, they will try to get others' possessions without confronting them directly. The best evidence of this transformation of open antisocial behavior to covert antisocial behavior is the development of indirect aggression (i.e., covert manipulative behaviors, such as spreading rumors, getting others to dislike a person, becoming friends with another person as a form of revenge, etc...). As the frequency of physical aggression decreases with age, the frequency of indirect aggression increases (Tremblay et al., 1996; Vaillancourt, in press). Thus the socialization process does have some impact, but the resilience of the jungle fabric is such that more sophisticated ways are developed to achieve the old "primitive" goals.

CONCLUSION

I have argued in this chapter that the "resilience" concept, which is possibly at the peak of its fashion, could not be applied to the development of disruptive behaviors unless we accept that it means the reverse of the meaning usually given to "resilience" by psychologists and psychiatrists, and sometimes by physical health specialists. This is because disruptive behavior is not an illness one catches and then attempts to get rid of in order to return to the initial state of health. Disruptive behaviors are rather something you are born with, an initial state, and you have to work hard at getting rid of them. In fact these behaviors are so "resilient" that you never get rid of them, you simply keep them in check by constant self-regulation. If the word "resilient" is used to mean "to recover an original form or state, after having been submitted to forces that could make you lose that original state," then saying that a child who has learned not to physically aggress others is "resilient" does not make sense. The whole exercise of education and growing up is to get rid of your original state. Children who do not learn *not* to cry and scream when they are angry are resilient, children who do not learn to talk are resilient, children who remain illiterate after having been taught to read and write are resilient.

From this perspective, prevention of disruptive behavior problems should not be seen as an effort to prevent innocent young children from learning from parents, siblings, peers or television how to aggress against others or how to refuse to obey rules. Prevention of disruptive behavior is, in fact, what used to be called "moral education": the process by which children learn how to behave in a way that will enable them to be accepted and even appreciated by their social environment. Since children are not born socialized, it is not a state they risk losing, it is a state they need to acquire, and the later they receive the proper support (education), the less likely they are to master these very sophisticated and terribly important skills for a citizen.

"I can say in my own favour that I was as a boy humane, but I owed this entirely to the instruction and example of my sisters. I doubt indeed whether humanity is a natural or innate quality." (Charles Darwin, 1876/1983, p. 11)

ACKNOWLEDGMENTS

The author wishes to thank the following persons who have made important contributions to the research and ideas presented in this chapter: Sylvana Côté, Éric Lacourse, Katia Maliantovitch, Daniel Nagin, Francisco Quiazua, Jean Séguin, Tracy Vaillancourt, and Frank Vitaro.

REFERENCES

Bandura, A. (1973). *Aggression: A social learning analysis.* New York: Holt.

Bandura, A., Ross, D., & Ross, S. A. (1961). Transmission of aggression through imitation of aggressive models. *Journal of Abnormal and Social Psychology, 63,* 575–582.

Broidy, L. M., Nagin, D. S., Tremblay, R. E., Brame, B., Dodge, K., Fergusson, D., et al. (2003). Developmental trajectories of childhood disruptive behaviors and adolescent delinquency: A six site, cross national study. *Developmental Psychology, 39,* 222–245.

Camp, B. W., Blom, G. E., Hebert, F., & Van Doorminck, W. J. (1977). Think Aloud: A program for developing self-control in young aggressive boys. *Journal of Abnormal Child Psychology, 5,* 157–169.

Campbell, F. A., Pungello, E. P., Miller-Johnson, S., Burchinal, M., & Ramey, C. T. (2001). The development of cognitive and academic abilities: Growth curves from an early childhood educational experiment. *Developmental Psychology, 47,* 231–242.

Campbell, F. A., Ramey, C. T., Pungello, E. P., Sparling, J., & Miller-Johnson, S. (2002). Early childhood education: Young adult outcomes from the Abecederian project. *Applied Developmental Science, 6,* 42–57.

Cartledge, G., & Milburn, J. F. (1980). *Teaching social skills to children. Innovative approaches.* New York: Pergamon Press.

Caspi, A., McClay, J., Moffitt, T., Mill, J., Martin, J., Craig, I. W., et al. (2002). Role of genotype in the cycle of violence in maltreated children. *Science, 297,* 851–854.

Côté, S., Tremblay, R. E., Nagin, D. S., Zoccolillo, M., & Vitaro, F. (2002). Childhood behavioral profiles leading to adolescent conduct disorder: Risk trajectories for boys and girls. *Journal of the American Academy of Child and Adolescent Psychiatry, 41,* 1086–1094.

Darwin, C. (1876/1983). *Autobiography.* Oxford, UK: Oxford University Press.

Dionne, G., Tremblay, R. E., Boivin, M., Laplante, D., & Pérusse, D. (2003). Physical aggression and expressive vocabulary in 19 month-old twins. *Developmental Psychology, 39,* 261–273.

Eron, L. D. (1982). Parent-child interaction, television violence, and aggression of children. *American Psychologist, 37,* 197–211.

Farrington, D. P., Loeber, R., & Van Kammen, W. B. (1990). The long term criminal outcomes of conduct problem boys with or without impulsive-inattentive behavior. In L. N. Robins & M. Rutter (Eds.), *Straight and devious pathways from childhood to adulthood* (pp. 62–81). New York: Cambridge University Press.

Goldstein, A. P., Sprafkin, R. P., Gershaw, N. J., & Klein, P. (1980). The adolescent: Social skills training through structured learning. In G. Cartledge & J. F. Milburn (Eds.), *Teaching social skills to children: Innovative approaches* (pp. 249–277). New York: Pergamon Press.

Goodenough, F. L. (1931). *Anger in young children.* Westport, CT: Greenwood Press.

Hobbes, T. (1641/1998). *On the citizen.* Cambridge: Cambridge University Press.

Huesmann, L. R., & Eron, L. D. (1986). *Television and the aggressive child: A cross-national comparison.* Hillsdale, NJ: Erlbaum.

Johnson, J. G., Cohen, P., Smailes, E. M., Kasen, S., & Brook, J. S. (2002). Television viewing and aggressive behavior during adolescence and adulthood. *Science, 295,* 2468–2471.

Kettlewell, P. W., & Kausch, D. F. (1983). The generalization of the effects of a cognitive-behavioral treatment program for aggressive children. *Journal of Abnormal Child Psychology, 11,* 101–114.

Lacourse, E., Côté, S., Nagin, D. S., Vitaro, F., Brendgen, M., & Tremblay, R. E. (2002). A longitudinal-experimental approach to testing theories of antisocial behavior development. *Development and Psychopathology, 14,* 909–924.

Lahey, B. B., Piacentini, J. C., McBurnett, K., & Stone, P. (1988). Psychopathology in the parents of children with conduct disorder and hyperactivity. *Journal of the American Academy of Child and Adolescent Psychiatry, 27,* 163–170.

Lahey, B. B., McBurnett, K., & Loeber, R. (2000). Are attention-deficit hyperactivity disorder and oppositional defiant disorder developmental precursors to conduct disorder? In A. Sameroff, M. Lewis, & S. Miller (Eds.), *Handbook of developmental psychopathology* (pp. 431–446). New York: Plenum Press.

Lavigueur, S., Saucier, J. F., & Tremblay, R. E. (1995). Supporting fathers and supported mothers in families with disruptive boys: Who are they? *Journal of Child Psychology and Psychiatry, 36,* 1003–1018.

Lavigueur, S., Tremblay, R. E., & Saucier, J. F. (1995). Interactional processes in families with disruptive boys: Patterns of direct and indirect influence. *Journal of Abnormal Child Psychology, 23,* 359–378.

Leblanc, M., McDuff, P., Charlebois, P., Gagnon, C., Larivée, S., & Tremblay, R. E. (1991). Social and psychological consequences, at 10 years old, of an earlier onset of self-reported delinquency. *Psychiatry, 54,* 133–147.

Lochman, J. E., Nelson, W. M., & Sims, J. E. (1981). A cognitive behavioral program for use with aggressive children. *Journal of Clinical Psychology, 10,* 146–148.

Loeber, R., & Schmaling, K. B. (1985). Empirical evidence for overt and covert patterns of antisocial conduct problems: A meta-analysis. *Journal of Abnormal Child Psychology, 13,* 337–352.

Magnusson, D. (1988). *Individual development from an interactional perspective: A longitudinal study.* Hillsdale, NJ: Erlbaum.

Magnusson, D., & Bergman, L. R. (1990). A pattern approach to the study of pathways from childhood to adulthood. In L. N. Robins & M. Rutter (Eds.), *Straight and devious pathways from childhood to adulthood* (pp. 101–116). New York: Cambridge University Press.

Magnusson, D., & Stattin, H. (1998). Person-context interaction theories. In W. Damon & R. M. Lerner (Eds.), *Handbook of child psychology: Vol. 1. Theoretical models of human development* (5th ed., pp. 713–749). New York: Wiley.

Magnusson, D., Dunér, A., & Zetterblom, G. (1975). *Adjustment: A longitudinal study.* New York: Wiley.

Magnusson, D., Klinteberg, B., & Stattin, H. (1992). Autonomic activity/reactivity, behavior, and crime in a longitudinal perspective. In J. McCord (Ed.), *Facts, frameworks, and forecasts. Vol. 3. Advances in criminological theory* (pp. 287–318). New Brunswick, NJ: Transaction Publishers.

McCord, J., Tremblay, R. E., Vitaro, F., & Desmarais-Gervais, L. (1994). Boys' disruptive behavior, school adjustment, and delinquency: The Montreal prevention experiment. *International Journal of Behavioral Development, 17,* 739–752.

Meichenbaum, D. (1977). *Cognitive-behavior modification: An integrative approach.* New York: Plenum Press.

Michelson, L., Sugai, D., Wood, R., & Kazdin, A. E. (1983). *Social skills assessment and training with children.* New York: Plenum Press.

Moffitt, T. E. (1993). The neuropsychology of conduct disorder. *Development and Psychopathology, 5,* 135–151.

Murray, B. (2003). Rebounding from losses: Psychologists share how they've applied resilience-building strategies from APA's public education campaign. *Monitor on Psychology, 34,* 42–43.

Nagin, D., & Tremblay, R. E. (1999). Trajectories of boys' physical aggression, opposition, and hyperactivity on the path to physically violent and nonviolent juvenile delinquency. *Child Development, 70,* 1181–1196.

Olds, D., Henderson, C. R., Cole, R., Eckenrode, J., Kitzman, H., Luckey, D., et al. (1998). Long-term effects of nurse home visitation on children's criminal and antisocial behavior: Fifteen-year follow-up of a randomized controlled trial. *Journal of the American Medical Association, 280,* 1238–1244.

Patterson, G. R. (1982). *A social learning approach to family intervention: Vol. 3. Coercive family process.* Eugene, OR: Castalia.

Patterson, G. R., Reid, J. B., Jones, R. R., & Conger, R. R. (1975). *A social learning approach to family intervention: Vol. 1. Families with aggressive children.* Eugene, OR: Castalia.

Patterson, G. R., Reid, J. B., & Dishion, T. J. (1992). *Antisocial boys.* Eugene, OR: Castalia.

Porges, S. W., Doussard-Roosevelt, J. A., Portales, A. L., & Greenspan, S. I. (1996). Infant regulation of the vagal "brake" predicts child behavior problems: A psychobiological model of social behavior. *Developmental Psychobiology, 29,* 697–712.

Potegal, M. (2000). Toddler tantrums: Flushing and other visible autonomic activity in anger-crying complex. In R. G. Barr, B. Hopkins, & J. A. Green (Eds.), *Crying as a sign, a symptom, and a signal: Clinical, emotional, and developmental aspects of infant and toddler crying. Clinics in developmental medicine, No. 152* (pp. 121–136). London: MacKeith Press.

Romano, E., Baillargeon, R., Wu, H. X., Robaey, P., & Tremblay, R. E. (2002). Prevalence of methylphenidate use and change over a two-year period: A nationwide study of 2- to 11-year-old Canadian children. *Journal of Pediatrics, 4,* 71–75.

Rowe, D. C., & Farrington, D. P. (1997). The familial transmission of criminal convictions. *Criminology, 35,* 177–201.

Sand, E. A. (1966). *Contribution à l'étude du développement de l'enfant. Aspects médico-sociaux et psychologiques.* Bruxelles, Belgium: Éditions de l'Institut de sociologie de l'Université libre de Bruxelles.

Schaal, B., Tremblay, R. E., Soussignan, R., & Susman, E. J. (1996). Male testosterone linked to high social dominance but low physical aggression in early adolescence. *Journal of the American Academy of Child and Adolescent Psychiatry, 35,* 1322–1330.

Schneider, B. H., & Byrne, B. M. (1987). Individualizing social skills training for behavior-disordered children. *Journal of Consulting and Clinical Psychology, 55,* 444–445.

Schweinhart, L. L., Barnes, H. V., & Weikart, D. P. (1993). *Significant benefits. The High/Scope Perry School Study through age 27.* Ypsilanti, MI: High/Scope Press.

Shaw, D., Lacourse, E., & Nagin, D. S. (2002, July). *Developmental trajectories of overt conduct problems and ADHD from ages 2 to 10.* Paper presented at the International Society for Research on Aggression XV World Meeting, Montréal, Canada.

Shaw, D. S., Gilliom, M., Ingoldsby, E. M., & Nagin, D. S. (2003). Trajectories leading to school-age conduct problems. *Developmental Psychology, 39,* 189–200.

Suomi, S. J. (in press). Genetic and environmental factors influencing the expression of impulsive aggression and serotonergic functioning in rhesus monkeys. In R. E. Tremblay, W. W. Hartup, & J. Archer (Eds.), *Developmental origins of aggressive behavior.* New York: Guilford Press.

Tisseron, S. (2003, August). "Résilience" ou la lutte pour la vie (⟨⟨Resilience⟩⟩ or the fight for life). *Le Monde diplomatique, 21.*

Tremblay, R. E. (2003). Why socialization fails?: The case of chronic physical aggression. In B. B. Lahey, T. E. Moffitt, & A. Caspi (Eds.), *Causes of conduct disorder and juvenile delinquency* (pp. 182–224). New York: Guilford Press.

Tremblay, R. E. (2004). The development of human physical aggression: How important is early childhood? In L. A. Leavitt & D. M. B. Hall (Eds.), *Social and moral development: Emerging evidence on the toddler years* (pp. 221–238). New Brunswick, NJ: Johnson and Johnson Pediatric Institute.

Tremblay, R. E., & Craig, W. (1995). Developmental crime prevention. In M. Tonry & D. P. Farrington (Eds.), *Building a safer society: Strategic approaches to crime prevention* (Vol. 19, pp. 151–236). Chicago: The University of Chicago Press.

Tremblay, R. E., & Nagin, D. S. (in press). The developmental origins of physical aggression in humans. In R. E. Tremblay, W. H. Hartup, & J. Archer (Eds.), *Developmental origins of aggression.* New York: Guilford Press.

Tremblay, R. E., Mâsse, B., Perron, D., LeBlanc, M., Schwartzman, A. E., & Ledingham, J. E. (1992). Early disruptive behavior, poor school achievement, delinquent behavior and delinquent personality: Longitudinal analyses. *Journal of Consulting and Clinical Psychology, 60,* 64–72.

Tremblay, R. E., McCord, J., Boileau, H., Charlebois, P., Gagnon, C., LeBlanc, M., et al. (1991). Can disruptive boys be helped to become competent? *Psychiatry, 54,* 148–161.

Tremblay, R. E., Pihl, R. O., Vitaro, F., & Dobkin, P. L. (1994). Predicting early onset of male antisocial behavior from preschool behavior. *Archives of General Psychiatry, 51,* 732–738.

Tremblay, R. E., Mâsse, L. C., Vitaro, F., & Dobkin, P. L. (1995). The impact of friends' deviant behavior on early onset of delinquency: Longitudinal data from 6 to 13 years of age. *Development and Psychopathology, 7,* 649–668.

Tremblay, R. E., Boulerice, B., Harden, P. W., McDuff, P., Pérusse, D., Pihl, R. O., et al. (1996). Do children in Canada become more aggressive as they approach adolescence? In Human Resources Development Canada & Statistics Canada (Eds.), *Growing up in Canada: National Longitudinal Survey of Children and Youth* (pp. 127–137). Ottawa: Statistics Canada.

Tremblay, R. E., Japel, C., Pérusse, D., McDuff, P., Boivin, M., Zoccolillo, M., et al. (1999). The search for the age of "onset" of physical aggression: Rousseau and Bandura revisited. *Criminal Behavior and Mental Health, 9,* 8–23.

Tremblay, R. E., LeMarquand, D., & Vitaro, F. (1999). The prevention of ODD and CD. In H. C. Quay & A. E. Hogan (Eds.), *Handbook of disruptive behavior disorders* (pp. 525–555). New York: Kluwer Academic/Plenum Publishers.

Tremblay, R. E., Vitaro, F., Nagin, D. S., Pagani, L., & Séguin, J. R. (2003). The Montreal longitudinal and experimental study: Rediscovering the power of descriptions. In T. Thornberry & M. Krohn (Eds.), *Taking stock of delinquency: An overview of findings from contemporary longitudinal stud*ies (pp. 205–254). New York: Kluwer Academic/Plenum Publishers.

Vaillancourt, T. (in press). Indirect aggression among humans: Social construct or evolutionary adaptation? In R. E. Tremblay, W. W. Hartup, & J. Archer (Eds.), *Developmental origins of aggressive behavior.* New York: Guilford Press.

Vitaro, F., & Tremblay, R. E. (1994). Impact of a prevention program on aggressive children's friendships and social adjustment. *Journal of Abnormal Child Psychology, 22,* 457–475.

Vitaro, F., Tremblay, R. E., Kerr, M., Pagani-Kurtz, L., & Bukowski, W. M. (1997). Disruptiveness, friends' characteristics, and delinquency: A test of two competing models of development. *Child Development, 68,* 676–689.

Vitaro, F., Brendgen, M., & Tremblay, R. E. (1999). Prevention of school dropout through the reduction of disruptive behaviors and school failure in elementary school. *Journal of School Psychology, 37,* 205–226.

Vitaro, F., Brendgen, M., & Tremblay, R. E. (2001). Preventive intervention: Assessing its effects on the trajectories of delinquency and testing for mediational processes. *Applied Developmental Science, 5,* 201–213.

Werner, E. E., & Smith, R. S. (1982). *Vulnerable but invincible: A study of resilient children.* New York: McGraw-Hill.

CHAPTER 4

The Resilience Revolution

A Paradigm Shift for Research and Policy?

BONNIE LEADBEATER, DAN DODGEN,
& ANDREA SOLARZ

As is clearly indicated in the chapters of this volume, research on resilience has sought to explain why some (often the majority) of individuals show adaptive functioning in the context of adverse circumstances. A central goal of resilience research is to increase knowledge
not only about the strengths or competencies of individuals, families,
and communities but also the conditions or *contexts* that are necessary
to maintain, promote, or enhance strengths and competent functioning
in the face of adversity. This research has also begun to identify the
protective *processes* that operate at individual, family, and community
levels to enable adaptive functioning over the long term. These contributions have lead to a shift in emphasis beyond (but not excluding)
the rich foundation of research that has illuminated the risks, problems,
and negative consequences that can result from the effects of living with
chronic stress, adversities or traumas.[1]

We will argue that research on the concept of resilience also demands a paradigm shift in our approaches to research, policy, and

[1]This chapter builds on the collaborative work of an American Psychological Association
Task Force that has joined resources from the Divisions of Child, Youth, and Family Ser-
vices (Division 37) and the Society for Community Research and Action (Division 27).
This union has produced an edited volume entitled *"Investing in Children, Youth, Fam-
ilies, and Communities: Strengths-Based Research and Policy"* (Maton, Schellenbach,
Leadbeater, & Solarz, 2004).

programs that seek to understand and alleviate the negative consequences of a wide range of social problems. This research raises questions about several time-honored and fundamental principles of scientific research and challenges our past, almost exclusive, emphasis on
large-scale generalizability; comparisons between groups of individuals with successful versus unsuccessful outcomes; and characteristics
of individuals. It focuses our attention on the diversity of responses to
adverse experiences, and we need to know more about the characteristics of the adversities themselves. We also need to undertake individual,
family, and community levels of analyses, and to investigate long-term
processes of change that support and sustain adaptive functioning in
the long term.

To make these differences in focus concrete in an example, we can
consider the research on domestic violence. This research has traditionally investigated the personality or behavioral characteristics of men
who assault their intimate partners in contrast to other men or of women
who remain in abusive relationships in contrast to women who leave.
From a resilience perspective, we need to know more about the competencies as well as the family and community resources of women
(actually the majority) who leave abusive relationships. One study of
women who left abusive relationships showed that they had made, on
average, 3.3 attempts before successfully leaving (Dutton, Goodman, &
Bennett, 1999). This suggests that we need to understand more about
the diversity in help-seeking efforts of these women and the supports
for and obstacles to their success. Recent research has shown that limited choices, financial insecurity, mental or physical health problems,
inadequate access to resources (transportation, child care, family support), police attitudes or inaction, and slow criminal justice responses
all compound the adversities experienced by women who are assaulted
by an intimate partner (Cook, Woolard, & McCollum, 2004). This work
suggests that we need to look both at and beyond individuals' and families' capacities for adaptive functioning in contexts of adversity towards
the systems and institutional responses that build on or serve to challenge these capacities. The long-term consequences of women's choices
for themselves and their children are also not well understood (Cook
et al., 2004; Leadbeater & Way, 2001).

In this chapter, we argue that the paradigm shift brought about by
resilience research requires changes in our approach to research, policy, and programs (see Table 4-1). While not ignoring problems, deficits,
or deviance of the individuals, there is a need for more research that
focuses our attention on a) the diversity of individual, family, and community responses to adverse circumstances rather than just generalized
population risks; b) the strengths, competencies, and resources needed

Table 4-1   The Scientific Revolution: Expanding the Focus of Risk Research

Risks-Based Focuses on	Strengths-Based Focuses on
Generalizable or population risks	Diversity of characteristics of adversities and responses
Deficits, deviance, and pathology	Strengths and competencies
Targets individuals and/or dysfunctional families	Targets individual, family, and community interrelations
Modeling multivariate risk and protective factors	Illuminating mechanisms of change
Immediate outcomes	Life-span pathways

for dealing with adversities rather than just the deficits, pathologies, and deviance that can result from them; c) the long-term pathways or life-span trajectories that are affected by variations in response to adversities rather than just the immediate outcomes; and d) on the inter-relations among individual, family, and community levels of development rather than just the characteristics of adapted individuals. It also requires policy decisions that take a strengths-based approach in supporting the resources of individuals, families, and communities and that anticipate and strive to affect the long-term consequences. Resilience research also requires that we rethink interventions aimed at solutions to societal problems. With a strengths-based gaze, our attention is broadened beyond the challenges of fixing individuals' deficits and pathologies or punishing their deviance towards the ways to support key protective processes and life-span, adaptive outcomes for individuals, families, and communities who are facing adverse circumstances. These outcomes depend on the collaboration of those affected by adversities as active decision makers and participants in change rather than as merely the recipients of services.

THE RESILIENCE REVOLUTION: HOW HAS RESEARCH CHANGED?

One more example sets the stage for understanding the nature of this scientific revolution as a paradigm shift from an exclusive focus on risks to an emerging focus on strengths. While teen parenting was, and often still is, considered to be a marker of a general problem behavior syndrome for girls that might also include promiscuity, school dropout, alcohol abuse, and delinquency (Woodward & Fergusson, 1999), recent research suggests that there is considerable diversity in both the precursors to unwanted teen pregnancies and the outcomes for adolescent mothers. Indeed, the majority of young mothers are not engaged in problem behaviors; they are working to complete high school and are competent parents. What we have overlooked in our focus on risk statistics particularly for minority group, poor, inner-city mothers is that many do not manifest the stereotypic negative outcomes (Furstenberg, Brooks-Gunn, & Morgan, 1980; Hamburg, 1986; Leadbeater & Way, 2001). Focusing on subgroup differences in outcomes illuminates the extent of the adversities that are experienced by some young mothers, as well as the strength-building processes that affect the outcomes for them. Becoming an adolescent parent can compound multiple, preexisting adversities (e.g., inner-city poverty, minority status, learning disabilities, school failure, and housing instability), or it can contribute to reduced problem behaviors as it inspires some young women to make something of themselves on behalf of their children (Leadbeater & Way, 2001). Lifespan outcomes are not static; rather, they follow pathways or trajectories that build on past experiences and anticipate the future. Developmental pathways can be affected positively or negatively by turning points (like having a baby while a teenager), but they are built on the context of past adversities and resources of individuals, their families, and their communities and they relate to the future opportunities that are available.

Understanding the Diversity of Individual Responses to Adversity

Difference in responses to adversities *within* populations challenge the generalizability and often the validity of risk-based statistics. Adversities can have very different effects for individuals, families, or communities with or without resources to deal with them. But how should research change? Focusing on within-group differences forces us to ask which individuals, families, or communities who are coping with what adverse circumstances will experience negative or positive outcomes. Finding appropriate comparison groups has long haunted research methodology in applied settings. Too often, comparisons of groups experiencing challenging circumstances (e.g., poor teenage mothers) are compared to apparently normative groups (e.g., poor women who delayed child bearing). Not surprisingly the "at-risk" group is found to be, on average, deficient or deviant in some way (such as having lower levels of education, income, or poorer parenting skills). This is problematic and can misguide public opinion and policy when, despite higher risk, the *majority* in the "defective" group are very similar to the normative one. While 1987 statistics (Alan Guttmacher Institute, 1994) showed that teen mothers are at risk for not finishing high school (29% did not finish) when compared to women who give birth at age 20 or over (9% did not finish), the large majority of teenage mothers (71%) did in fact earn a high school diploma. With our emphasis on risk, we know very little about the experiences of the majority of young mothers who graduate or about the one in five teen mothers who go on to college. What supports would be needed to make these normal transitions to adulthood possible for all young mothers? Both adversities (e.g., welfare status, school dropout) and competencies (e.g., social skills, acquiring human capital) are not static events even for teenage mothers (Schellenbach, Leadbeater, & McCollum, 2004).

The status of risks, protective factors, and outcomes changes over time. In the New York study of teenage mothers (Leadbeater & Way, 2001), 41% of the mothers had continuously attended school throughout the pregnancy and the first year postpartum; 21% dropped out during the pregnancy or early postpartum period but returned by the time their child was one year old; 12% of mothers dropped out before the pregnancy and did not return; 26% of mothers dropped out of school during the pregnancy or early postpartum period and did not return. At 3 years postpartum, there was considerable stability in these groupings: 78% of the mothers remained in the group they had been in at 12-months postpartum (Leadbeater, 1996). The effects of several variables including whether the teen lived with her mother, the quality of their relationship, the presence of support from friends and boyfriends, levels of self-reported stress and depressive symptoms, the number of repeat pregnancies, and occupational aspirations or commitment helped to predict school outcomes for these mothers. However, when the teen's grade placement before the delivery (ideal grade for age minus last grade completed; i.e., an assessment of prior school performance) was entered into this equation, it was found to be the *only* independent predictor of the mothers' delayed grade placement at 1 and 3 years postpartum (Leadbeater, 1996) and it remained a strong predictor of educational achievement at the 6-year follow-up (Leadbeater, 1996, 1998; Way & Leadbeater, 1999). Trajectories for school engagement and school outcome expectations are established in elementary school, and these may be better targets for policy and programming hoping to affect long-term welfare use than targets that focus on reducing benefits for teenage mothers.

Understanding the Complex Nature of Adversities

Findings of within-group differences also require that we refine our understanding of the nature of adversities. What constitutes adversity? What constitutes exposure? Establishing the magnitude of risks or thresholds of exposure has not been the focus of much attention.

We know that contexts of adversity are not static or unidimensional. Family violence can range from a single episode to long-term abuse. Divorce can have negative or positive effects on children's development, for example, by increasing the likelihood of living in poverty or providing relief from family conflict, respectively (Braver, Hipke, Ellman, & Sandler, 2004).

Definitions of adversities have emphasized their differential impact on individuals' competencies, but variations in the adversities themselves are often not addressed. Adversities comprise either a significant threat to an individual (e.g., urban poverty, teenage parent) or exposure to severe adversity or trauma (e.g., parental illness, abuse, divorce) (Masten & Coatsworth, 1998). What Ann Masten (2001, p. 30) has called the "ordinary magic" of resilience that emerges from "the normal operation of ordinary protective systems" is compromised under the extraordinary conditions created by *simultaneous* exposure to multiple risks, or severe traumas. Sandler, Ayers, Suter, Schultz, and Twohey-Jacobs (2004) also focus our attention on the influence of person-environment relations in defining adversities. They argue that adversities refer to environments in which individuals' basic human needs, motivations, and goals are not satisfied and in which competencies to carry out valued social roles are not developed.

Adversities, like strengths, are not present or absent. Developmental outcomes for individuals, families, or communities involve feedback loops in which adversities are affected by and affect ongoing processes of changes in both individual competencies and the circumstances in which they function. These processes create multiple chances for competent functioning or recovery and suggest points for interventions that target not only individuals but also adversities and protective systems. For example, maternal mental illnesses, like depression, may affect children's development, but its impact can be mediated through family education and enhanced supports (e.g., child care) that enable positive parenting and reduce stresses that trigger depressive episodes (Beardslee & Knitzer, 2004). We need to know more about these ordinary protective systems, including how they are disabled and how they can be supported.

Also of concern when defining adversity are the points at which individual, family, or community levels of competence are overwhelmed. Research has demonstrated that the negative effects of multiple risk factors increase factorially, rather than additively, in creating challenges to children's development (Gorman-Smith, Tolan, & Henry, current volume; Sandler et al., 2004; Tolan, Sherrod, Gorman-Smith, & Henry, 2004). The effects of resilient personal characteristics (such as intelligence, optimism, internal locus of control, and interpersonal skills) or even family characteristics (such as parenting warmth) can be blunted by the extreme stress associated with living in inner-city, economically deprived neighborhoods (Tolan et al., 2004). Multiple forms of stresses including negative life events, daily hassles, chronic stresses, and role strain are founded in the social, educational, and economic base of inner-city communities. These adversities intersect with developmental outcomes for children in these communities through their experiences as victims of, and witnesses to, high levels of violence; less than adequate access to conventional levels of classroom instruction, school supplies, safe buildings, and after-school activities; daily encounters with family economic strains and resulting parenting stress; isolation from supportive networks of neighbors or extended family; lack of opportunities for success; inadequate adult supervision; health compromising or disorganized environments; and insufficient access to health care (Gorman-Smith et al., this volume; Perkins, Florin, Rich, Wandersman, & Chavis, 1990; Tolan et al., 2004). Exposure to unconventional peer socialization can also add to the cycling of adversities for inner-city youth (Kupersmidt, Coie, & Howell, 2004). Individual efforts to cope with or adapt to the challenges of these stresses in order to meet basic needs for safety, food, affiliation, and housing (e.g., through illegal activities or gang involvement) can take priority over actions that may be more effective in the long term in diminishing these stressors (e.g., college attendance). Without clearly identifying and addressing the adversities that characterize many poor, inner-city communities, individual coping capacities must deal with short-term goals. The possibilities for long-term adaptive functioning are compromised. One of the young mothers in the New York study explains this difference between living day-to-day and building a rock to stand on in the future as she describes what it means to her to grow up and become "independent." Quoted in Leadbeater and Way (2001, pp. 47–48), Charise says;

> I'm not helpless and ... in order to go somewhere you have to come from somewhere and you have to make a rock for yourself to stand on. Basically, I feel I've done that ... Like, if you're not independent, you have no worries, no plans for tomorrow, nothing to look forward to, like, you're just living on a day-to-day basis. And basically, I'm not. I know what the future holds and I know what everyday life is and basically I can see that this is for today, but I know I'm going to need this for tomorrow.

Focusing on Developmental Trajectories and Processes of Long-Term Changes

The extensive study of characteristics of resilient individuals (intelligence, optimism, social supports) has created the foundation for current research on the developmental processes or mechanisms that modify person-environment responses to adverse circumstances. The acquisition and maintenance of competence is a function of the risk and protective processes that are encountered by individuals, families and communities over time. From a process-oriented perspective, the concept of resilience must be set in motion to address intra-individual continuities and discontinuities in adaptive behaviors over the life-span. Variations reflect the multiple, co-occurring risk and protective processes created by changing individual, family, and community circumstances (see Leadbeater, Schellenbach, Maton, & Dodgen, 2004). Families and communities also follow predictable trajectories in their responses to the adversities or risks and protective processes that they encounter over time. Understanding the continuities, discontinuities, and individual differences in strengths and competencies, as well as the resources that maintain or promote adequate functioning in the face of adversity, all need to be the focus of more targeted research efforts.

However, the complexity of the co-occurring and transacting processes that promote individual, family, and community strengths often challenges the ability of individual researchers to investigate or understand them. No one university discipline or community organization can develop the understanding and skills needed to promote individual, family, and community strengths. Interdisciplinary, community-based collaborations need to be fostered by universities, communities, and funding agencies (see Peters, this volume). These collaborations can bring together researchers with expertise in many different disciplines and methodologies (e.g., public health surveys, longitudinal and quasi-experimental designs, and ethnography) that are needed to illuminate within-group differences and resilience processes. Professional workshops are also needed for researchers to feel comfortable with and responsible for the translation of research evidence into action (e.g., talking to the media, preparing research briefs, and educating the public).

THE POLICY REVOLUTION: WHAT DOES RESILIENCE MEAN FOR POLICY MAKERS?

Policy making both marches ahead of scientific research and lags behind it. Public policy often sets agendas and priorities for research questions and funding but it may also set agendas for programming before there is adequate scientific knowledge. Why? Gaps in policy and research stem from differences in their settings, goals, priorities, orientations, methods, and time schedules (e.g., see Shonkoff, 2000). Institutionalizing the gaps between the two worlds, the major players in research and policy are segregated into separate spheres of practice (universities versus government agencies), where they utilize different sources of information and develop divergent sets of terminology. Policy makers make decisions that have immediate effects on such things as the distribution of tax dollars in ways intended to advance public welfare or serve a particular constituency. Plights of individuals, bottom lines, popular opinion, and economic concerns weigh in heavily in their decision-making processes. Policy dialogue takes the form of verbal debates, often among strongly held views and competing interests.

Although many policy makers would agree that scientific research is important to their decision making, their access to scientific knowledge is limited by the very scientific processes that are designed to ensure its validity. Research is oriented toward the generation, and frequently regeneration, of knowledge in changing social circumstances. Paradigmatic research methods are time consuming and focus on the verification or certainty of knowledge claims. Research dialogue is fueled by funding decisions, data collection, systematic analyses, and peer reviews of written findings. Despite these differences, however, a reconciliation of the disparate research and policy universes is overdue.

Policy and program efforts directed at supporting family, community, or institutional strengths can also have effects on individuals (Duncan & Brooks-Gunn, 2000; Zigler & Hall, 2000). Research on the consequences of the quality of school environments (Smith, Boutte, Zigler & Finn-Stevenson, 2004) and the timing of middle school transitions (Eccles, Lord, Roeser, Barber, & Hernandez Jozefowicz; 1997; Seidman, Aber, & French, 2004) provide salient examples of how institutional polices can have direct effects on children's development. For example, decisions about when children move from elementary schools to middle schools have been largely based on economic, space, and staffing concerns. These transitions vary from as early as 5th grade to as late as 8th grade. Declines in academic competence and engagement that are frequently observed at the time of middle school transitions were previously thought to be a consequence of individual students' inability to handle a more difficult curriculum. Characteristics of the school setting (such as teacher attitudes and support, classroom size, community involvement, and school climate) and curriculum (such as cultural relevance of instructional methods and content) were rarely considered (Smith et al., 2004). However, the match (or mismatch) of school transitions with developmental concerns of early adolescence appears to be important. Early transitions that coincide with the biological, cognitive, and interpersonal changes that are also occurring at different rates among children ages 10 to 14 can set in motion processes of disengagement from schools for some children that can have long-term negative consequences. Research shows that some children who make the transition to middle school in early adolescence show decrements in academic performance, and are more likely to drop out of school and to have declines in self-esteem compared to students who attended schools with a kindergarten to 8th and 9th to 12th grade organization (Seidman et al., 2004; Smith et al., 2004). Solutions to student problems historically focused exclusively on remedial programs for affected children or prevention programs to prepare most children for these transitions. However, recent research suggests that organizational and structural changes that create smaller, more holistic social units or school communities within schools are more responsive to students' needs and are able to sustain their engagement and competence across school transitions (Seidman et al., 2004). Similarly, changes in classroom levels of victimization can affect individual differences in children's behavioral and emotional problems (Leadbeater, Hoglund, & Woods, 2003). Although children's voices are rarely heard by policy makers, children's developmental pathways are influenced by policy decisions about health care, family support, parental leaves, media regulation and so on (Zigler & Hall, 2000).

What Is Needed to Incorporate Scientific Research into Strengths-Based Policy?

Bridges Are Needed to Cross the Communication Gaps Between Researchers and Policy Makers

Research that exists to guide policy on major social problems is frequently jargon-ridden, hard to access, and ignored by those in positions to make policy decisions. Traditional avenues for gaining access to scientific research through hearings that solicit short testimonies from experts are costly and often target issues suddenly drawn to public attention by newspaper headlines, for example, about epidemics, youth violence, or environmental disasters. However, research-based knowledge is hard to access and crisis-driven responses can leave policy makers and the public believing that nothing is known about a social problem and that we are starting from ground zero. For example, in the panic that followed the shooting of 12 students and one teacher in Littleton, Colorado, researchers were barraged with newspaper reports of unpredictable and out-of-control youth violence that seemed to have no solutions, despite the existence of knowledge addressing youth violence that is founded on more than 50 years of research (Elliott, Hamburg, & Williams, 1998). Legislation that follows such anecdotes can lead to the passage of laws that have disastrous, unintended consequences. For example, juvenile transfer laws, which were intended to move older teenagers convicted of murder into adult prisons, have also lead to increased numbers of young offenders convicted of drug or property offenses who are in adult prisons—at a time when youth crime is on the decline and the public costs of prisons is rising.

Policy based on research can decrease the risks of misplaced investments of public funds. As well said by Sherrod (quoted in Tolan, et al., 2004. p. 24),

> Research-based policy leads to increased effectiveness through the objectivity and enduringness of research that transcends highly charged political environments … It promotes investment in youth capital, addresses core causes rather than treating symptoms, promotes a long-term perspective, and acknowledges that it's never too late to invest in children (i.e., investment need not be early).

Collapsing the differences in specific interests of academics, lobbyists, and policy makers may diminish the value of their independent contributions to public policy. However, generating opportunities for more open discussions among these groups is essential to generating science-based solutions. More joint conferences and networking among policy makers, lobby groups, the media and academics needs to be funded and instituted. Websites could provide accessible links among academic centers, governments, and lobby groups, but funding for monitoring and maintaining specific sites is typically not available in academic centers. Researchers must become more skilled at translating their research findings into formats that are both understandable by, and easily transferred to, policy makers. Funding for research and policy development needs to be directed to academic settings for the preparation and distribution of readable policy briefs from relevant research.

Policy Makers Should Seek to Identify and Build on the Knowledge about Supporting Resilience or Strengths in Individuals, Families, and Communities

This research frequently cuts across isolated social problems such as reducing teenage pregnancy, school dropout, or youth violence. Models stemming from resilience research can elaborate the transactions among vulnerabilities, ongoing adversities, protective factors and the development of competence. These suggest integrated targets for policy and programming that are critical for promoting child, youth, family, institutional, and community strengths. The expected rippling effects of policy decisions across specific societal problems needs to be specified. Since perturbing or vitalizing the development of competence at one level has direct and indirect effects on others, integrated approaches to promoting adequate functioning should have benefits across a range of specific social problems. For example, there is little doubt that creating processes and contexts that support the capacity for parenting warmth or the school engagement of young adolescents would have widespread effects on children's and teenager's problem behaviors, educational achievements, health, interpersonal skills, and pregnancy rates (Leadbeater & Way, 2001; McLoyd, 1998; McLoyd & Hernandez Jozefowicz, 1996; Sandler et al., 2004). Parenting skills and warmth could be affected by measures that decrease the stresses of work for parents, increase flexibility of work schedules, increase funding for the treatment of depression or other mental health problems, or increase educational opportunities and incomes of single-parent heads-of-households. Similarly, school engagement can be enhanced by creating favorable, non-violent school climates, equalizing resources available to inner-city and rural neighborhoods, instituting co-op programs to integrate schools and communities, reducing the mismatch of timing for transitions to middle school, or creating schools-within-schools to better address individual students' needs for adult attachments and opportunities for developing their competencies (Connell, Spencer, & Aber, 1994).

Policy Makers Need to be Held Accountable for Delineating the Expected Long-Term Consequences of Their Current Decisions

A strengths-based or resilience perspective draws attention to the need to consider not only immediate changes and innovative approaches but also how to sustain positive trajectories of individual, family, or community development. How are funds spent on innovative programs going to support the maintenance of successful programs? How are welfare reforms going to reduce not only the number of people on welfare but also the number of families living in poverty? Understanding apparently negative "outcomes" as points in a trajectory that connect past experiences with anticipated future opportunities again demands longer-term commitments to sustaining development.

What conclusion can we draw from the resilience revolution? The foundations for a paradigm shift in research, policy, and program are evident. This shift modifies our beliefs about the nature of risk and protective factors and the inter-related processes of change. Our optimism about the possibilities for real changes in the developmental trajectories of individuals, families, or communities dealing with adversities is warranted as we consider the many integrated targets that make intervention possible. Our optimism is tempered, however, by the complexity of the challenge to make the needed shifts in research, policy, and programming to reflect a strengths-building perspective and help to guide this new direction for social change.

REFERENCES

Alan Guttmacher Institute. (1994). *Sex and America's teenagers*. New York: Author.

Beardslee, W., & Knitzer, J. (2004). Mental health services: A family systems approach. In K. I. Maton, C. J. Schellenbach, B. J. Leadbeater, & A. L. Solarz (Eds.), *Investing in children, youth, and families: Strengths-based research and policy* (pp. 157–171). Washington, DC: American Psychological Association.

Braver, S. L., Hipke, K. N., Ellman, I. M., & Sandler, I. N. (2004). Strengths-building public policy for children of divorce. In K. I. Maton, C. J. Schellenbach, B. J. Leadbeater, & A. L. Solarz (Eds.), *Investing in children, youth, and families: Strengths-based research and policy* (pp. 53–72). Washington, DC: American Psychological Association.

Connell, J. P., Spencer, M. B., & Aber, J. L. (1994). Educational risk and resilience in African-American youth: Context, self, action, and outcomes in school. *Child Development, 65*, 493–506.

Cook, S., Woolard, J. L., & McCollum, H. C. (2004). The strengths of women facing domestic violence: How can research and policy support them? In K. I. Maton, C. J. Schellenbach, B. J. Leadbeater, & A. L. Solarz (Eds.), *Investing in children, youth, and families: Strengths-based research and policy* (pp. 97–115). Washington, DC: American Psychological Association.

Duncan, G., & Brooks-Gunn, J. (2000). Family poverty, welfare reform, and child development. *Child Development, 71*, 188–196.

Dutton, M. A., Goodman, L. A., & Bennett, L. (1999). Court-involved battered women's responses to violence: The role of psychological, physical, and sexual abuse. *Violence and Victims, 14*, 89–104.

Eccles, J. S., Lord, S. E., Roeser, R. W., Barber, B. L., & Hernandez Jozefowicz, D. M. (1997). The association of school transitions in early adolescence with developmental trajectories through high school. In J. Schulenberg, J. Maggs, & K. Hurrelmann (Eds.), *Health risks and transitions during adolescence* (pp. 283–320). New York: Cambridge University Press.

Elliott, D. S., Hamburg, B. A., & Williams, K. R. (1998). *Violence in American schools*. New York: Cambridge University Press.

Furstenberg, F. F., Brooks-Gunn, J., & Morgan, S. P. (1987). *Adolescent mothers in later life*. Cambridge: Cambridge University Press.

Hamburg, B. (1986). Subsets of adolescent mothers: Developmental, biomedical, and psychosocial issues. In J. Lancaster & B. Hamburg (Eds.), *School-age pregnancy and parenthood: Biosocial dimensions* (pp. 115–146). Hawthorne, NY: Aldine de Gruyter.

Kupersmidt, J., Coie, J., & Howell, J. (2004). Resilience in children exposed to negative peer influences. In K. I. Maton, C. J. Schellenbach, B. J. Leadbeater, & A. L. Solarz (Eds.), *Investing in children, youth, and families: Strengths-based research and policy* (pp. 251–268). Washington, DC: American Psychological Association.

Leadbeater, B. J. (1996). School outcomes for minority group adolescent mothers at 28 to 36 months postpartum: A longitudinal follow-up. *Journal of Research on Adolescence, 6*, 629–648.

Leadbeater, B. J. (1998). The goals of welfare reform reconsidered: Supporting the transition to work for inner-city adolescent mothers. *Children's Services: Social Policy, Research and Practice, 2*, 23–44.

Leadbeater, B. J. & Way, N. (2001) *Growing up fast: Early adult transitions of inner-city adolescent mothers.* Mahwah, NJ: Erlbaum.

Leadbeater, B., Hoglund, W., & Woods, T. (2003). Changing contexts? The effects of a primary prevention program on classroom levels of peer relational and physical victimization. *Journal of Community Psychology, 31,* 397–418.

Leadbeater, B. J., Schellenbach, C. J., Maton, K. I., & Dodgen, D. (2004). Research and policy for building strengths: Processes and contexts of individual, family, and community development. In K. I. Maton, C. J. Schellenbach, B. J. Leadbeater, & A. L. Solarz (Eds.), *Investing in children, youth, and families: Strengths-based research and policy* (pp. 13–30). Washington, DC: American Psychological Association.

Masten, A. S. (2001). Ordinary magic: Resilience processes in development. *American Psychologist, 56,* 227–238.

Masten, A. S., & Coatsworth, J. D. (1998). The development of competence in favorable and unfavorable environments: Lessons from research on successful children. *American Psychologist, 53,* 205–220.

McLoyd, V. (1998). Socioeconomic disadvantage and child development. *American Psychologist, 53,* 185–202.

McLoyd, V. C., & Hernandez Jozefowicz, D. M. (1996). Sizing up the future: Predictors of African American adolescent females' expectations. In B. J. Leadbeater & N. Way (Eds.), *Urban girls: Resisting stereotypes, creating identities* (pp. 355–379). New York: New York University Press.

Perkins, D. D., Florin, P., Rich, R. C., Wandersman, A., & Chavis, D. M. (1990). Participation and the social and physical environment of residential blocks: Crime and community context. *American Journal of Community Psychology, 18,* 83–113.

Sandler, I. N., Ayers, T. S., Suter, J. C., Schultz, A., & Twohey-Jacobs, J. (2004). Adversities, strengths, and public policy. In K. I. Maton, C. J. Schellenbach, B. J. Leadbeater, & A. L. Solarz (Eds.), *Investing in children, youth, and families: Strengths-based research and policy* (pp. 31–49). Washington, DC: American Psychological Association.

Schellenbach, C. J., Leadbeater, B. J., and McCollum, H. C. (2004). Enhancing the developmental outcomes of adolescent parents and their children. In K. I. Maton, C. J. Schellenbach, B. J. Leadbeater, & A. L. Solarz (Eds.), *Investing in children, youth, and families: Strengths-based research and policy* (pp. 117–136). Washington, DC: American Psychological Association.

Shonkoff, J. P. (2000). Science, policy, and practice: Three cultures in search of a shared mission. *Child Development, 71,* 181–187.

Seidman E., Aber, J. L., & French, S. E. (2004). Adolescent school transitions: Risky situations in need of restructuring. In K. I. Maton, C. J. Schellenbach, B. J. Leadbeater, & A. L. Solarz (Eds.), *Investing in children, youth, and families: Strengths-based research and policy* (pp. 233–250). Washington, DC: American Psychological Association.

Smith, E. P., Boutte, G. S., Zigler, E., & Finn-Stevenson, M. (2004). Opportunities for schools to promote resilience in children and youth. In K. I. Maton, C. J. Schellenbach, B. J. Leadbeater & A. L. Solarz (Eds.), *Investing in children, youth, and families: Strengths-based research and policy* (pp. 213–231). Washington, DC: American Psychological Association.

Tolan, P., Sherrod, L., Gorman-Smith, D., & Henry, D. (2004). Building protection, support, and opportunity for inner-city children and youth and their families. In K. I. Maton, C. J. Schellenbach, B. J. Leadbeater, & A. L. Solarz (Eds.), *Investing in children, youth, and families: Strengths-based research and policy* (pp. 193–211). Washington, DC: American Psychological Association.

Way, N., & Leadbeater, B. J. (1999). Pathways toward educational achievement among African American and Puerto Rican adolescent mothers: Reexamining the role of social support from families. *Development and Psychopathology, 11*, 349–356.

Woodward, L. J. & Fergusson, D. M. (1999). Early conduct problems and later risk of teenage pregnancy in girls. *Development and Psychopathology, 11*, 127–141.

Zigler, E. F., & Hall, N. W. (2000). *Child development and social policy.* New York: McGraw-Hill.

PART II

Resilience Enhancement Programs for High-Risk Children, Families, and Youth

CHAPTER 5

Creating Effective School-Based Interventions for Pregnant Teenagers

VICTORIA SEITZ & NANCY H. APFEL

In this chapter, we examine how a comprehensive program, addressing medical, educational, and social needs, offered to pregnant and parenting teens in a public school can help them have healthy pregnancies, remain in school, and delay subsequent childbearing. We discuss research evidence from our 18-year longitudinal study of a program that shows both short- and long-term benefits to teen mothers and their children, and we consider components of the program that appear to be responsible for the different kinds of success. Finally, we discuss policy implications, recommending that communities elsewhere would benefit from implementing similar programs.

Teenage parents and their offspring are very appropriate populations to consider in a volume on risk and resilience. Adolescent parenthood, often described as "children having children," creates parents who have problems adapting to adult responsibilities. Nevertheless, many show remarkable recovery from early difficulties, and demonstrate considerable resiliency.

Understanding what leads to success or failure for this high-risk group should ideally be based on longitudinal studies. However, few studies of teenage mothers and their children have continued until the children became adolescents themselves. One of these was a groundbreaking study begun in the late 1960s by Frank Furstenberg, a sociologist, who identified a Baltimore population of 404 women who were younger than 18 when they became pregnant with their firstborn child. Furstenberg and his colleagues reported results for them and their children when the children were 5 years old (Furstenberg, 1976) and again when the children were 16–17 years old (Furstenberg, Brooks-Gunn, & Morgan, 1987). Two epidemiologists, Lorraine Klerman and James Jekel in New Haven, CT began a second longitudinal study, also in the 1960s, with a group of teenagers attending a special prenatal program at Yale-New Haven Hospital (Klerman & Jekel, 1973). Horwitz and her colleagues reported results for a 20-year follow-up of this population (Horwitz, Klerman, Kuo, & Jekel, 1991a, b). Emmy Werner's longitudinal study of all children born in Kauai County, Hawaii in 1955, has also yielded information about long-term outcomes for the adolescents in the study who became teenage mothers (see Werner & Smith, 1992, chapter 5).

In agreement with many shorter-term studies (Hofferth, 1987), these studies showed that common problems for the mothers included failing to complete high school, having another child quickly, failing to establish a lasting marriage, and remaining welfare-dependent for many years. Long-term outcomes for young mothers were quite variable however, with most of them showing a gradually improving pattern over time. In Baltimore, for example, Furstenberg reported that mothers often resumed their education after their children had entered school. Seventeen years after they gave birth, two-thirds had become high school graduates or earned a GED certificate, a result similar to findings for the New Haven sample. Werner and Smith (1992) reported that all of their former teenage mothers had graduated from high school or earned a GED by their early thirties.

The long-term studies also revealed that—contrary to the stereotype that teenage mothers usually bear numerous children—most adolescents limited their total family size to two or three children. In the New Haven sample, only about one-quarter had large families of 4 or more children, and the Hawaiian results were similar; in Baltimore only about one-eighth had had large families. Furstenberg and his colleagues concluded that, "many teenage parents seem to stage a recovery of sorts in later life. Most do not fit the popular image of the poorly educated, unemployed woman with a large number of children living on public assistance" (1987, p. 133).

Given this picture of apparent resiliency, one might ask whether this population needs special programs or intervention efforts. For at least two reasons the answer is yes. Despite gradual improvement for many mothers, those who have numerous children and remain welfare dependent for many years are extremely costly to society. Burt (1986) has estimated that more than half of total U.S. federal outlays for AFDC, Medicaid, and food stamps are expended on families begun by teenage mothers. There is a principle, attributed to the Italian economist Pareto, that for many events, 80% of the costs are generated by 20% of the persons concerned (e.g., 20% of the drivers cause 80% of the accidents). Welfare costs arising from teenage mothers probably fit Pareto's principle, and it is worth intervening with adolescent mothers to try to improve outcomes for even a small percentage of them.

A second major concern is that outcomes for the children of teenage mothers are much less encouraging than the outcomes for their mothers. Problems are likely to begin at birth: pregnant adolescents are at well-documented risk of delivering a low-birthweight baby (Institute of Medicine, 1985; Strobino, 1987), and such children often have later health problems and difficulties in school. Whether or not they are born healthy, children of teenage mothers are at risk for poor health, cognitive, and social outcomes (Brooks-Gunn & Furstenberg, 1986; Osofsky, Eberhart-Wright, Ware, & Hann, 1992). Studies that have continued into adolescence have also revealed problems, some of them very serious. Furstenberg and his colleagues reported finding "massive school failure," as did the researchers in the New Haven study. Delinquency and early parenthood were also frequent. In both studies, between 25% and 40% of the adolescent boys reported engaging in assault or theft, and approximately 25% of the girls became adolescent parents themselves. These are disturbing findings, and they lead to the observation that programs for adolescent parents need to be mounted with the intention of eventually benefiting the children as well as their mothers.

Many communities have established special programs for pregnant teenagers in hospitals or health clinics, often resulting in better birth outcomes for them. Because teenagers often delay seeking prenatal care until late in pregnancy, some communities have attempted to improve early outreach by establishing school programs for pregnant students. Evaluations of such programs have consistently reported better educational outcomes for attendees and better birth outcomes for their babies; however, most school programs have been evaluated with such weak research designs that their findings are not conclusive. In the present chapter, we will describe how one community, New Haven, CT, has developed a school-based program for pregnant teenagers and how we have been able to take advantage of conditions that approximate naturally-occurring random assignment to evaluate the program's effects. After examining these effects, we will discuss broader policy implications.

DESCRIPTION OF THE POLLY T. McCABE
CENTER IN NEW HAVEN, CT

The Polly T. McCabe Center is a public school for pregnant students. This school was established in 1966 as an outgrowth of one of the earliest specialized hospital programs for pregnant adolescents, the Young Mothers Program (YMP), initiated at Yale-New Haven Hospital in 1965. Two physicians, an obstetrician and a pediatrician, had established the YMP after observing that pregnant teenagers often needed more care and services than regular prenatal clinics were providing. After the YMP clinic was established, its social workers quickly recognized that the educational needs of its young patients were often unmet, and the program's creators approached the New Haven Public Schools about this problem. Along with community grassroots organizers, their efforts led to the creation of a school program, the Polly T. McCabe Center, aimed at improving the educational and medical outcomes for inner-city teenagers who become pregnant before they have graduated from high school.

The McCabe Center, operated by the New Haven Board of Education, follows the same daily schedule, academic curriculum, and 4-quarter September through June calendar of the other New Haven schools. Students are enrolled by referral from their regular schools when their pregnancy becomes apparent or when they notify a teacher or counselor that they are pregnant. (Pregnant New Haven students can choose either to remain in their regular schools or to attend the McCabe Center). Typically, an enrolled student remains at the McCabe Center to complete the academic quarter in which her baby is born, then returns to her regular school the following quarter. Over the years, there usually have been about 100 students attending at any given time.

The students in our long-term study attended McCabe in its early days (late 1970s through early 1980) when the program was housed in the basement level of a church, with minimal space available. There were several small offices, a large multi-purpose room divided by partitions for classes, two small classrooms, and an open area outside the offices with exercise mats for the students. About a decade ago, the program was relocated to a more spacious and brighter facility. This new building has 11 classrooms, a baby-care room, five smaller offices, and a cafeteria that serves a daily hot lunch. Although the program was moved, its characteristics remained the same. Staff continuity is remarkable with many having taught at McCabe for well over a decade. The program had the same director for 25 years until her retirement in 1992.

The Triad of Services

In an analysis of the effectiveness of programs for pregnant and parenting adolescents, Lorraine Klerman and her colleagues emphasized the need for programs to be comprehensive. That is, it is usually necessary to provide a triad of services—educational, social, and medical—to effectively address the problems that such teenagers experience (Klerman & Horwitz, 1992).

The McCabe Program was designed to provide services in all three domains. As a school program, the educational aspects of the services are the most obvious. The program offers courses from the public school curriculum, taught by public school teachers, which can be applied for credit toward high school graduation. A typical day for a McCabe student is to attend six 40-minute classes. Class size varies from a low of 6 in nurse-taught classes to a high of 20 in regular academic courses. Entering a McCabe classroom, a visitor would notice that the classrooms have tables instead of desks and chairs in a row. As one teacher describes the classes, "You can't get lost here, and you can't skip classes either." The program staff also offers transitional support for the student to help her return to her regular school program.

Unlike the average urban school, the McCabe program offers substantial supportive social services to address the home and school-life issues of the students. In one form, this involves a personalized follow-up on absences. If a student is absent, a staff person telephones her to ask how she is and why she is not in school. If there is no compelling medical or other reason for her absence, she is urged to come in. If there is a problem, the staff person attempts to solve it. The McCabe social worker provides help, if needed, to address problems such as dealing with a substance-abusing parent or helping to find affordable housing. In some cases, outreach services are provided, with home visits.

Thirdly, many medical services are provided in this school setting. These mostly take the form of educational efforts to supplement and reinforce information that the teenagers are receiving in their regular prenatal care at hospitals or clinics. The services therefore resemble what David Olds has called "enhanced prenatal care" (Olds, et al., 1986), as provided by the nurses in his program who make regular home visits to pregnant women. (We will describe McCabe medical services more extensively below). In sum, the Polly T. McCabe Center is an excellent example of what Klerman and her colleagues have labeled a "comprehensive" program.

Using Schools as Part of the Health-Care System

The fact that it is possible to use schools effectively to provide health care is so important that it is worth examining carefully how such services are delivered. One unique medical aspect of the McCabe program is the ongoing observation of students by nurses, teachers, and other personnel, all of whom are attuned to health issues. If a student does not look well, or has symptoms of problems with the pregnancy, such as swollen ankles, the staff alerts the student and refers her for evaluation. Thus the program provides personalized day-to-day health monitoring of the teens.

Three times a week, pregnant students go to a prenatal education class taught by a registered nurse. This class presents information about fetal development, the importance of nutrition and prenatal care, women's health, and preparation for labor and delivery. The instructors have developed specialized curricula designed to help the teenagers begin to bond with their babies. For example, they draw life-sized pictures of developing fetuses matched to the teenager's current stage of pregnancy and encourage the teens to place these pictures over their abdomens and look into the mirror so that they can better visualize their baby. The nurses have reported to us, "They love it. The more they can bond with their baby during pregnancy, the less likely they are apt to abuse it later on."

The nurses encourage the teens to eat a well-balanced diet, not to smoke, not to use over-the-counter medications without specific approval by their doctors, and to avoid street drugs. In addition to providing Lamaze training so that the teens will be prepared for labor and delivery, at an appropriate stage of the pregnancy, the nurse takes her students on a tour of the hospital labor and delivery rooms. She tells us, "That's when reality sets in. It is important to help them with the experience." Evidently, this preparation is very effective, and the nurses are proud of reports from the hospitals about how well the students handle labor and delivery.

After their babies are born, the students continue to attend this class once a week, but begin to attend classes taught by a perinatal fitness specialist and a pediatric nurse practitioner who specializes in postpartum health care for the other two days a week. Although the nurses who teach the different classes specialize in different phases of the students' health education, there is crossover and continuity, with both nurses available to counsel and teach the students during and after pregnancy.

The nurse who teaches the postpartum education class addresses the new mother's concerns about how to care for her baby. Students are taught basics of feeding, bathing, dressing, and safety as well as information about normal infant development. Discussions are also held about arranging suitable childcare for the baby while the young mother attends school. Each student is helped by a personalized, case-by-case review of her available childcare options.

The teenager's own personal medical concerns are also a focus. The nurse provides a "hands-on" discussion about contraception, passing around an array of contraceptive devices and medications and encouraging discussions about their use and any fears or concerns the teens may have about them. She also provides individual counseling about contraception, placing this information within the context of the teenager's short- and long-term educational goals.

The nurses have told us that the first month after the baby is born is typically a kind of "honeymoon period" for the teen and her family, when all are highly enthusiastic about the new baby. After this, however, the troublesome demands of caring for a new baby must be met, and family stresses reappear. At the same time, as the new mother recovers from the delivery, issues of resuming sexuality begin to emerge. Thus, the second month after the baby is born is an opportune time to address the issue of repeat pregnancy. At this critical "teachable moment" a new mother's attention can be focused on her future and how to avoid having another child quickly, and information about contraception becomes most meaningful to her. The discussions at McCabe occur under the guidance of persons whom the teenager has learned to trust during her pregnancy and in a group of other teenagers who are facing the same issues. The postpartum medical services are thus a continuation of the same kind of services begun during pregnancy. As we will now see, this innovative blend of medical and educational services in a school setting has important consequences for the teenagers and their children.

EVALUATION OF THE EFFECTS
OF THE POLLY T. McCABE CENTER

In the best research design, persons are assigned randomly either to receive a program or to be part of a comparison group. This is rarely feasible in evaluating a public school. However, program rules sometimes mimic random assignment when they do not allow attendees choice about how long to attend. We found that, if we limited our analyses to students who attended the McCabe Center as long as the rules permitted, we were able to create good comparison groups. We will explain how we did this for each of the outcomes we measured.

Question #1: How Well Did the McCabe Program Reach Its Target Population?

To answer this question, we used hospital birth records to identify all the first-time school-aged mothers who were New Haven city residents and who gave birth from March 1979 through February 1980. We then searched city school records to determine the school status of the teens. We discovered that almost three-quarters of the first-time school-aged mothers in the city were African-American, and almost three-quarters of this group (72%) were successfully served by the Polly T. McCabe Center. Many of the Latina and White school-aged mothers had dropped out of school before they became pregnant. In general, our findings suggest that a public high school can successfully reach a majority of the ethnic group of students that most commonly become adolescent mothers in the city but that other ethnic groups may perhaps feel out of place in such a school and choose not to attend.

Question #2: Did Attending the McCabe Center Improve the Students' Birth Outcomes?

To study this question, we looked at all teens, not just African-American teens. As noted above, students were allowed to enroll at McCabe when they were pregnant and to remain until the end of the school quarter in which their baby was born. Because of summer vacation, the school did not accept new students after May first, so that from May through August each year, the school was closed to admission. This created two groups of students, those who were able to enroll as soon as they wished, and those who were forced to wait until the school re-opened in September.

Their medical records showed that the teenagers were slow to acknowledge and seek medical help with their pregnancy, typically waiting about four months until their first prenatal checkup. As Table 5-1 shows, the result was that students who became pregnant in the months of January through April were the ones most likely to have to wait until late in their pregnancy before they could attend McCabe.

Very few students who conceived in January through April began attending the McCabe Center in the first half of their pregnancy, whereas many students who conceived in the rest of the year did so. This difference in timing made a substantial difference in whether the teens then had a successful pregnancy (i.e., were able to carry their pregnancy to full term). Among teenagers enrolled in public school when they became pregnant who conceived in the months of January through April,

Table 5-1 Time of Entry into McCabe for Pregnant Teenagers Who Were Enrolled in Public School at Conception ($N = 158$)

	Approximate Time of Conception	
	January–April ($N = 43$)	May–December ($N = 115$)
Before mid-pregnancy	14%	43%
After mid-pregnancy	58%	31%
Didn't attend or dropped out	28%	26%

an alarming 12% delivered a preterm, low-birthweight infant; only 1% of teens who conceived in the other months of the year did so.

We looked for time-of-conception effects in the rest of the teenage mothers in the city that year (i.e., those who were not enrolled in public school when they became pregnant), and found that the time they became pregnant did not affect their birth outcomes. Thus, the findings for the students did not indicate some kind of citywide seasonal effect. As we had expected, the practice of denying program availability during the summer months led to the existence of two groups of teenagers who appeared to be equivalent except in their probability of receiving early intervention and in their birth outcomes. David Olds and his colleagues have shown that a comprehensive program of prenatal nurse home visitation that is begun prior to mid-pregnancy can improve birth outcomes for pregnant adolescents (Olds, Henderson, Tatelbaum, & Chamberlin, 1986). The results of our evaluation suggest that a comparable program provided by nurses in a school setting can be similarly effective. (For a full description of our study, see Seitz & Apfel, 1994).

Question #3: Did Attending McCabe Improve the Students' Educational Outcomes?

To answer this question, we looked at the students who were motivated enough to remain at McCabe until they delivered their baby and to earn passing grades in at least one subject while they were there. Because almost all such students were African-American, we limited our final analyses to the African-American students (there were 106 students who met this study's criteria). Examining these students' academic records, we found that most had been poor students before they became pregnant. We thought it likely that McCabe might have different effects for poorer than for better students, so we divided the sample approximately in half. We defined students who had not earned at least a C average in any marking period for the year before they became pregnant as poorer students (there were 49 of them). The remaining students, who had earned a C average or better at least once, we defined as better students prior to pregnancy (there were 55 such students).

The McCabe Center had a very powerful educational effect on poorer students. As we described above, the length of attendance at McCabe was not a matter of choice for the students, and those who attended only one quarter were no different in any way that we could measure from those who were able to attend for four quarters. But the differences in outcome were striking. Only 16% of poor students who attended one quarter were educationally successful by the time their baby was two years old, whereas 80% of poor students who were able to attend for four quarters were educationally successful. (The percentage of successful outcomes for two-quarter and three-quarter attendees fell in between, with 40% and 60% of such students, respectively, becoming educationally successful.) For students who had previously had better academic achievement, approximately two-thirds were educationally successful, no matter how long they remained at the McCabe Center.

For school outcomes, the McCabe program thus appeared to operate in two different ways, depending upon the previous academic success of its students. For better students, it offered a safe environment in which to continue their educational progress without a potentially dangerous interruption. For poorer students, however, it actually turned their academic careers around, raising them to the same level of educational success as students who had previously been academically competent. In a specialized program such as McCabe, more individual attention is possible due to the small class sizes. Also, support is available to help a student overcome personal problems that could interfere with academic success. In such a setting, the marginal student who is able to attend for a longer time may be able to establish an increasingly strong sense that she is capable of being an adequate student. This positive response of poorer students to a smaller, personalized setting agrees with evidence from many studies of scholastically at-risk students. In an analysis of such studies, both Dryfoos (1990) and Hodgkinson (1985) have noted that a small student-teacher ratio is consistently one of the most important factors in preventing marginal students from becoming school dropouts. A full description of our study of the educational effects of the McCabe Center in our study is available in Seitz, Apfel, and Rosenbaum (1991).

Question #4: Did Attending McCabe Help Students Postpone Additional Childbearing?

To answer this question, we looked at the same group we studied for educational outcomes (question #3), except that we did not include 4 students who dropped out of school after delivering their baby. Students who delivered their baby in the summer months were unable to attend McCabe after their babies were born, and those who delivered their babies near the end of a marking period also received little or no time at McCabe postnatally. They did not choose to leave so quickly, but being forced to do so had serious consequences for them.

We divided the group in half at the median length of time that students remained at McCabe after their baby was born (7.1 weeks). We found that students who were able to continue attending at the McCabe Center for more than 7 weeks after their baby was born were much less likely to have a second baby within the next 5 years than were students who had been required to leave by the time their baby was 7 weeks old. Surprisingly, more than half of the young mothers who had stayed more than 7 weeks postnatally (55%) still had not had a second child when their first child was 5 years old, whereas this was true for only 30% of the mothers who had had to leave McCabe quickly. As we describe more fully elsewhere (Seitz & Apfel, 1993), the two groups of students were similar in age, the amount of family support they received, the kind of students they were, their measured cognitive ability, and in every other way we examined, but they had very different patterns of later childbearing. As we will now show, these differences in childbearing had profound consequences for both the adolescent mothers and their firstborn children.

Consequences of Delaying Childbearing for the Teenage Mother

Approximately one-quarter of the mothers had a second baby before their first child's second birthday. This led to negative educational and economic outcomes for them, and they were likely to have larger families. As Table 5-2 shows, only one quarter of the mothers who had another child quickly became high school graduates and they were mostly still welfare dependent by the time their first child was 18 years old.

Table 5-2 Consequences of Rapid Repeated Childbearing for Young African-American Mothers ($N = 115$)

	New Delivery Within 2 Years of First		
	No (73%)	Yes (27%)	
High school graduate at 18 yrs	55%	25%	$p < .01$
AFDC within last year at 18 yrs	55%	83%	$p = .02$
Number of living children	3	4.4	$p < .04$

Consequences of Delaying Childbearing for the Firstborn Children of the Teenage Mothers

Eighteen years later, the length of time mothers had waited before having a second child varied from 8.5 months (a prematurely born second child) to 18 years (for mothers who had never had a second child). The length of time that children remained an only child was an important protective factor for them. Interestingly, boys needed to remain an only child longer (at least 5 years) than did girls, who needed to be an only child for only 2 years to show benefits. Table 5-3 shows the results for the firstborn daughters of the African-American mothers in our study.

As Table 5-3 shows, remaining an only child for at least 2 years led to better school achievement for teenage daughters of the teen mothers and to a higher likelihood they would graduate from high school or be expected to do so by age 18. It also reduced the likelihood that the girls would have a police record and sharply decreased the likelihood of following in their mothers' footsteps by becoming school-aged mothers themselves. (Almost half the girls who had a sibling by age 2 became school-aged mothers, whereas this was true for only 20% of those who remained an only child for at least 2 years.) We present the original teenage mothers' scores on the Peabody Picture Vocabulary Test to show that those who waited to have a second child did not have higher cognitive ability than those who had a second child quickly. Thus, the good results for their daughters did not occur simply because their mothers were brighter.

Table 5-4 shows the results for the sons of the school-aged mothers in our study. As was true for the girls, being an only child for a sufficient time (in this case, throughout the entire preschool period), led to much

Table 5-3 Consequences of Short Sibship Interval (<2 years) for Daughters of Young African-American Mothers ($N = 58$)

	New Sibling by Age Two		
	No (71%)	Yes (29%)	
Age 6 Stanford-Binet IQ	83.5	75.8	$p < .08$
Age 12 Reading Percentile Rank	45th	22nd	$p < .04$
Age 12 Math Percentile Rank	37th	14th	$p < .01$
Age 18 Good Educational Outcome	74%	41%	$p < .02$
Police record by Age 18	0%	12%	$p < .03$
Ever in jail by Age 18	8%	12%	n.s.
Parent by Age 18	20%	47%	$p < .05$
[Mothers' PPVT IQ Score]	70.5	70.1	n.s.

Table 5-4 Consequences of Short Sibship Interval (<5 Years) for Sons of Young African-American Mothers ($N = 58$)

	New Sibling by Age Five		
	No (28%)	Yes (72%)	
Age 6 Stanford-Binet IQ	87.0	78.7	$p = .03$
Age 12 Reading Percentile Rank	48th	22nd	$p = .05$
Age 12 Math Percentile Rank	40th	18th	$p = .05$
Age 18 Good Educational Outcome	56%	34%	n.s.
Police record by Age 18	12%	34%	n.s.
Ever in jail by Age 18	31%	62%	$p < .05$
Parent by Age 18	0%	30%	$p < .02$
[Mothers' PPVT IQ Score]	67.9	67.0	n.s.

better school achievement for the boys. In fact, the reading performance for such boys was nearly at national norms for 12-year-old children in the United States, an astonishing performance for boys born to poor, African-American teenage mothers. Sadly, good school performance at age 12 did not translate into a higher likelihood of educational success by age 18. Nevertheless, by age 18, boys with this protective factor were less likely to have spent any time in jail and they were unlikely to have become teenage fathers. Again we present their mothers' scores on the PPVT vocabulary test to show that the better outcomes for the boys did not occur simply because their mothers were brighter.

To summarize, the effects of the McCabe program in helping mothers postpone having a second child were of immense importance for both the young mothers and their children. In addition, these effects were evident many years after program participation, when the children were nearly adults themselves.

Question #5: What Features of the McCabe Program Contributed to Its Success?

In Table 5-5, we summarize the factors that are probably responsible for the McCabe Program's success.

Interviews with former students years later revealed the powerful effect that the personalized, nurturant attitude of the staff had on these vulnerable teens. (We use substitute names in the following quotes to protect privacy.) As one young woman, Donna, told us, "They have the sweetest teachers there, and you get to eat free." Adrienne told us, "It was easy to have excuses about school. McCabe helped me keep motivated to go back to school. The one-on-one counseling got you thinking about

Table 5-5   Features of the Polly T. McCabe Program Probably Contributing to Its Success

- Low student-staff ratio and high personalized attention: Staff available for counseling and follow-up on student absences
- Education about prenatal development, and preparation for childbirth and delivery taught by a nurse or health care professional
- Academic courses for which a student receives credit toward graduation (the primary motivation for attendance for many students)
- A daily nutritious lunch
- Continuity of staff from pregnancy through the postnatal period
- Nurse/health educator-taught postnatal education continued for at least two months after delivery
- Postnatal support in establishing childcare to prevent school dropout.
- A totally voluntary approach to attendance at the program

what to do after high school. I didn't want to be on welfare." (Adrienne went to business school after her high school graduation.) For many teens, McCabe represented their first positive experience with school in many years, and it was hard for them to leave. Stephanie told us, "I wanted to say at McCabe. I did not want to go back. I cried like a baby." Twelve years after leaving McCabe, one student asked during her interview whether the poem she had written there was still mounted on the bulletin board. This young mother, who had had few academic successes before McCabe, wistfully remembered the recognition she had received there for her creative writing efforts—evidently an extremely meaningful event for her.

Special Considerations in Using Schools to Provide Services to Pregnant Adolescents

Advantages

Public schools offer numerous advantages as a service delivery model. Because schools are already available in all communities, the task is one of modifying existing services rather than building entirely new programs. From the point of view of medical services, schools permit a much more intensive intervention than do specialized clinics or home visitation programs. Students attend for about 25 hours a week, in which they receive health education, counseling, and monitoring. Free transportation typically is available through school buses, or, as at McCabe, can be arranged by providing vouchers for students to ride city buses. Nutrition can be improved by providing at least one meal (lunch), and possibly two per day. Schools would obviously not be the model of choice for reaching pregnant teens who have dropped out of school. Our study showed, however, that at least for some ethnic groups within the city, most pregnant teens were still enrolled in school when they became pregnant. Public schools, especially if the program policies are inviting and inclusive ones, can reach a surprisingly high proportion of at least some groups of pregnant teens. Finally, peer group support is intrinsic within school programs and can be capitalized upon to strengthen the effectiveness.

The McCabe Center was a separate school for pregnant students, a characteristic that not all communities might be willing to consider. Nevertheless, it may have been a key feature in its effectiveness. One young mother, Gail, spoke for many when she told us, "I didn't want to go to school. I was embarrassed. I wanted to hide my head in the sand. There was no way I was going back to high school pregnant. I would have dropped out of school (without McCabe)." And, as Adrienne observed in commenting favorably on the all-girl atmosphere, "There were no boys there. That's why we were there (in the first place). That's what brought us there." Many teens expressed relief in not having to contend with the often-chaotic setting of public school hallways and stairwells when classes change. They indicated that they would have felt vulnerable to jostling and even injury, especially late in their pregnancy.

Potential Problems

Summer vacation is the most obvious concern when schools are used as a service delivery model for pregnant adolescents. As we saw in our evaluation, the long vacation adversely affected birth outcomes by making it impossible for some teens to enter the program early in pregnancy. Teens who delivered their babies in the summer were unable to receive postnatal intervention and were at higher risk of having another child quickly. Although a remedy might be to provide school services on a year-round basis, such a strategy might not be popular with students and might therefore be ineffective. More promising options might be to supplement schools with other approaches, as needed. The school nurses, for example, might make postnatal home visits to teens who deliver during the summer, and specialized clinics in hospitals might provide enhanced prenatal care to teenagers who become pregnant during the late winter months and who are unable to attend a school program early in pregnancy. School programs could also adopt a very liberal entrance policy, allowing admission even very late in the school year, recognizing the health advantages of beginning participation early in pregnancy.

More subtle problems with school programs can arise when the philosophy of the service providers differs from that of the successful McCabe Center. As noted above, the original director of the program had a very liberal approach to enrollment, recognizing that many of these students were highly troubled prior to their pregnancy, and she did not expect them to be exemplary students. High absenteeism, poor grades, and aggressive behavior were shown by many McCabe students before they entered. Nevertheless, the program philosophy was that such students were welcome, nurtured, and helped to behave in more appropriate ways. In response to such expectations, many of these seemingly impossible students became able to function in the McCabe environment and, as noted earlier, were able to return to their regular programs and eventually graduate from high school.

A change in philosophy occurred when the original director retired and a new director adopted a more restrictive enrollment policy, discouraging the more troubled population of students (those with a history of poor grades, high absenteeism, or fighting) from enrolling. The result has been that the program now enrolls a smaller, better-behaved population. In all likelihood, however, the many who are not being served by McCabe are now dropping out of school or enrolling in alternative GED programs. Whether such students are having their educational needs met is not clear, but they are almost certainly not receiving the medical and social services that they need. This example illustrates that even when a program is in place and functioning well it can be vulnerable to shifts in operating philosophy.

POLICY IMPLICATIONS IN REPLICATING NEW HAVEN'S MODEL

Many communities have established special programs for pregnant adolescents and for those who have become parents. Such programs are rarely evaluated because ethical considerations make it difficult to establish comparison groups to show what happens when the program's services are not available. Our evaluation of the McCabe Center suggests that many programs existing elsewhere are probably far more effective than their staffs realize.

A reasonable implication of our findings is that other communities should be encouraged to implement programs similar to McCabe with the expectation of reaping substantial immediate and long-term benefits. A community could begin with a school program, supplemented by more expensive outreach interventions for the minority of high-risk teenagers who are missed by the schools. If, for financial or philosophical reasons, communities are not able to implement all aspects of the McCabe model, a modified approach that builds on its strengths might still be effective, retaining the elements we summarized in Table 5-5.

We suggest that communities give serious consideration to a full-scale program like the McCabe model. This program is a popular choice among pregnant students. Given that many of these students are in serious academic difficulty by the time they become pregnant, their improved performance has been striking, as well as their subsequent determination to return to school after birth, and to finish high school. The majority of these students become high school graduates before their firstborn goes to school, overwhelmingly they deliver healthy babies, and, with only about 2 months of attendance after their baby is born, more than half of them are able to avoid having a second child over the next 5 years. Their children, who remain only children for several years, have much better life outcomes, including the avoidance of teen parenthood themselves. We recommend this totally voluntary approach to improving the lives of high-risk students to other urban community leaders and policymakers.

REFERENCES

Burt, M. R. (1986). Estimating the public costs of teenage childbearing. *Family Planning Perspectives, 18*, 221–226.

Brooks-Gunn, J., & Furstenberg, F. F., Jr. (1986). The children of adolescent mothers: Physical, academic, and psychological outcomes. *Developmental Review, 6*, 224–251.

Dryfoos, J. (1990). *Adolescents at risk: Prevalence and prevention.* New York: Oxford University Press.

Furstenberg, F. F., Jr. (1976). *Unplanned parenthood.* New York: Free Press.

Furstenberg, F. F., Jr., Brooks-Gunn, J., & Morgan, S. P. (1987). *Adolescent mothers in later life.* NY: Cambridge University Press.

Hodgkinson, H. (1985). *All one system: Demographics of education, kindergarten through graduate school.* Washington, DC: Institute for Educational Leadership.

Hofferth, S. L. (1987). Social and economic consequences of teenage childbearing. In S. L. Hofferth & C. D. Hayes (Eds.), *Risking the future: Adolescent sexuality, pregnancy, and childbearing* (Vol. 2, pp. 123–144). Washington, DC: National Academy Press.

Horwitz, S. M., Klerman, L. V., Kuo, H. S., & Jekel, J. F. (1991a). School-aged mothers: Predictors of long-term educational and economic outcomes. *Pediatrics, 87*, 862–868.

Horwitz, S. M., Klerman, L. V., Kuo, H. S., & Jekel, J. F. (1991b). Intergenerational transmission of school-age parenthood. *Family Planning Perspectives, 23*, 168–172, 177.

Institute of Medicine, Committee to Study the Prevention of Low Birthweight. (1985). *Preventing low birthweight.* Washington, DC: National Academy Press.

Jekel, J. F., & Klerman, L. V. (1982). Comprehensive service programs for pregnant and parenting adolescent. In E. R. McAnarney (Ed.), *Premature adolescent pregnancy and parenthood* (pp. 295–310). New York: Grune & Stratton, Inc.

Klerman, L. V., & Horwitz, S. M. (1992). Reducing the adverse consequences of adolescent pregnancy and parenting: The role of service programs. *Adolescent Medicine: State of the Art Reviews, 3*, 299–316.

Klerman, L. V., & Jekel, J. F. (1973). *School-age mothers: Problems, programs, and policy.* Hamden, CT: Shoe String Press.

Olds, D. L., Henderson, C. R., Jr., Tatelbaum, R., & Chamberlin, R. (1986). Improving the delivery of prenatal care and outcomes of pregnancy: A randomized trial of nurse home visitation. *Pediatrics, 77*, 16–28.

Osofsky, J. D., Eberhart-Wright, A., Ware, L., & Hann, D. (1922). Children of adolescent mothers: A group at risk for psychopathology. *Infant Mental Health Journal, 13*, 49–56.

Seitz, V., & Apfel, N. H. (1993). Adolescent mothers and repeated childbearing: Effects of a school-based intervention program. *American Journal of Orthopsychiatry, 63*, 572–581.

Seitz, V., & Apfel, N. H. (1994). Effects of a school for pregnant students on the incidence of low-birthweight deliveries. *Child Development, 65*, 666–676.

Seitz, V., Apfel, N. H. & Rosenbaum, L. K. (1991). Effects of an intervention program for pregnant adolescents: Educational outcomes at two years postpartum. *American Journal of Community Psychology, 19*, 911–930.

Strobino, D. M. (1987). The health and medical consequences of adolescent sexuality and pregnancy: A review of the literature. In S. L. Hofferth & C. D. Hayes (Eds.), *Risking the future: Adolescent sexuality, pregnancy, and childbearing* (Vol. 2, pp. 93–122). Washington, DC: National Academy Press.

Werner, E., & Smith, R. S. (1992). *Overcoming the odds.* Ithaca, NY: Cornell University Press.

CHAPTER 6

Dating Relationships among At-Risk Adolescents

An Opportunity for Resilience?

KATREENA SCOTT, LAURA-LYNN STEWART,
& DAVID WOLFE

Childhood maltreatment is a potent risk factor for psychological and social difficulties across the life span. Relationship difficulties, in particular, are associated with experiences of abuse and neglect. Maltreated children show high rates of hostility and aggression in relationships (Brown, Cohen, Johnson, & Smailes, 1999; Wolfe, Wekerle, Reitzel-Jaffe, & Lefebvre, 1998) and are more likely than non-maltreated children to be rejected by their peers (Dodge, Pettit, & Bates, 1994). In adolescence, these individuals are less likely to report close, supportive friendships (Bolger & Patterson, 2001) and are at elevated risk of becoming involved in violent dating partnerships (Wolfe, Scott, Wekerle, & Pittman, 2001). Patterns of relationship dysfunction continue into adulthood, where childhood maltreatment is associated with both domestic violence (Bevan & Higgins, 2002) and child abuse in the next generation (Kaufman & Zigler, 1987; Newcomb & Locke, 2001; Pears & Capaldi, 2001).

Despite the multiple negative outcomes associated with childhood maltreatment, it is important to recognize that such outcomes are not inevitable or consistent. Some abused and neglected individuals seem able to overcome some of the initial harm stemming from maltreatment, and develop normally or with few impairments. Such "unexpected" outcomes may be due to the relatively brief or minor abuse they received, the benefits of early intervention, correction of the problems associated with maltreatment (e.g., parental conflict; alcohol abuse, etc.), or the inherent resources of the individual. A study by Wolfe and colleagues (2001), for example, involved non-clinically referred, high school adolescents who reported a history of moderate to severe child maltreatment experience. They found, on the one hand, that a history of childhood maltreatment was strongly associated with elevated risk of negative outcomes such as anger, depression, post-traumatic stress, delinquency, abuse perpetration or victimization. However, between 60% and 90% of teens reporting prior maltreatment did not exhibit clinically significant symptoms. These latter individuals who experience adversity but avoid developing clinically or socially significant difficulties are often described as "resilient." They have caught the attention of researchers attempting to find strategies to prevent problems and promote healthy outcomes in high-risk populations.

Over the past decade, we have focused on adolescence as an important window of opportunity for interventions that break the cycle of violence and promote healthy, resilient functioning (Wolfe, Wekerle, & Scott, 1997). We have studied normative adolescent transitions and development, and have designed and evaluated a prevention and promotion program targeting high-risk youth, the Youth Relationships Project (YRP). In this chapter we review previous studies on prevention with adolescents at high risk for problematic outcomes due to a history of child maltreatment. We also present results that support intervention at this stage for reducing rates of violence perpetration and victimization in adolescent intimate relationships. We then explore the role adolescent relationships may play in promoting these positive outcomes. Our aim is to try to identify whether particular aspects or patterns of dating may be related to resilient functioning among at-risk youth.

THE CONTEXT OF ADOLESCENT
RELATIONSHIPS

In adolescence, a key developmental task is the establishment of healthy, non-familial intimate relationships. Progress towards this goal begins in early adolescence, with the development of close-knit groups of same-sex peers and small groups of mixed-sex friends. These groups form a springboard for dating involvement, and by age 14 or 15, about half of all adolescents move from mixed-friend groups to single- or group-dating experience (Connolly & Johnson, 1996; Feiring, 1996). Dating at this early age is a short-term, rapidly shifting affair, as adolescents learn methods of interpersonal and sexual relatedness and experiment with romantic identities. For example, the average length of relationship among 15 year-olds in one study was approximately four months (Feiring, 1996). After a period of experimentation in multiple casual relationships, youth generally progress to more serious, exclusive dating relationships that become increasingly important sources of support relative to parents and peers (Furman & Buhrmester, 1992). By 18 years of age most adolescents have had at least one steady relationship (Thornton, 1990), and dyadic relationships are the norm (Brown, 1999; Connolly & Goldberg, 1999). Romantic relationships at this age are more intense, committed, and satisfying and, it is theorized, form an important basis for later intimate, long-term partnerships (Brown, 1999).

During this rapidly shifting developmental period, youth are consistently challenged to negotiate conflicting family, peer and partner pressures and develop new means of relating interpersonally, all while managing the sometimes intense emotions that arise during this time of life (Larson & Ham, 1993). Given the difficulties inherent in these tasks, it is perhaps not surprising that rates of intimate partner aggression and abuse are particularly high. Approximately 1 in 5 to 1 in 10 teens report being a victim of a relatively severe form of physical aggression or sexual coercion from a dating partner (Centers for Disease Control, 2000; Coker et al., 2000; Silverman, Raj, Mucci, & Hathaway, 2001). When behaviors such as verbal and psychological intimidation, isolation and degradation are included, rates are much higher with as many as one half of adolescents reporting experiences as a victim, perpetrator or both (Malik, Sorenson, & Aneshensel, 1997; Wolfe et al., 2001).

Due to their history of relationship disadvantage, youth with a history of childhood maltreatment are at particular risk for becoming involved in violent and abusive adolescent dating relationships. Wolfe and colleagues (2001) found that male adolescents who had experienced moderate or severe childhood maltreatment were 1.8 times as likely to report experiencing sexual abuse and 2.8 times as likely to report being threatened. Female adolescents reported even higher risk, with odds of abuse perpetration and victimization for girls who had been maltreated 2.1 to 3.3 times higher than those with no maltreatment history.

YOUTH RELATIONSHIPS PROJECT

Program Description

Given the convergence of developmental pressures and vulnerability, we reasoned that adolescence may offer an important window of opportunity for altering the developmental course of youth at-risk for abusive intimate relationships (Wolfe et al., 1997). Adolescents are interested in exploring a variety of models of intimacy and are actively engaged in experimenting with different dating partners and patterns of relatedness. Moreover, we reasoned that lessons learned at this stage will likely have a rippling effect, shaping the patterns of later, long-term intimate partnerships. As such, this stage may represent an opportune time for promoting youths' entry onto a healthy trajectory of relationship functioning.

The YRP is a prevention program designed to capitalize on this opportunity for prevention. Targeted at male and female youth aged 14 to 16 who are considered to be at-risk of developing abusive relationships due to their own history of maltreatment experiences, this 18-session, psychoeducational program aims to both prevent abusive behavior and promote healthy nonviolent relationships (Wolfe, et al., 1996). The program is based on aspects of attachment theory, social learning theory and feminist explanations of relationship violence. The YRP is also youth-centered in that it aims to partner with adolescents to assist them in making informed choices and in enhancing their relationship competencies, rather than "treat" deficiencies. Youths were involved in the development and planning of this program and are active participants in facilitating groups and planning a social action activity. Groups are operated in community locations and are attended voluntarily.

The YRP curriculum is organized around four major objectives: 1) Understanding the relationships of power to interpersonal violence; 2) Considering the role of choice in abusive and healthy relationships; 3) Appreciating the societal contexts of relationship violence; and 4) Making a difference in abuse through community action. Education and awareness sessions focus on helping adolescents recognize and identify abusive and healthy behavior across a variety of relationships (e.g., woman abuse, child abuse, sexual harassment). Equality is emphasized as a major component of relationship health. Program participants are directed to consider the "power" that they have gained through access to resources, jobs, education, family income, race, sexual orientation, etc., and to be attentive to responsibilities inherent in having this power. They consider the nature of choices made around relationships through open cross-sex discussion of desirable and less desirable characteristics of dating partners. Societal pressures to choose and act in stereotypically male and female roles and the relation of these roles to dating violence are explored through analyses of video and print material. Finally, explicit information about gender-based violence, sexual assault and its impact is presented through guest speakers, videos and discussion sessions.

The YRP program complements education and awareness sessions with skills development and social action. Healthy and unhealthy listening, empathy, emotional expressiveness and problem solving are modeled and practiced. Teens are then encouraged to apply these skills to both hypothetical and real situations and to share these experiences with the group.

Finally, social action activities provide adolescents with information about resources in their community and with an empowering community development experience. In this section of the program, pairs of youth are given hypothetical problems related to dating violence and are challenged to find social service agencies that may be helpful. With the support and assistance of co-facilitators, they call agencies and arrange a visit to gain information that they then report back to the group. This exercise helps teens overcome their prejudices or fears of community agencies and develop help-seeking competencies. In addition, program participants plan and implement a social action fund-raising event (e.g., walk to end violence against women) or community awareness event (e.g., mall poster display) that allows youth to be part of the solution to ending violence in relationships (Grasley, Wolfe, & Wekerle, 1999).

YRP Program Evaluation

Evaluation of the impact of the YRP was recently completed (Wolfe et al., 2003). One hundred and ninety one adolescents (92 boys and 99 girls) randomly assigned to either the YRP program or to a non-treatment control group were followed over a period of 2 years. Participants completed assessment measures during intake and on completion of the intervention/control period. They were then contacted bi-monthly by telephone. Adolescents who were, or had been, dating during the previous 2-month period were scheduled to complete assessment questionnaires that included information on their dating relationship and activities, abuse perpetration and victimization, relationship competencies, and symptoms of emotional distress. In addition, face-to-face assessment interviews were scheduled with all youths at 6-month intervals. At this time, participants were interviewed about their current life situations, patterns of dating involvement, emotional distress and help-seeking competencies.

Growth modeling was used to compare the progress over time of adolescents who did and did not receive preventative intervention. Briefly, growth modeling is a powerful method for analysis of individual change over time (Willett, Singer, & Martin, 1998). In using this method, all available data is used to estimate each individual's trajectory of change over time on a target outcome variable. For our purposes, for example, we estimated the trajectory of youths' dating violence perpetration and victimization from the data we collected each 2-month period that youths were dating. Due to the flexibility of this method of data analysis, trajectories could be estimated regardless of the number and timing of assessments. For example, the trajectory for one youth could be estimated on the basis of data collected at 18, 20, 24, and 30 weeks after program initiation. If a youth delayed romantic involvement, his or her trajectory could be estimated from data collected 52, 60, 68, and 80 weeks following program initiation. Once these trajectories are estimated, it is then possible to examine whether healthier patterns of change in abuse perpetration and victimization were due to program involvement and/or other variables, such as gender.

Results of analyses showed a number of positive effects of YRP group participation. In terms of abuse perpetration, all adolescents showed an overall reduction in physical and emotional abuse perpetration over time. Importantly though, the decline in physical abuse rate was greater for both male and female adolescents who had participated in the YRP than for youth randomly assigned to non-intervention (see Figure 6-1). To put these results in perspective, we compared the rates of violence among youth during the follow-up period to a normative sample. Among treatment youth, follow-up rates of physical abuse were similar to those found in a normative sample (21% and 11% for

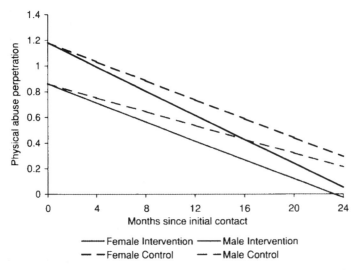

Figure 6-1 Growth curves for physical abuse perpetration for males and females in the intervention and control condition.

Table 6-1   Rates of Victimization by a Dating Partner among
Youth Randomly Assigned to Intervention or Control as
Compared to Rates in a Normative Sample

	Normative ($N = 1419$)	Intervention ($n = 96$)	Control ($n = 62$)
Boys			
Physical abuse victimization	28%	29%	33%
Emotional abuse victimization	15%[1]	10%	29%
Threatening victimization	24%	7%	43%
Girls			
Physical abuse victimization	19%	18%	18%
Emotional abuse victimization	15%	21%	32%
Threatening victimization	21%	24%	27%

[1] Cut-off point set at the 85th percentile in a large independent normative sample
of youth (Wolfe et al., 2001).

girls and boys, respectively). In contrast, 41% of girls and 19% of boys
in the comparison group reported physical abuse perpetration during
their final assessment.

Results were even more striking when victimization was considered. In this case, adolescents who participated in the YRP showed
significantly greater reductions in all forms of victimization than non-
intervention youth. The resulting growth curve lines were similar to
those shown in Figure 6-1. Female adolescents tended to report higher
levels of victimization than male adolescents and rates of abuse victimization declined for all adolescents over time. However, for both boys
and girls, the rate of decline was significantly steeper for intervention
youths as compared to control. Once again, we can put these results in
perspective by comparing rates of abuse victimization at follow-up to reported rates in a normative sample. As shown in Table 6-1, rates of abuse
reported by intervention youths at follow-up were generally similar to
or lower than those reported in a normative sample. Youths from the
control group, in contrast, tended to report rates of abuse victimization
that were considerably higher than the norm. The most striking of these
results is the rate of emotional abuse and threat reported by boys in the
control group, both of which are over 19% higher than normative rates.

This reduction in self-reported victimization is important for a
number of reasons, even beyond reduced victimization itself. Studies
with adolescents and adults have consistently shown that intimate violence most often occurs in relationships that are mutually hostile and
aggressive (Burman, John, & Margolin, 1992; Cordova et al., 1993). This
is not to say that the likelihood of injury or degree of responsibility to

both partners is equal—females are clearly more likely to be the victims of serious and physically harmful assaults (Rennison, 2001; Scott, Finkelhor, & Ormrod, in press). Nevertheless, a reduction in victimization reported by male and female adolescents may be indicative of a relationship that is less hostile overall, and one where perpetration may also be expected to be relatively low.

A second reason that reductions in self-reported victimization are important concerns the potential cognitive biases associated with reporting these events. Among boys who have been maltreated, there is a clear tendency to attribute hostile intent to others in ambiguous situations (Price & Glad, 2003), and the same process likely occurs in adolescents. This cognitive bias also corresponds with male batterers' tendency to see themselves as "victims" of their partners' hostile and aggressive actions (Dutton, 1998). Reductions in self-reported victimization may, then, also reflect more realistic processing of intimate partner intent in ambiguous situations.

In summary, results suggest that adolescents who participated in the YRP program showed trajectories of decreasing frequency and severity of abuse as compared with the control group across several types of violence. Over the 2 years of follow-up, YRP youth were less physically abusive towards their dating partners and reported less physical, emotional and threatening forms of abuse by their partners towards themselves. These results are significant as they suggest that youth who received intervention are on a less abusive relationship trajectory. Cumulative effects may include better self-image and confidence in relationships, healthier expectations and choices with regards to dating partners, greater emotional support from intimate partners and eventually, better marriages and healthier, less-abusive parent-child relationships. From the perspective of resilience then, intervention may have been effective in preventing the development of problems and potentially promoting healthy, "resilient" relationship functioning.

MECHANISMS OF ADOLESCENT RESILIENCE

Although the results from the YRP are promising, several issues remain of concern. How can an 18-week intervention change a trajectory of relationship dysfunction that has taken 14 to 16 years to establish, even if adolescence is a period of normative development and change in this area? What components of the program are most important—increased knowledge and awareness, skills development, feelings of empowerment generated though participation in social action, or aspects of the group experience that are not directly targeted in the intervention, such as the support received from other adolescents? What changes go along with reductions in abuse perpetration and victimization? Human behavior is multi-determined and complex, and finding any single explanation for change is likely impossible. Thus, it is intriguing to begin to "unpack" the development of these adolescents in an effort to identify those factors that relate to positive change.

In our past work we have found that one important factor for change in the trajectory of relationships is trauma symptomatology, especially youths' trauma-related anger (Scott, Wolfe, & Wekerle, 2003). A secondary finding of the study of the YRP was that intervention youth showed greater reductions in trauma symptomatology than non-intervention youth. In an independent study, we have found that level of trauma symptomatology mediates the relationship between a childhood history of abuse and involvement in an abusive dating relationship in adolescence (Wekerle & Wolfe, 1998). Finally, we have presented data to suggest that there is a reciprocal relationship between trauma and dating violence, with each more likely in the presence of the other (Scott et al., 2003). In combination, these results suggest that trauma is one driving factor for continuity and change in patterns of adolescent dating relationships.

Herein we consider another potential mechanism of resilience among these youth—choices made with regard to entering and remaining in relationships. We examine if there is a difference in the frequency or intensity of dating relationships among at-risk adolescents who move into a generally healthy, or less healthy, trajectory in terms of overall adaptation. Two relationship patterns, in particular, are associated with resilience in popular literature and academic scholarship—development of a committed relationship and avoidance of romantic connections.

Escape through Romance: Relationships as Resilience

As long idealized in movies and books, romantic relationships are often seen as a way to escape from disadvantaged and at-risk circumstances. In this respect, romantic relationships in adolescence may function to help at-risk youth shift from patterns of unhealthy family and peer relationships to healthy intimacy and generally adaptive functioning in other life domains. In the developmental literature, adolescent dating is generally considered as a subset of peer relationships (Zimmer-Gembeck, Sienberuner, & Collins, 2001) and part of the normative transition from peer friendships to adult romantic relationships. In childhood and adolescence, peer relationships are seen to influence development positively in that they help to promote social competence, provide emotional security and social support, act as an impetus for amicable conflict resolution, and prepare individuals for later romantic attachments and adult love relationships (Shaffer, 1994). During adolescence, peer relations become more intense and help to fulfill developmental goals such as identity development, socialization into heterosexual behavior, and peer status structuring (Zani, 1993). As adolescents transition to dating relationships, they are potentially provided with additional sources of support and companionship. In addition, these relationships provide the context for youths' developing romantic identities and confidence with intimate sharing. If dating partners provide adolescents with support, companionship, and intimacy, is it possible that opportunities for resilience exist within these relationships?

Empirical research has shown some support for the relationships as resilience theory. Early studies revealed that adolescents considered at risk for unhealthy parenting or criminal involvement were often able to escape negative pathways after forming close intimate relationships. For example, in a longitudinal study of women raised in institutional settings, Quinton, Rutter, and Liddle (1984) found that support from a non-deviant spouse provided a moderating protective effect from negative outcomes. Specifically, women who formed healthy and supportive relationships showed an increased likelihood of exhibiting good parenting in comparison to the women who did not engage in such relationships. Similarly, researchers have shown that young offending males who enter early, cohesive marriages, or marriages with a non-deviant spouse, show decreases in their criminal behavior, suggesting that an adolescent's investment in a socially cohesive marriage has a potentially preventive effect on criminal offending over time (Laub, Nagin, & Sampson, 1998; Quinton, Pickles, Maughan, & Rutter, 1993). Taken together, these findings are important in that they show the potential for romantic relationships to help ameliorate the negative trajectories of at-risk individuals.

There is a limitation of the above studies for understanding adolescent relationships, given the focus on marital relations. The question remains as to whether the shorter-term relationships typical of adolescence can also lead to healthier functioning among at-risk youth. Recent empirical work has provided evidence supporting the potentially positive impacts of dating in adolescence. Davies and Windle (2000), for example, followed a sample of 701 middle to late adolescents over 1 year to explore the correlates of dating. They found that although increased involvement in casual dating was associated with rising trajectories of problem behavior, steady relationships were associated with fewer problematic outcomes. In fact, adolescents who became involved in steady relationships saw themselves as more attractive, showed declines in depressive symptoms, reported more self-disclosure in close friendship dyads and exhibited decelerating trajectories of problem behavior, such as delinquency and alcohol use. Thus, they suggest that greater involvement in steady dating relationships in adolescence may facilitate social and self-development, and may lead to early "maturing out" of the somewhat deviant norms of teen subcultures. Similar findings were also reported by Zimmer-Gembeck, Sienberuner, and Collins (2001), who found that adolescents who engaged in steady relationships perceived themselves as being more socially accepted, physical attractive, and romantically appealing than did their peers who reported lower levels of dating involvement. Again, these results were not found among adolescents with shorter relationships. If dating relationships function in a similar way for at-risk youth, then, steady romantic partnerships during adolescence may be able to provide adolescents with opportunities for resilience.

Avoiding the Pitfall of Adolescent Romance: Relationships as Risk

An alternate model of resilience in adolescent relationships suggests just the opposite—that the best strategy for at-risk adolescents is to delay serious romantic involvement. This recommendation follows from research on the negative correlates of adolescent dating. Failure to delay dating activities and, in particular, the early establishment of committed relationships, is generally thought to be a source of considerable risk for adolescent social and emotional development. From a theoretical perspective, premature stability in romantic relationships is thought to preclude healthy exploration and commitment to the process of identity formation with resultant effects on the adolescents' perusal of other important developmental goals, such as the attainment of education and employment (Erikson, 1968; Samet & Kelly, 1987). In addition, it is reasoned that demands for intimacy and commitment at this age may overwhelm adolescents and restrict autonomous social and emotional growth, so that early dating adolescents fail to develop a full range of negotiation, disclosure, and emotional regulation skills (Samet & Kelly, 1987). Finally, theorists have pointed to the importance of dating as a catalyst for greater affiliation with peer culture, so that adolescents involved in dating may be increasingly at-risk for involvement in normative adolescent misconduct, such as delinquency and experi-mentation with alcohol and drug use (Davies & Windle, 2000; Furman & Buhrmester, 1992).

Research has provided considerable support for theorized risks of early adolescent dating involvement. Early dating initiation has been associated with adolescent problem behaviors, such as teen pregnancy, decline in academic grades, smoking, drinking, and delinquency (Billy, Landale, Grady, & Zimmerle, 1988; Ostrov, Offer, Howard, Kaufman, & Meyer, 1985; Neemann, Hubbard, & Masten, 1995). On the basis of a summary of data, Miller and Benson (1999) suggest that delaying dating long enough to develop a close friendship first increases the chance of engaging in responsible sexual behavior, thereby decreasing the risk of sexually transmitted diseases and teen pregnancy. There is also some evidence that dating itself, rather than just the initial pre-dictors of early involvement, predicts negative outcomes. Neemann, Hubbard, and Masten (1995) followed a sample of 205 students over childhood and adolescence to explore correlates of dating. They found that involvement in dating in late childhood and early to middle adoles-cence was associated with increases in conduct problems and decreases in academic and job achievement. Dating involvement in late adoles-cence did not have these negative associations.

Evaluating the Hypotheses

Follow-up data from adolescents involved in the YRP program al-lowed us to examine these contrasting ideas and to determine if there is a path to resilience through either involvement in or avoidance of com-mitted intimate relationships. To evaluate these two potential paths to healthy functioning in adolescence, we examined the dating patterns of the 96 youth who were involved in the YRP program (48% male) over the 2-year follow-up period, and their relation to negative outcomes. Focus was placed only on negative outcomes that are generally agreed to be severe deviations from a path of healthy development; specifically, the number of adolescents who reported regular or daily use of alcohol, regular or daily use of illegal drugs, who dropped out of or were ex-pelled from school or who reported being arrested or convicted for a criminal offense. In this high-risk sample, a full 44% of youth reported at least one of these outcomes over the follow-up period.

We next examined whether youths' dating patterns were associated with their risk of these severe outcomes. Teens were grouped according to greatest level of reported dating involvement over follow-up. Three groups resulted—those who reported no dating at all over follow-up

Table 6-2 Percentage of Youth Reporting Severe Problems at Least Once during Follow-Up According to Their Pattern of Dating Involvement

Dating Pattern	Percent Reporting Severe Problems at Least Once During Follow-Up
Not dating ($n = 20$)	22%
Some dating ($n = 11$)	27%
Steady dating ($n = 41$)	58%

Note: $\chi^2 = 8.22$, $p < .05$. Differing levels of background risk and initial presenting difficulties did not predict dating pattern. Moreover, steady dating involvement was related to greater risk for youth even controlling for these background factors.

(26%), those who reported dating either periodically or regularly as their greatest involvement (16%), and those who reported going steady on at least one follow-up assessment (58%). A chi-square analysis was then used to determine if the chance of someone reporting a serious negative outcome was associated with his or her dating pattern. Results, as shown in Table 6-2, clearly indicated that steady dating, though not casual dating, was associated with a higher rate of problematic outcomes. About one quarter of youth who reported no dating or some dating also reported at least one serious negative outcome over follow-up, compared to a full 58% of those youth reporting steady dating.

In addition to information about youths' general adaptation and development, we collected data about negative outcomes in relationships—specifically, teenage pregnancy, and experiences of dating violence perpetration or victimization (Victimization and perpetration experiences were self-reported, but then verified with an interview to screen out incidents that were "teasing" and not upsetting to either dating partner). With these data we could examine whether patterns of dating (i.e., some dating or steady dating) were also associated with these negative outcomes. Results showed that overall, negative outcomes were relatively common among adolescents who reported dating—29% reported experiencing dating violence, 29% reported perpetrating dating violence, and 17% reported being pregnant. In combination, 54% of adolescents reported at least one of these negative outcomes.

The association of these negative dating outcomes with youths' dating patterns was next examined. Here, some important sex differences were suggested. For girls, results showed the same pattern of greater risk with greater dating involvement. Among girls who reported casual dating, 50% reported experiencing at least one serious negative outcome, compared to 60% of girls who reported going steady. Among boys this pattern was reversed—among those reporting causal dating,

57% reported at least one serious negative outcome as compared to 39% of male adolescents reporting steady relationships. Limited confidence can be placed in these results however, due to the relatively low number of at-risk male and female adolescents available and the resulting instability in estimates.

In summary, evidence from this high-risk sample of youth suggests that greater dating involvement is not associated with resilience in adolescence. In contrast, greater involvement in dating may be associated with significantly greater risks for negative outcomes at this age. The exception may be for males; although non-dating is still the best option, for boys who are dating, steady commitment may lead to healthier outcomes than casual dating. If there is a path towards resilience, then, it may be by helping youth to think carefully about delaying dating and serious commitment until adulthood (Irwin, Burg, & Cart, 2002).

As a final note around these findings, it is important to recognize that the optimal developmental trajectory of at-risk youth may differ from that of youth more generally. Specifically, the finding that non-dating is associated with better outcomes for at-risk youth does not necessarily imply that all adolescents should avoid committed relationships. Adolescents with a childhood history of maltreatment may be particularly at-risk for negative correlates of dating, whereas adolescents with a firm history of supportive relationships may avoid these pitfalls. Adaptive progression through phases of romantic involvement is predictable from adolescents' past relational experiences, primarily those with peers and family members. In general, successful romance follows from peer competence, which follows from healthy and secure parent-child relationships (Cicchetti & Rogosch, 2002; Connolly, Pepler, Craig, & Taradash, 2000; Shulman & Scharf, 2000). Further research is clearly needed on patterns of dating in normative and at-risk youth and on their correlates for negative and healthy outcomes.

SUMMARY AND CONCLUSIONS

The pervasiveness of relationship difficulties among individuals who have been maltreated points to the need for theory-based relationship violence prevention strategies across the life span (Chalk & King, 1998). In this chapter, we have provided evidence that adolescence is a viable time to offer preventative interventions. At-risk youth who participated in a high-quality, theory-driven intervention group reported lower rates of dating violence over a 2-year follow-up period.

Identifying at-risk youth who do and do not avoid problematic outcomes is a first step towards considering resilience. In our work, rather than try to identify those individuals who are resilient, we are trying to uncover processes and changes that place youth on a healthier developmental trajectory. In the current chapter, we explored the possibility that youths' pattern of relationship involvement may be related to healthy or less healthy functioning. We found that adolescents who avoided steady romantic relationships were also more likely to avoid negative outcomes, such as school dropout and criminal involvement. These results add to the growing evidence that for at-risk youth, in any case, becoming involved in serious intimate relationships does not generally lead to positive outcomes, as often portrayed in popular media. Rather, these relationships may strain the limited capacity of at-risk youth to achieve healthy adaptation.

Continued research is needed to identify those processes most associated with healthy development in at-risk populations. Adolescence remains an important period for change in developmental trajectories, and for interventions to help youth avoid the potentially serious negative outcomes associated with deviations from a healthy developmental path.

REFERENCES

Bevan, E., & Higgins, D. J. (2002). Is domestic violence learned? The contribution of five forms of child maltreatment to men's violence and adjustment. *Journal of Family Violence, 17*, 223–245.

Billy, J. O., Landale, N. S., Grady, W. R., & Zimmerle, D. M. (1988). Effects of sexual activity on adolescent social and psychological development. *Social Psychology Quarterly, 51*, 190–212.

Bolger, K. E., & Patterson, C. J. (2001). Developmental pathways from child maltreatment to peer rejection. *Child Development, 72*, 549–568.

Brown, B. (1999). "You're going out with who?" Peer group influences on adolescent romantic relationships. In W. Furman, B. Brown, & C. Feiring (Eds.), *The development of romantic relationships in adolescence* (pp. 291–329). New York: Cambridge University Press.

Brown, J., Cohen, P., Johnson, J. G., & Smailes, E. M. (1999). Childhood abuse and neglect: Specificity of effects on adolescent and young adult depression and suicidality. *Journal of the American Academy of Child and Adolescent Psychiatry, 38*, 1490–1496.

Burman, B., John, R. S., & Margolin, G. (1992). Observed patterns of conflict in violent, nonviolent, and nondistressed couples. *Behavioral Assessment, 14*, 15–37.

Centers for Disease Control and Prevention (June 9, 2000). Youth Risk Behavior Surveillance—United States 1999. *Morbidity and Mortality Weekly Report, 49*(5), 1–96.

Chalk, R., & King, P. A. (Eds.) (1998). *Violence in families: Assessing prevention and treatment programs.* Washington, D.C.: National Academy Press.

Cicchetti, D., & Rogosch, F. A. (2002). A developmental psychopathology perspective on adolescence. *Journal of Consulting and Clinical Psychology, 70*, 6–20.

Coker, A. L., McKeown, R. E., Sanderson, M., Davis, K. E., Valois, R. F., & Huebner, E. S. (2000). Severe dating violence and quality of life among South Carolina high school students. *American Journal of Preventive Medicine, 19*, 220–227.

Connolly, J., & Goldberg, A. (1999). Romantic relationships in adolescence: The role of friends and peers in their emergence and development. In W. Furman, B. B. Brown, & C. Feiring (Eds.), *The development of romantic relationships in adolescence* (pp. 266–291). New York: Cambridge University Press.

Connolly, J. A., & Johnson, A. M. (1996). Adolescents' romantic relationships and the structure and quality of their close interpersonal ties. *Personal Relationships, 3*, 185–195.

Connolly, J., Pepler, D., Craig, W., & Taradish, A. (2000). Dating experiences of bullies in early adolescence. *Child Maltreatment: Journal of the American Professional Society on the Abuse of Children, 5*, 299–310.

Cordova, J. V., Jacobson, N. S., Gottman, J. M., Rushe, R., & Cox, G. (1993). Negative reciprocity and communication in couples with a violent husband. *Journal of Abnormal Psychology, 102*, 559–564.

Davies, P. T., & Windle, M. (2000). Middle adolescents' dating pathways and psychosocial adjustment. *Merrill-Palmer Quarterly, 46*, 90–118.

Dodge, K. A., Pettit, G. S., & Bates, J. E. (1994). Effects of physical maltreatment on the development of peer relations. *Development and Psychopathology, 6*, 43–55.

Dutton, D. G. (1998). *The abusive personality: Violence and control in intimate relationships*. New York: Guilford Press.

Erikson, E. H. (1968). *Identity: Youth and crisis*. Oxford, England: Norton & Co.

Feiring, C. (1996). Concepts of romance in 15-year-old adolescents. *Journal of Research on Adolescence, 6*, 181–200.

Furman, W., & Buhrmester, D. (1992). Age and sex differences in perceptions of networks of personal relationships. *Child Development, 63*, 103–115.

Grasley, C., Wolfe, D. A., & Wekerle, C. (1999). Empowering youth to end relationship violence. *Children's Services: Social Policy, Research, and Practice, 2*, 209–223.

Irwin, C. E., Burg, S. J., & Cart, C. U. (2002). America's adolescents: Where have we been, where are we going? *Journal of Adolescent Health, 31*(Suppl6), 91–121.

Kaufman, J., & Zigler, E. (1987). Do abused children become abusive parents? *American Journal of Orthopsychiatry, 57*, 186–192.

Larson, R., & Ham, M. (1993). Stress and "storm and stress" in early adolescence: The relationship of negative events with dysphoric affect. *Developmental Psychology, 29*, 130–140.

Laub, J. H., Nagin, D. S., & Sampson, R. J. (1998). Trajectories of change in criminal offending: Good marriages and the desistance process. *American Sociological Review, 63*, 225–238.

Malik, S., Sorenson, S., & Aneshensel, C. (1997). Community and dating violence among adolescents: Perpetration and victimization. *Journal of Adolescent Health, 21*, 291–302.

Miller, B.C., & Benson, B. (1999). Romantic and sexual relationship development during adolescence. In W. Furman, B. B. Brown, & C. Feiring (Eds.), *The development of romantic relationships in adolescence.* (pp. 99–121). New York: Cambridge University Press.

Neeman, J., Hubbard, J., & Masten, A. S. (1995). The changing importance of romantic relationship involvement to competence from late childhood to late adolescence. *Development and Psychopathology, 7*, 727–750.

Newcomb, M. D., & Locke, T. F. (2001). Intergenerational cycle of maltreatment: A popular concept obscured by methodological limitations. *Child Abuse and Neglect, 25*, 1219–1240.

Ostrov, E., Offer, D., Howard, K.I., & Kaufman, B. (1985). Adolescent sexual behavior. *Medical Aspects of Human Sexuality, 19*, 28–36.

Pears, K. C., & Capaldi, D. M. (2001). Intergenerational transmission of abuse: A two-generational prospective study of an at-risk sample. *Child Abuse and Neglect, 25*, 1439–1461.

Price, J. M., & Glad, K. (2003). Hostile attributional tendencies in maltreated children. *Journal of Abnormal Child Psychology, 31*, 329–343.

Quinton, D., Pickles, A., Maughan, B., & Rutter, M. (1993). Partners, peers, and pathways: Assortative pairing and continuities in conduct disorder. *Development and Psychopathology, 5*, 760–783.

Quinton, D., Rutter, M., & Liddle C. (1984). Institutional rearing, parenting difficulties and marital support. *Psychological Medicine, 14*, 107–124.

Rennison, C. M. (2001). *Intimate partner violence and age of victim, 1993–1999.* Washington, DC: U.S. Department of Justice, Bureau of Justice Statistics.

Samet, N., & Kelly, E. W. (1987). The relationship of steady dating to self esteem and sex role identity among adolescents. *Adolescence, 22*, 231–245.

Scott, K. L., Finkelhor, D., & Ormrod, R. (in press). *Juvenile victims of intimate partner violence.* Bulletin. Washington, DC: U.S. Department of Justice, Office of Justice Programs, Office of Juvenile Justice and Delinquency Prevention.

Scott, K. L., Wolfe, D. A., & Wekerle, C. (2003). Maltreatment and trauma: Tracking the connections in adolescence. *Child and Adolescent Psychiatric Clinics of North America, 12*, 211–230.

Shaffer, D. R. (1994). *Social and personality development.* Pacific Grove, CA; Brooks/Cole Publishing.

Shulman, S., & Scharf, M. (2000). Adolescent romantic behaviors and perceptions: Age-and gender-related differences, and links with family and peer relationships. *Journal of Research on Adolescence, 10*, 99–118.

Silverman, J. G., Raj, A., Mucci, L. A., & Hathaway, J. E. (2001). Dating violence against adolescent girls and associated substance use, unhealthy weight control, sexual risk behavior, pregnancy, and suicidality. *Journal of the American Medical Association, 286*, 572–579.

Thornton, A. (1990). The courtship process and adolescent sexuality. *Journal of Family Issues, 11*, 239–273.

Wekerle, C., & Wolfe, D. A. (1998). The role of child maltreatment and attachment style in adolescent relationship violence. *Development and Psychopathology, 10*, 571–586.

Willett, J. B., Singer, J. D., & Martin, N. C. (1998). The design and analysis of longitudinal studies of development and psychopathology in context: Statistical models and methodological recommendations. *Development and Psychopathology, 10*, 395–426.

Wolfe, D. A., Wekerle, C., Scott, K., Straatman, A., Grasley, C., & Reitzel-Jaffe, D. (2003). Dating violence prevention with at-risk youth: A controlled outcome evaluation. *Journal of Consulting and Clinical Psychology, 71*, 279–291.

Wolfe, D. A., Scott, K., Reitzel-Jaffe, D., Wekerle, C., Grasley, C., & Straatman, A. (2001). Development and validation of the Conflict in Adolescent Dating Relationships Inventory. *Psychological Assessment, 13*, 277–293.

Wolfe, D. A., Scott, K., Wekerle, C., & Pittman, A. (2001). Child maltreatment: Risk of adjustment problems and dating violence in adolescence. *Journal of the American Academy of Child and Adolescent Psychiatry, 40*, 282–298.

Wolfe, D. A., Wekerle, C., Reitzel-Jaffe, D., & Lefebvre, L. (1998). Factors associated with abusive relationships among maltreated and non-maltreated youth. *Development and Psychopathology, 10*, 61–85.

Wolfe, D. A., Wekerle, C., Reitzel-Jaffe, D., Grasley, C., Pittman, A., & MacEachran, A. (1997). Interrupting the cycle of violence: Empowering youth to promote healthy relationships. In D. A. Wolfe, R. J. McMahon, & R. DeV. Peters (Eds.), *Child abuse: New directions in prevention and treatment across the lifespan* (pp. 102–129). Thousand Oaks, CA: Sage Publications.

Wolfe, D. A., Wekerle, C., & Scott, K. (1997). *Alternatives to violence: Empowering youth to develop healthy relationships.* Thousand Oaks, CA: Sage Publications.

Wolfe, D. A., Wekerle, C., Gough, R., Reitzel-Jaffe, D., Grasley, C., Pittman, A., et al., (1996). *The youth relationships manual: A group approach with adolescents for the prevention of woman abuse and the promotion of healthy relationships.* Thousand Oaks, CA: Sage Publications.

Zani, B. (1993). Dating and interpersonal relationships in adolescence. In S. Jackson & H. Rodriguez-Tome (Eds.), *Adolescence and its social worlds* (pp. 95–119). Hillsdale, NJ: Erlbaum.

Zimmer-Gembeck, M., Siebenbruner, J., & Collins, W. A. (2001). Diverse aspects of adolescent dating: Associations with psychosocial functioning from early to middle adolescence. *Journal of Adolescence, 24,* 313–336.

CHAPTER 7

Building Strengths and Resilience among At-Risk Mothers and Their Children

A Community-Based Prevention Partnership

Cynthia J. Schellenbach, Kathleen Strader, Francesca Pernice-Duca, & Marianne Key-Carniak

Research on the developmental impact of adolescent pregnancy has proliferated during the recent past (Coley & Chase-Lansdale, 1998; Zazlow, Dion, Morrison, Weinfield, Ogawa, & Tabors, 1999). Reviews of the research have underscored the multitude of risks of parenting for the development of both the young mothers and their children. However, few studies have offered viable conceptual frameworks for assessing the impact of interactive risk and protective factors. Social programs designed to remediate these risks have often produced disappointing results. There are several reasons for these findings.

First, these mothers often have multiple problems. For example, they may lack education, have inadequate social support, have limited access to transportation, or be living in high-violence neighborhoods. Accumulating risks make it even more challenging for young mothers to access interventions that may alleviate these conditions. Moreover, it is often difficult to assess the benefits of intervention if outcomes are evident only in the long-term (e.g., increased job opportunities that may only result from school retention). Finally, research has mainly focused on the negative outcomes associated with the stress of adolescent parenting—although there is growing emphasis on the diversity of outcomes, including positive outcomes, in the scientific literature on adolescent mothers and their children (Schellenbach, Leadbeater, & Moore, 2004).

This chapter extends earlier research on risk and protective factors in several unique ways. First, the present work shifts beyond a focus on individuals (usually the mothers) to include dyadic, social, and community levels of analysis. Second, we move from an examination of single risk factors and outcomes to an examination of multiple factors that interact to predict developmental outcomes. Third, we introduce a strengths-based approach and highlight the diversity in outcomes for young mothers and their children. Finally, we assess a community-based, collaborative approach to the development and implementation of a preventive home visitation program for young mothers and their children.

The first unique aspect of the community collaboration was its basis in theory and its focus on an integrated approach to the multiple components of stress that these mothers confront: individual, dyadic, and social contextual. The program was also based on a multisystemic approach to prevention. It targeted not only mothers and children, but also the social systems (staff systems, services systems, community collaborative systems) that contain these mothers and their children.

Previous research on risk and protective factors has been guided mainly by the use of a causal model of cumulative risk and protection to predict single aspects of behavior intervention (Masten & Coatsworth, 1998). For example, additive main effect models suggest that action of an asset on a single positive outcome is measurable as an additive main effect of the outcome (e.g., the presence of a supportive and involved mother of an adolescent has a positive effect when present but no effect when absent). Alternatively, risk and protective factors may interact so that the impact of a specific risk factor depends on another variable that is activated when risk is experienced (e.g., a young mother may have access to a preventive parenting program when she gives birth to a low birthweight infant, but only if the infant is healthy). Preventive assets can also function to avert risk in a child. For example, early and high quality prenatal care is likely to prevent specific types of risk in the child. Although these frameworks have proven useful in understanding the impact of risk on developmental outcomes, transactional models that account for multivariate risk and outcomes are needed to better understand the function of risk and protective factors in long-term developmental processes.

DIVERSITY OF OUTCOMES
FOR ADOLESCENT MOTHERS
AND THEIR CHILDREN

Past research has typically emphasized the negative correlates of early pregnancy and parenting. For example, research suggested that girls who became pregnant were more likely to have experienced maternal rejection, have poor self-esteem, and have poor problem-solving skills in comparison to those who did not experience early pregnancy. Adolescents with lower school performance were at greater risk for pregnancy than those with higher school achievement (Moore, Miller, Morrison, & Glei, 1995). Adolescent pregnancy also tended to be associated with a pattern of risk-taking behavior that included substance use, risky sexual behavior, and early sexual activity (Moore et al., 1995). Studies have also reported that early pregnancy tends to be related to behavioral characteristics such as aggression. For example, Underwood, Kupersmidt, and Coie (1996) found that half of the aggressive girls within a group of lower-income, African American adolescents became pregnant, compared to 25% of the girls rated as non-aggressive.

However, evidence of diversity within groups of young mothers is accumulating. The importance of school success, individual personality characteristics, and support are documented in the literature. Mothers who have more positive outcomes following birth tend to be older, on grade level for their age, and more socially competent and involved with their peers (Leadbeater & Way, 2001; Whitman, Borkowski, Keogh, & Weed, 2001).

Resilience has been defined by Masten and Coatsworth (1998) as "manifest competence in the context of significant challenges to adaptation or development" (p. 205). Competence has been defined as a pattern of effective adaptation in the environment either broadly defined as the achievement of developmental tasks or specifically defined in terms of domains of competence. Developmentally appropriate indicators of competence vary for younger and older adolescents. For younger adolescents, school engagement, academic achievement, and the development of positive peer relationships are all normative tasks. For older adolescents, the successful transition to young adulthood includes high school graduation, post-secondary school training, and economic

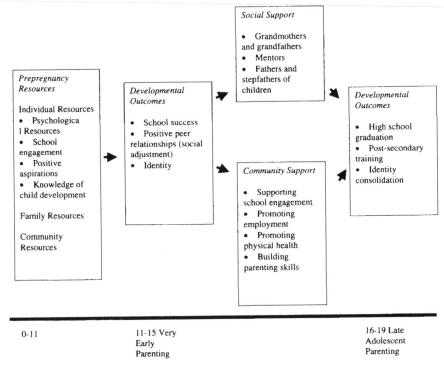

Figure 7-1   A developmental competence model of adolescent parenting.

independence. The competence model for adolescent mothers is depicted in Figure 7-1 (Schellenbach et al., 2004).

A HOME VISITATION PROGRAM TO ENHANCE RESILIENCE AMONG AT-RISK MOTHERS AND CHILDREN

The state of Michigan ranked 39th in indicators of child health and wellbeing, as indicated by high rates of infant mortality and child poverty. These trends were causes for concern in the target Midwestern city. The city had infant mortality rates twice the national average of 9 per 1000, and its residents accounted for 38% of the births to adolescents in the county. The city had the lowest per capita income in the county, and the poverty rate for children under the age of 5 was 39%.

The Healthy Families Oakland Community Partnership

In the early 1990's, Oakland County in general, and the inner-city area of the target city in particular, were primed for a change in its service delivery system. Although numerous service agencies offered support to vulnerable families, there was no unifying connection or bridge among the agencies. Services provided in this traditional way (especially in large communities) are often perceived as confusing to families and difficult to access. Over time, they can become increasingly disjointed, communication between providers becomes limited, and organizations become highly competitive in their respective bids to obtain the scant funding resources that exist to support them. The all-too-frequent results, evidenced in communities throughout the country, are duplication of services to families, failures to assess and connect with families that are harder to reach, and a discouraging inability to improve community-wide indicators of family and child wellbeing.

In 1992, the national child abuse prevention organization in Chicago, illinois entitled *Prevent Child Abuse* secured funding to form a national network of researchers and practitioners that became known as Healthy Families America. A local collaboration secured funding from the Skillman Foundation of Detroit, Michigan for the Healthy Families Oakland program and developed a unique program that was targeted to serve some of the most needy families in a lower-income, high-risk urban area. A local hospital system, human service agencies, and Oakland University were committed to deliver services and to conduct an initial evaluation of the project. The goal was to improve child health and development and family wellbeing by providing an individualized, structured, and strength-based approach of intensive, long-term, home-based family support to vulnerable new families.

The components of this ongoing program include family assessment services that are provided systematically to all families in the target community to enable the connection of families most in need with intensive home-based support as well as home visits by a specially trained family support specialist. Families receive weekly visits during the initial six to twelve months of the life of the child—and which can be extended if family needs warrant. As family stability improves, visits are tapered to twice monthly, monthly, and then quarterly over a three to five year period.

The service delivery team is comprised of bachelor-degreed and non-degreed family support specialists who provide regular and ongoing home-visiting services to families and are employed with the various human service agencies within the community, master-degreed family assessment specialists who provide initial outreach and connection of families to the program and who are employed by the hospital, master-degreed infant mental health specialists who augment home-based support to the family when clinically indicated, and master-degreed supervisors who provide centralized support to the entire collaborative ensuring program accountability, professional support, and skill development for all staff.

Healthy Families Oakland adheres to the standards of practice that are grounded in a series of critical elements, which represent current knowledge about implementing successful home visiting. Family support services are intensive, comprehensive, long-term, flexible, and culturally sensitive and begin prenatally or at birth. The objectives are to: a) provide parenting education through use of standardized curriculum materials on child development, health and safety, as well as activities to promote positive parent-child interaction; b) develop parenting skills through parent-initiated goal setting, observation, and guided interventions that build confidence and competence; c) support the parent-child relationship through the development of a consistent, trusting, and caring relationship between the parent and the family support specialist; and d) advocate on behalf of each family and child by providing linkage to health, education, and community services and to do so in such a way that builds the family's ability to advocate for these services on their own behalf. The home visitation program was designed to promote maternal and child health, improve quality of parenting, improve child and maternal well-being, and increase and integrate the level of community collaboration to provide higher-quality and more accessible services to young mothers and their children.

Sustaining and Growing the Partnership

From 1992 to 2002, the Healthy Families Oakland initiative grew from four organization partners to 10, from serving families citywide to countywide, and from one funding source to 22 private foundation and public funding sources. Funding also came from partner organizations and private community donations.

The implementation and decade-long growth of the program required more than what was anticipated in the momentum that propelled the program's launch. It required a willingness on the part of each agency to take risks as well as the steadfast commitment at all levels, from direct services providers to management and administrative leadership. For example, specialists in family assessment, family support, infant mental health, and parent-group facilitation all worked as members of the Healthy Families Oakland team, while employed at 10 different organizations. Centralized support and supervision was provided by one agency. This required the development of a uniform job description for program positions across agencies. Staff needed to be motivated to increase their contribution to the team and remain engaged with the program, as staff retention is often a challenge in the human services field. When it became evident that the differential salary range for similar positions across agencies was causing some staff to consider moving to another agency, the collaborative partnership agreed on a common salary range to promote stability. Although these system changes may appear minor, the ability and willingness of organizations to alter their systems of staff supervision and human resources and to increase rates of compensation was of paramount importance to the strength and survival of this collaborative.

Evaluating Our Success

While formal evaluation research was not possible at the beginning of the program, a social action research approach was possible. There are many indicators that together suggest the Healthy Families Oakland program has been successful. The collaborative partnership on two occasions (1998 and 2002) underwent an accreditation site visit that required the coordinated involvement of all organizations. Both times, outside assessors recommended and accredited the program and this resulted in securing a four-year national credential as a Healthy Families America program on each occasion.

The collaborative has also annually measured the quality of the workplace and studied the engagement of all staff (representing all 10 agencies) with assistance from the Gallup Organization. The findings have been highly positive and clearly show the commitment of each organization partner and their staff. The Gallup Organization assesses engagement scores across four stages of an engagement hierarchy (The Gallup Organization, 2000). The program's scores have consistently fallen well into the top quartile in comparison to Gallup's extensive national database. In Gallup's meta-analysis of engagement hierarchy, organizations that rank in the top quartile have higher productivity, better employee retention, increased customer satisfaction, better cost efficiencies, and improved employee safety.

Clearly also indicating its success, the Healthy Families Oakland collaborative has sustained itself and grown in numerous ways. However, even in the face of this maturity and relative funding stability, this is not to say that the process becomes easier. The partnerships continuously require devout attention and energy to resist the regular pull that each agency naturally feels from time to time to return to more traditional, single-agency service delivery systems. The stabilizing force during these times is a renewed commitment to the purpose of our shared work.

ASSESSING THE EFFECTS OF A COMMUNITY-BASED PREVENTION PROGRAM

The impact of the Healthy Families Oakland program on the families it served was informally assessed and findings suggest positive outcomes. A more formal evaluation would have given more reliable evidence of the value of the program, but this is not always feasible in a broad-based community program—where the use of even a wait-list control group over many years can be seen as a restriction of services that could excessively burden needy individuals. Large-scale, costly comparisons with communities without the program would provide useful comparison through fully-funded large-scale evaluations.

Analysis of the Process of Service Delivery

In an effort to assess the relationship between services and issues raised by the mothers and the topics actually covered during the home visits, concerns were coded from the Home Visit Process Records that were written at each home visit. Concerns were categorized according to maternal life course issues (e.g., employment, housing, and return to school), intrapersonal and interpersonal relationship issues, and instrumental support issues. During the first 3 months of service, mothers raised concerns regarding interpersonal relationships and instrumental support. Mothers began to initiate a focus on their own life course issues between the 6th and 9th month of service.

The types of services provided by each family support specialist to mothers were summarized from home-visit records to check on the validity of the implementation of the model. Four categories were used to check which program components were implemented at home visits: a) use of a standardized curriculum; b) resources and guided intervention to enhance parenting skill; c) emotional support through the development of a caring relationship with the family support specialist; and d) advocacy to provide referrals and links to community services. The summary showed that the family support specialists utilized each component at each of the home visits, but the greatest amount of time was devoted to professional support from the family support specialist to the young mother. The next highest amount of time was devoted to the use of the standardized curriculum and modeling or guided parenting interventions. Providing advocacy services remained high during the year of participation.

Healthy Families Oakland participants consisted of a sample of 193 mothers and their children who were recruited from two major hospitals in a metropolitan area. The mothers ranged in age from 13 years to 39 years of age. The majority of the participants were young (mean age of 19.6 years), single (95.4%), and low in education. The mean level of educational attainment was 10.6 years at the time of the child's birth. The mothers also tended to be poor, as 89% were below poverty level. There was some diversity in the ethnicity of the sample, with 46.4% Caucasian, 43.7% African-American, 9.4% Latino, and .5% of Asian-American origin.

The infants in the sample (50.7% male) were healthy and of average birth weight (6.86 pounds) and gestational age (38.78 weeks). Scores on Apgar assessments at birth were in the normal range (8.11 at 1 minute following birth, 8.82 at 5 minutes following birth).

Levels of risk and demographic variables within the hospital setting were assessed in individual interviews within 48 hours following birth. The quality of care giving, physical health of the child, and child developmental status were assessed at home visits scheduled when the infant was four months of age. The data collected on the Healthy Start Oakland project were based on a multi-method approach utilizing interviews, standardized assessments, behavioral observations, questionnaires, and self-report data. The variables focus on structural, individual, and dyadic risk and protective factors and the dynamic interplay of these factors in predicting resilient outcomes among the at-risk mother-infant dyads.

Risk and Protective Factors

The hospital record screen consisted of a checklist for the presence or absence of specific psychosocial and mental health factors that are associated with poor parenting and negative child outcomes. Screening was based on an 18-item review of current social contacts and emotional health (e.g., family supports, family problems) and history of mental distress (e.g., substance abuse or depression). Mothers are referred to the second level of the screening process if records indicate risk on any 2 of the 18 items or if the records indicate that the mother meets any of the following criteria: a) single parent; b) late or no prenatal care; or c) mother considered an abortion for the present birth.

The second tier of the assessment involves an in-person interview of the mother. The Family Stress Checklist (Orkow, Murphy, & Nicola, 1985) is a structured interview which assesses the parent's perceptions of his/her strengths and needs in 10 specific areas: childhood experience; lifestyle, behaviors and mental health (including substance use history); previous contact with protective services; coping skills and social support system; stresses; anger management; expectations of children's developmental milestones and behaviors; plans for discipline; perception of child; and bonding and attachment. Each factor is assigned a "0" if no risk is present, a "5" if mild risk is present, and a "10" if severe risk is present. Total scores range from 0 to 100; a total score of 25 or over indicates that the mother is at high risk for problems in parenting. Typically, data indicate that approximately 50% of those interviewed are offered services, or 20% of all mothers originally screened, are offered services.

Four-Month Postpartum Follow-Up Measures

The Child and Maternal Health Record was a tool used by Family Support Specialists to record whether the mother is linked to a primary care physician, immunizations, well-child care visits, and sick-child care visits.

The HOME Scale (The Home Observation Measure of the Environment) (Caldwell & Bradley, 1985) was used to assess the quality of the child's caregiving environment. The scale is an observational and report measure completed during a home visit by the trained family support specialist. The HOME consists of six subscales including responsivity, acceptance of child behavior, organization of the environment, parental involvement with the child, provision of play material, and opportunities for variety. The HOME Scale is widely used and accepted home observation and parental report measure.

The MSSI (Maternal Social Support Index) was used to assess the mother's social support system. Twenty questions are used to tap seven categories of support: help with daily tasks, visits with relatives, individuals the mother can count on in time of need, emergency child care, satisfaction/communication with male partner, community meetings, and community group work involvement. The MSSI has strong test-retest reliability after 9 months and good internal consistency (Pascoe, Ialongo, Horn, & Reinhardt,1990).

The Ages and Stages Questionnaire (Squires, Potter, & Bricker, 1995) was used to assess the development of the infants. Each questionnaire includes 30 items that assess development in five domains: communication, gross motor skills, fine motor skills, problem solving, and personal-social development. Reading level of each questionnaire ranges from fourth to sixth grade. For each of the items, trained staff members assist parents in an observation of whether or not the child performs the specific behavior, coded "yes"; performs the specific behavior on an occasional basis, coded "sometimes"; or does not yet perform the behavior, coded "not yet."

Characteristics of the Families and Findings

The total scores and subscale scores for *risk and protective factors* are depicted in Figure 7-2. Major risks that were reported included multiple family crises and stresses, lack of support and coping skills, and substance abuse or history of depression. Many mothers also reported problems in bonding and attachment to their infants, as well as coping and self-esteem issues. Twenty-four percent of the sample scored within the extremely high-risk domain on an item of the Family Stress Checklist.

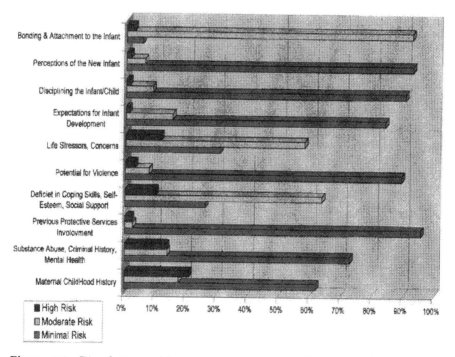

Figure 7-2 Distribution of level of risk across Family Stress Checklist risk scales: Initial assessment subscale scores.

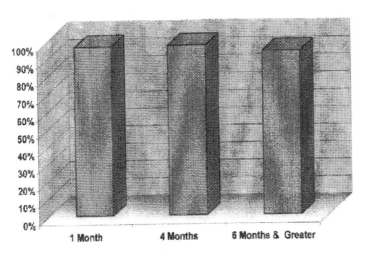

Immunization Rates of Healthy Start Participants During the First Year of Life

Infant's Age

Figure 7-3 Analyses based on total number of open and closed cases during reported month intervals.

The results indicated that the mothers were responsible for many of the household and parenting tasks such as paying bills, housework, preparing the child for bed, and feeding the child. In 33.9% of the cases, the mothers received assistance with these tasks. Most (84%) of the mothers reported that they received instrumental support (food, money, and clothing) from their relatives. Young mothers believed that they could depend on a partner for instrumental support; however, only 15% of the mothers reported that they received instrumental support from their partners. Moreover, many of the young mothers (47.4%) believed that their partners would be able to provide care on a regular basis; however, individuals who provided childcare were most often neighbors (63.2%) or relatives (36.8%).

Health-promotion behaviors were assessed as: engagement in the preventive health care system through successful linkage to the primary health care physician, successful compliance with immunization schedule of the National Academy of Pediatrics, and decreased use of emergency room care. The Health Record for each child was typically completed through the use of a hospital-based computerized recording system to improve the accuracy of the data collection. Data indicated that 100% of the participants were successfully linked to a primary care physician within the system, and 99% of the sample were up-to-date on well-child care visits (documenting engagement with the preventive health care system) and on immunizations at 1 month and 4 months of age. The use of emergency room care was low during the first year of life (6.2 visits) compared to the mean number of visits for a comparable group (21 visits per year).

Analyses of the Effects of Co-Occurring, Multi-Level Risk and Protective Factors

Since one of the major goals of the project was to improve the quality of parenting of the at-risk mothers, several analyses were conducted to assess the relationship of structural, familial, and individual risk and protective factors influencing quality of parenting. Identification of the relative influence of these variables could provide information about the variables that affect program outcomes. Structural variables of educational attainment, income, age, and employment status were derived from the demographic record. Data on intrapersonal risk and maternal coping skills and depression were obtained from the standardized risk assessment administered within 48 hours of birth. Quality of parenting was derived from the HOME scale administered in the mothers' homes 4 months following birth.

In multiple regression analyses, a model using both structural and intrapersonal variables was significant, with income, parent coping skills, and maternal depression independently predicting quality of parenting. Overall, mothers with higher income, better coping skills, and lower levels of depression at time of birth showed higher quality of parenting 4 months following birth.

Perhaps not surprisingly, given that the sample included infants who were healthy at birth, 95% exceeded the cutoff point for positive development on the screening tool (the ASQ) at four months of age. However, based on a developmental competence model of adolescent parenting, parental resources (personal coping skills or maternal depression) and community support (average contact hours with Healthy Families Oakland) were expected to predict developmental outcomes (ASQ scores) at 4 months of age. The results of the multiple regression were significant. However, the influence of contact with the program varied by risk status of the mother. Mothers who had lower risk (more positive coping skills) received average contact and had infants with higher developmental scores. Mothers who were at higher risk (fewer coping skills) received higher than average contact but had infants with lower developmental scores.

DISCUSSION AND IMPLICATIONS

The mothers who participated in this strengths-based community prevention program showed high levels of preventive health-promotion behaviors, as well as enhanced parenting and home environment. Anecdotally, positive gains in the health-promotion behaviors showed in the transition from a more crisis-oriented and distrusting approach to a preventive and trusting approach among the young mothers. Indeed, all of the mothers succeeded in linking to a primary care physician for their preventive health care needs and the mothers were highly successful in achieving age-appropriate immunizations (99%–100%). Moreover, the limited use of emergency room care and the regular use of office-visit medical care were important to providing more effective and earlier medical intervention. Decreased use of emergency room care also results in more cost-effective use of the medical care system.

Mother–infant adaptation was influenced by both structural and intrapersonal variables. Consistent with previous research indicating the negative effects of poverty associated with parenting (McLoyd, 1990), the quality of parenting in this sample was influenced by an individual's economic resources, despite their program involvement. Moreover, personal variables such as the coping skills of the mother also influenced the quality of parenting. In addition, exploratory analyses indicated that the risk level of the mother influenced her interaction with the community-based prevention program and its success in enhancing the children's early development. Programs need to be sensitive to the needs of subgroups of mothers with specific intrapersonal and structural profiles that can interact with program variables to affect outcomes.

Many prevention programs for young mothers focus on a deficits-based approach regarding knowledge, motivation, skills, or support. The findings from this community-based prevention program suggest that a strengths-based approach that builds on the personal resources of the mother and the goals that she has for herself and her child can be effective in influencing positive outcomes for her child. Although all of the mothers in the prevention program were lower income, single, and experiencing personal risks, it was evident that diversity existed within the group. Using a strengths-based model of adolescent competence, individual differences in personal attributes were explored. Higher levels of personal coping skills were related to more positive outcomes for the participants. These findings are consistent with results from previous research suggesting that maternal personality characteristics influence participant outcomes in home-based intervention programs (Olds et al., 1999). Future research should assess the contribution of the individual characteristics of the infant (such as premature births or low birth weight) to program use and outcomes.

The findings also have important implications for funding agencies and public policy programs. These organizations need to rely more on comprehensive programs that address goals for both the mothers and the children within a strengths-based perspective. The Healthy Families Oakland program was effective in increasing community collaboration from 4 partners to 10 partners over a 4-year period and in expanding the number of mothers served from city-wide to county-wide. Finally, the program has been successful in institutionalizing services and increasing funding sources from a single source to more than 22 public and private sources of financial support. In summary, the success of this community-based program demonstrates what can be accomplished within a decade-long, university-community collaboration. The collaboration was successful because of the strong commitment to sustained effort and because of the unique strengths of each of the partners in joining to accomplish a mutual goal: to make a difference in the lives of these young mothers and their children.

REFERENCES

Caldwell, B. M., & Bradley, R. H. (1985). *HOME observation for the measurement of the environment.* Little Rock: University of Arkansas.

Coley, R., & Chase-Landsdale, P. (1998). Adolescent pregnancy and parenthood: Recent evidence and future directions. *American Psychologist, 53,* 152–166.

Gallup Organization. (2000). *Q-12 IMPACT Momentum Training Manual.* Unpublished manuscript. Princeton, NJ: Author.

Leadbeater, B. J., & Way, N. (2001). *Growing up fast: Transitions to early adulthood of inner-city adolescent mothers.* Mahwah, NJ: Erlbaum.

Masten, A. S., & Coatsworth, J. D. (1998). The development of competence in favorable and unfavorable environments: Lessons from research on successful children. *American Psychologist, 53,* 205–220.

McLoyd, V. C. (1990). The impact of economic hardship on Black families and children: Psychological distress, parenting, and socioemotional development. *Child Development, 61,* 311–346.

Moore, K. A., Miller, B. C., Morrison, D. R., & Glei, D. A. (1995). *Adolescent sex, contraception, and childbearing: A review of recent research.* Washington, DC: Child Trends.

Olds, D., Henderson, C., Jr., Kitzman, H., Eckenrode, J., Cole, R., & Tatelbaum, R. (1999). Prenatal and infancy home visitation by nurses: Recent findings. *The Future of Children, 9,* 44–65.

Orkow, B., Murphy, S., & Nicola R. M. (1985). Implementation of a family stress checklist. *Child Abuse and Neglect, 9,* 405–410.

Pascoe, J. M., Ialongo, N., Horn, W., & Reinhardt, M. A. (1990) The reliability and validity of the Maternal Social Support Index. *Family Medicine, 20,* 228–230.

Schellenbach, C. J., Leadbeater, B. J., & Moore, K. A. (2004). A strengths-based approach to enhancing the developmental outcomes of adolescent parents and their children. In K. I. Maton, C. J. Schellenbach, B. J. Leadbeater, & A. Solarz (Eds.), *Strengths-based research and policy: Investing in children, youth, families, and communities* (pp. 117–136). Washington, DC: American Psychological Association.

Squires, J., Potter, L., & Bricker, D. (1995). *The Ages and Stages user's guide.* Baltimore: Brookes Publishing.

Underwood, M. K., Kupersmidt, J. B., & Coie, J. D. (1996). Childhood peer sociometric status and aggression as predictors of adolescent childbearing. *Journal of Research on Adolescence, 6,* 201–223.

Whitman, T., Borkowski, J., Keogh, D., & Weed, K. (2001). *Interwoven lives: Adolescent mothers and their children.* Mahwah, NJ: Erlbaum.

Zazlow, M., Dion, M. R., Morrison, D., Weinfield, N., Ogawa, J., & Tabors, P. (1999). Protective factors in development of preschool-aged children of young mothers receiving welfare. In E. M. Hetherington (Ed.), *Coping with divorce, single parenting, and remarriage* (pp. 193–223). Mahwah, NJ: Erlbaum.

PART III

Expanding Resilience Programs to Include Neighborhoods and Communities

The Social Transformation of Environments and the Promotion of Resilience in Children

KENNETH I. MATON

The risk and protective factors that affect children's development are embedded within multiple levels of the social environment (e.g., setting, community, societal). Unless fundamental changes occur at these varied environmental levels, our interventions to promote resilience in children seem destined to fall short. Specifically, deeply embedded features of setting, community, and societal environments can influence critical risk and protective processes, nullify person-focused, "inoculation" programs, make it difficult to sustain and disseminate promising intervention approaches, and prevent the large-scale mobilization of resources that are necessary for making a substantial difference. It is proposed that successful social transformation requires simultaneous engagement of four key, interrelated processes: capacity building, group empowerment, relational community-building, and culture-challenge. These processes and related intervention approaches at setting, community, and societal levels are identified as potential targets for effective social action. Two intervention approaches, whole school reform and comprehensive neighborhood revitalization, are selected for review in more detail. Directions for future social transformation efforts to promote resilience in children are proposed.

Unless fundamental changes occur in the critical social environments which directly and indirectly affect children's lives, our efforts to promote resilience in children are destined to fall short (e.g., Levine, 1998; Maton, Schellenbach, Leadbeater, & Solarz, 2004). There are four reasons why it is critical to transform multiple levels of the social environment, including the setting (e.g., a local school), community (e.g., school system), and societal (e.g., national educational policy) levels. First, consistent with an ecological perspective, characteristics of social environments are viewed as critical aspects of the risk and protective processes linked to resilience. Deeply troubled schools, violent neighborhoods, and family poverty, for instance, are key proximal environmental risk factors linked to negative youth outcomes; natural support systems, opportunities for school engagement, and community-based programs, in turn, represent some of the key proximal environmental protective factors linked to positive youth outcomes and resilience (e.g., Black & Krishnakumar, 1998; Booth & Crouter, 2001; Garbarino, 1995; Sampson, 2002; Schellenbach & Trickett, 1998; Wandersman & Nation, 1998). Furthermore, each of these proximal social environments is directly influenced by the larger community social systems in which they are embedded (e.g., school, human service, and political systems). Each of these, in turn, is embedded in still larger societal, economic, political, and cultural environments (e.g., Caughy, O'Campo, & Brodsky, 1999; Kelly, 2000; Pilisuk, McAllister, & Rothman, 1996; Sarason, 1996; Thompson & Kline, 1990).

Influencing and ultimately transforming these multiple levels of the environment are thus essential, especially for children confronted with multiple, major risk factors. Transforming environments enhances resilience in part by reducing the number of environmental adversities impacting the child, thereby increasing the odds of a child's resilience in dealing with a smaller number of remaining adversities. The transformation of social environments also significantly increases available protective processes in the family, neighborhood, school, community, and the larger society (Maton et al., 2004).

A second reason for focusing on the transformation of environments is that person-centered intervention programs developed to promote resilience and wellness are often limited in their impact due to the powerful, countervailing nature of the local social environments in which daily life and social problems are embedded (cf. Levine, 1998). For instance, a school-based intervention program that enhances the competencies of inner-city youth may not be sufficient to prevent, or reverse, negative trajectories sustained through the neighborhood, family, and peer group environments. In public health terms, the interventions may not be sufficiently potent to "inoculate" youth against the noxious influence of powerful environmental forces.

Third, when promising programs are developed, fundamental features of social environments often do not allow sustained program operation at the initial host site, or effective dissemination and adoption in new host settings or communities (e.g., Elias, 1997). At the initial development site, demonstration projects may disband or lose effectiveness when demonstration funding ends, program champions move on, and changing priorities result in reductions in resources. In new host settings or communities, the promising conditions present in the initial program development may not be present, including knowledgeable and influential program advocates, active staff collaboration in program development, and the resources necessary for full, high-quality implementation.

Finally, our attempts to influence large numbers of children, and especially those at highest risk, are fundamentally limited due to a lack of social, economic, and political resources. Large-scale, ongoing mobilization across governmental, voluntary, and business sectors is necessary to harness sufficient financial and social resources to develop, disseminate and "bring to scale" effective approaches to promote wellness and resilience. Such a large-scale mobilization is ultimately dependent on major changes at the societal level—that is, in our national priorities, norms, and values.

In summary, deeply embedded features of setting, community, and societal environments influence critical risk and protective processes, can nullify person-focused "inoculation" programs, make it difficult to sustain and disseminate promising intervention approaches, and prevent the large-scale mobilization of resources necessary for making a substantial difference. In order to enhance the resilience of children and families, we need to focus on and transform social environments.

If it is imperative to influence and ultimately transform complex social environments, how should we proceed to do so? Four foundational processes for social transformation appear especially important: capacity-building, group empowerment, relational community-building, and culture challenge (Maton, 2000). These processes are interrelated and interdependent. Indeed, given the difficulty of transforming social environments, any one of these processes, if it does not engage the others, may not bring about enduring change. Rather, as indicated in Figure 8-1, it is the emergent, mutual influences between and among these processes which constitute the heart of social transformation. As depicted in the figure, these influences span levels and domains of the social environment. Below, these transformation processes are described. Then, two intervention approaches, one at the setting level (whole school reform) and one at the neighborhood level (comprehensive neighborhood revitalization) are detailed, and in each case the interrelationships among the four transformational processes depicted.

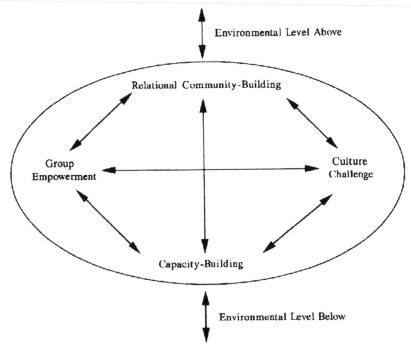

Figure 8-1 Model of social transformation process.

The chapter concludes with suggestions for future social transformation efforts to promote resilience in children.

TRANSFORMING SOCIAL ENVIRONMENTS

The four processes that guide social transformation—capacity building, group empowerment, relational community-building, and culture challenge—are shown in Table 8-1. Each focuses primarily on a particular facet of the social environment—respectively, the instrumental (e.g., tasks, activities), structural (e.g., power relationships), relational (e.g., interpersonal and intergroup relationships), and cultural (e.g., norms and values) facets. A variety of intervention approaches at setting, community, and societal levels exist related to each process.

Capacity Building

Capacity building emphasizes a participatory, grass-roots, strengths-based approach to change (e.g., Briggs, 2002; French & Bell, 1999).

Table 8-1   Four Transformational Processes[1]

	Transformational Processes			
	Capacity Building	Group Empowerment	Relational Community-Building	Culture-Challenge
Facet of Environment Targeted	Instrumental	Structural	Interpersonal	Cultural
Focus	Core methods Resources Problem-solving capability Leadership	Opportunity structure Distribution of resources and power	Connectedness Inclusiveness Shared mission Support Belonging	Belief systems Values Social norms Traditions Practices
Sample Intervention Approach:				
Setting Level	Participatory organizational development	Empowering setting development	School restructuring	Alternative norms development
Community Level	Community-building	Community organizing	Inter-group relationship building	Social activism
Societal Level	Strengths-based social policy	Distributive public policies	Shared national mission development	Social movements

[1]Modified from Maton (2000).

It assumes that the mobilization of setting and community resources from within is the essential foundation for effective and enduring change. Capacity building represents an alternative to the external, top-down, expert-dominated approaches to solving problems with which there has been increasing disillusionment over the years.

Substantively, capacity building focuses on the instrumental facet of the social environment, including the tasks and activities to be performed. Specifically, it attempts to enhance the ability of a setting, community or society to accomplish its core mission. This may involve fundamental changes which enhance core methods (e.g., type of pedagogical approach in education), resources, problem-solving capability, or leadership.

At the setting level, a capacity-building approach with transformational potential necessarily involves the active participation of major constituents in analyzing problems and devising solutions—this might be termed participatory organizational development. In the realm of education, for example, whole school transformation through a capacity-building process marks the work of well-known school reformers such as Comer (Comer, Haynes, Joyner, & Ben-Avie, 1996) and Levin (Finnan & Levin, 2000). Enhanced school engagement is a major protective factor for children which can result from school transformation initiatives.

At the community level, attention to community building has greatly expanded in recent years (cf. Ferguson & Stoutland, 1999). A range of community-building techniques can be employed to increase community capacity, including coalition building, community-based economic development, and comprehensive neighborhood revitalization (e.g., Perkins, Crim, Silberman, & Brown, 2004). Enhanced community-based job opportunities, safer neighborhoods, and an enhanced array of family supports are examples of resilience-promoting factors that can stem from such efforts.

At the societal level, strengths-based social policies have a critical role to play in the capacity-building process (cf. Maton et al., 2004). These policies view citizens as valuable assets and self-determining agents; this contrasts with a deficits-based approach which often views citizens as in need of remediation, punishment, control, or guidance provided by external experts. Strengths-based approaches, for example, direct resources to citizen and community groups via programs which support child, family, school, and community development, thus promoting resilience in children.

Group Empowerment

Group empowerment as a transformational process seeks to enhance the access of marginalized and oppressed families and communities to resiliency-related economic, psychological, and political resources. Economic resources are strongly linked to health, child development, and a vibrant community (e.g., McLoyd, 1998; Taylor, Repetti, & Seeman, 1997; Wilson, 1987). Psychological resources, such as self-esteem and self-efficacy, are also linked to a diversity of resiliency outcomes (cf. Dalton, Elias, & Wandersman, 2001). Political power enables marginalized groups to garner both economic and psychological resources.

Group empowerment focuses on the structural facet of the social environment, including power relationships, control over resources, and relative status. As such, change aims to enhance the opportunity structures (e.g., educational and occupational opportunity) for marginalized groups, and reduce inequalities in the distribution of resources and power at setting, community, and societal levels (Fisher et al., 1996; Rappaport, 1981).

At the setting level, one approach to group empowerment is the development and strengthening of local empowering community settings, such as social action groups, faith communities, self-help organizations, and voluntary associations. Consultation and coalition building efforts can contribute to the ability of such groups to empower their members (cf. Dalton et al., 2001).

At the community level, a key empowerment strategy is community organizing, which strives to influence access to decision making, local policies, and resources. Grass-roots citizen organizing and mobilization of community-based organizations represent two primary community organizing approaches (e.g., Pilisuk et al., 1996), potentially enhancing resilience in children through reducing economic, social, and political adversity affecting families and communities.

At the societal level, distributive public policies contribute to group empowerment through enhancing the resources and opportunity structures available to low-income families, thus reducing adversities and mobilizing protective processes (cf. Briggs, 2002; Lotz, 1998; Saegert, Thompson, & Warren, 2001). Partnerships with allied disciplines, advocacy organizations, and citizen groups enhance our capacity as social scientists to generate policy-relevant research and contribute to policy advocacy in this arena (Maton, 2000).

Relational Community Building

Relational community building represents a third key transformational process. Within local settings (e.g., school, church, neighborhood), within communities, and in the larger society, it speaks both to a vital process, bringing people and groups together, and to critical resilience resources for children and families, including connectedness, support, and meaning.

Relational community building addresses the interpersonal facet of the environment. Thus, it encompasses the quality and nature of personal and intergroup relationships. Environments characterized by high levels of connectedness, inclusiveness, shared mission, support and belonging contribute to positive socio-emotional and behavioral outcomes (e.g., Henderson & Milstein, 1996; Moos, 1996). Relatedly, social analysts posit that a basic cause of many social problems, and a contributing factor to their apparent intractability, is a weakening in the overall social-relational fabric—i.e., the erosion of community (e.g., Putnam, 1996).

At the setting level, various approaches are used to enhance relational community. For example, within school settings, two promising approaches are development of school-wide pro-social norms (e.g., Solomon, Battistich, Watson, Schaps, & Lewis, 1996) and secondary school restructuring (e.g., Felner & Adan, 1988). As key protective processes, enhanced support and community in school and related settings directly contribute to resilience for at-risk children.

At the community level, varied approaches to enhancing relationships in communities are also being undertaken. These include intergroup relationship building through intergroup action coalitions, multicultural training and recruitment initiatives, and community dialogue techniques (e.g., Bond, 1999; Rossing & Glowacki-Dudka, 2001).

At the societal level, there is a critical need for leaders who are capable of shaping a sense of shared purpose and mission. Also essential are concrete practices and policies which are inclusive, bringing together rather than polarizing subgroups within a society. Enhanced inclusion and connectedness at the community and societal levels can reduce discriminatory and related adversities for marginalized populations, and directly enhance resource mobilization for resilience-related efforts.

Culture Challenge

Challenging and transforming extant cultural norms, beliefs and values is the fourth, critical social transformational process. Extant peer norms may curtail resilience for youth either through enhancing risk processes (e.g., norms which support substance use, aggression, teen pregnancy) or impeding protective processes (e.g., norms which discourage school engagement and academic success) (cf. Kupersmidt, Coie, & Howell, 2004). Cultural beliefs which devalue targeted, marginalized groups (e.g., ethnic minorities) similarly impede development and resilience (Weinstein, 2002). Finally, mainstream cultural values linked to self-absorption and individual materialism severely limit the mobilization of the economic and social resources sorely needed to truly make a difference for those children most in need.

Culture challenge addresses the cultural facet of the social environment, encompassing belief systems, values, norms, traditions, and practices. Settings, peer groups, ethnic or population groups, communities, and societies all have unique and vibrant cultures with the potential to promote, or curtail, resilience in children (Martin, 1992; Sarason, 1971).

At the setting level, maladaptive peer norms which directly influence youth behavior can be targeted in various ways. For example, school-based interventions can promote alternate peer norms (e.g., anti-bullying; Olweus, 1994). Also at the setting level, mainstream cultural norms which support problematic adult priorities can be targeted. One strategy is the creation and strengthening of local settings that promote alternative cultural values (e.g., progressive social action or political groups; some self-help, spiritual, or religious organizations).

At the community level, problematic peer norms guiding youth behavior can be addressed via community-wide promotion programs that include media and community-outreach components (e.g., Jason, 1998). Concerning problematic mainstream cultural values, social activism through grass-roots campaigns and coalition-development represent viable strategies at the community level (Saegert et al., 2001).

At the societal level, federal policies can transform extant norms through the creation of new behavioral options or constraints (e.g., nonsmoking areas; seat-belt use). Equally important, problematic cultural norms can be effectively challenged by emergent social movements (e.g., women's and civil rights movements, a needed children's movement), in part inspired by countervailing social science ideas and writings and support for social movement organizations (cf. Etzioni, 1993; Ryan, 1971; Wilson, 1987).

SOCIAL ENVIRONMENT TRANSFORMATION INTERVENTIONS: TWO EXAMPLES

As delineated above, there are many different intervention approaches that have potential to transform important social environments and promote resilience. Below, two of these approaches are examined in more detail. The first, at the setting level, focuses on transforming schools. This is an area where current empirical evidence indicates promising outcomes. The second, at the community level, aims to revitalize impoverished urban neighborhoods. Perhaps not surprisingly, efforts in this domain have a way to go to achieve their transformational goals. Taken together, these two examples illustrate both the potential and the challenges of environmental transformation in two critical domains that affect the well-being and resilience of children and families.

Whole School Reform

In the 1990s, a number of comprehensive approaches to reform schools with high proportions of at-risk students emerged. Often termed "whole school reforms," these efforts aim to transform the school environment in order to enhance student engagement and academic success—key protective processes for at-risk children. Well-known efforts supported by empirical findings include the School Development Program, aiming to transform relationships among educators, students, and parents (Comer et al., 1996); the Child Development program, targeting the creation of a caring school climate (Solomon et al., 1996); the School Transitional Environmental Project, focusing on a transformation of the structure of 9th grade (Felner & Adan, 1988); and Success for All, aiming to transform core classroom pedagogy (Slavin & Madden, 2001).

An additional whole school reform program, Levin's Accelerated Schools Project (ASP), represents a good example of whole school reform with an ambitious social environment transformation agenda. ASP incorporates an in-depth, empowerment-oriented process of change in an attempt to turn around low-achieving elementary and middle schools, many in urban areas. As Finnan and Levin (2000) describe it:

> "The project introduces a process by which the school takes over its own destiny and that of its students. This process includes fundamental explorations of all dimensions of the school, the construction of a living vision and goals, a setting of priorities, a governance system in which all participate, and a systematic approach to action research and problem solving" (pp. 93–94).

ASP, over time, comprehensively targets instrumental, structural, relational, and cultural facets of the school environment. It does so through the four transformational processes of capacity building, group empowerment, relational community building, and culture challenge. For example, the ASP facilitators explicitly work to challenge and transform the culture of low expectations in the school. The assumption is that all students can be fully incorporated, and will respond positively to an enriched learning environment—the type reserved for students identified as gifted and talented (Finnan & Levin, 2000). Such a shift in belief systems helps open the door to new core methods (i.e., a student-centered, action-learning teaching approach). In addition, the opportunity structure allows empowered teachers and parents to contribute productively to educational planning. Furthermore, enhancing capacity-building processes appears to contribute to greater relational community (i.e., a sense of connectedness and shared purpose). In synergistic fashion, the emerging capacity building, group empowerment, relational community, and culture-challenging processes appear to mutually reinforce and contribute to each other.

ASP has been introduced into more than 1,000 elementary and middle schools. Evaluations to date, albeit preliminary, have been positive (e.g., Bloom, Ham, Melton, & O'Brien, 2001). Longitudinal studies of ASP, and the other whole school reform efforts noted above, are needed. There is no reason to believe that systematic attempts to transform individual inner-city schools—much less entire school systems—will be easy. Nonetheless, whole-school reform, with its potential to enhance the critical protective factors of school engagement and school success, exemplifies the resilience-enhancing potential of a focus on transforming local settings.

Comprehensive Neighborhood Revitalization Efforts

At the community level, comprehensive neighborhood revitalization efforts aim to transform poor, urban neighborhoods. A primary goal is to bring about changes in the community environment through reforming multiple community systems, including those in the economic, health, housing, family support, and education arenas. Such efforts would enhance resilience in children by decreasing risk factors and enhancing protective processes. These large-scale, privately-publicly funded initiatives generally take place over extended periods of time— i.e., 5–10 years (Connell & Kubisch, 2001; Kubisch et al., 2002).

A key element of these initiatives is a commitment to long-term community capacity building. The capacity-building emphasis is a direct response to the unsuccessful history of previous top-down, externally driven approaches. The participatory, capacity-building process aims to develop community leadership, personal networks, and social capital. Representatives from multiple citizen groups and multiple sectors take part.

The community capacity-building process is meant to result in more effective, better-functioning community institutions (schools, human services, health agencies, etc.). In addition to these changes in the instrumental domain, changes in the structural, relational, and cultural domains are expected as well. In the structural domain, economic empowerment is the focus, based in part on living-wage job and business creation. Relational community-building, in turn, is expected to result in part from citizens working together to enhance the community and in part from activities such as local newspaper development, community celebrations, and block watches. Finally, culture challenge is reflected in the strengths-based view of the positive potential of inner-city residents and institutions.

A representative example is the Sandtown-Winchester Neighborhood Transformation Initiative (Brown, Butler, & Hamilton, 2001). Sandtown-Winchester is a West Baltimore neighborhood of 10,000 residents. It is characterized by high rates of housing abandonment, unemployment, substance abuse, and violent crime. In 1990, the mayor of Baltimore appointed a task force to design a "neighborhood-driven" planning process that could transform the neighborhood. A local foundation made a long-term commitment of resources and staff to the initiative. Town meetings were held, resident-led planning groups created, and a vision for change developed in multiple substantive areas (e.g., economic development, family support, health, education). A new community-based organization was formed to coordinate partnerships across private and public sectors, including citizen and community groups.

From 1991 to 1999, over 20 new projects across community sectors were initiated. These include Healthy Start (1991, to reduce low birth weight), Family Assistance Network (1993), Home Instructional Program for Preschool Youngsters (1994), Compact Schools Summer Institutes (1995), and direct instruction curriculum in area elementary schools (1997).

Evaluations of the Sandtown-Winchester and other comprehensive neighborhood initiatives have primarily focused on the overall capacity-building process (cf. Brown et al., 2001; Kubisch et al., 2002). Thus, they do not directly reveal the extent to which specific protective factors have enhanced resilience in children and families. However, the studies do reveal a number of valuable contributions, including bringing new resources (e.g., funding, staff) into poor neighborhoods, developing new capacities and relationships, physical improvements, enhancing the quality and quantity of social services, and increased economic activity.

These positive effects notwithstanding, it is clear that this generation of comprehensive neighborhood initiatives did not lead to the complete transformation of neighborhoods, as had been hoped (e.g., Kubisch et al., 2002). Limitations in outcome are due to multiple factors, including difficulties in implementation and the economic, social, and political forces and policies external to inner-city neighborhoods that constrain the potential for change. Analysts propose that future efforts involve more intensive and aggressive efforts focused in part within poor neighborhoods, and efforts extending beyond the neighborhood to the external, surrounding region and to national policies (Kubisch et al., 2002).

FUTURE DIRECTIONS

A variety of intervention approaches will be necessary to influence, and ultimately transform, the facets of the social environment that are critical for child development and the promotion of resilience in children. These approaches must include organizational restructuring, neighborhood and community development, and social policy initiatives. The transformational processes which need to be mobilized include capacity building, group empowerment, relational community building, and culture challenge. As the efforts reviewed in this chapter reveal, much work remains, and many challenges will need to be overcome, to successfully alter environments in ways that truly make a difference in the lives of children who are most at risk.

One key question for our field that arises in environment transformation efforts is whether the research and intervention foundation for such work resides in disciplines external to psychology. After all, psychology's area of expertise traditionally has resided at the level of persons, not environments. Should research and intervention in organizational restructuring be left to organizational development fields, neighborhood revitalization efforts to community development fields, and social policy initiatives to fields with policy expertise?

No one discipline has the knowledge base to understand the various facets and levels of the social environments within which children, families, and our interventions are embedded. Relevant subfields of anthropology, political science, psychology, sociology, urban studies, and others, have important theoretical and methodological knowledge to offer. Indeed, in most cases, research foundational to the transformation of environments will necessarily be multidisciplinary in nature. Thus, at the level of both individual investigators and research disciplines, numerous bridges will need to be built, spanning psychology and other fields (Maton, 2000).

Similarly, in most cases intervention efforts will prove maximally successful and sustainable if they draw upon the expertise and participation of diverse practitioner fields. Early childhood education, community development, government, public education, public health, social work, and youth development are but a sampling of relevant fields. Collaborative partnerships with multiple practitioners and stakeholders will enhance our potential to bring about substantive change across environmental levels. Much knowledge about the challenges and benefits of developing such coalitions has emerged in the past decade (e.g., Briggs, 2002; Wolff, 2001).

The distinctive contributions of psychology to larger, comprehensive efforts to transform environments are critical. We bring to bear expertise on established child-centered, family-centered, and, increasingly, community-centered intervention programs that can be integrated into, or aligned with, larger reform efforts. In addition, we possess invaluable, experience-based knowledge about the important proximal environments within which children and families are embedded.

Although we cannot do it alone, we are important partners in comprehensive, multi-level efforts to promote resilience in children.

Given the difficulty in bringing about change in complex environments and the extensive resources needed in comprehensive, multi-level change efforts, a second major question involves the wisdom of placing too much emphasis on social transformation approaches, in contrast to more narrowly focused efforts. For example, would the wellness and resilience of the children in inner-city neighborhoods addressed by the neighborhood revitalization efforts of the 1990s have been better served by investing those resources in high quality, child- and family-centered promotion efforts? More generally, should incremental change, beginning with person-centered and single-setting programs, serve as the primary strategy, with the expectation that when successful they are our best hope for mobilizing resources for further work in the field?

Research is needed to shed insight on the relative contribution of person-centered versus comprehensive, multi-level change efforts. Important outcomes to examine include enhanced resilience in the population of children at large, and levels of change in the environments that affect children's lives. In part, this research needs to focus on the relative sustainability over time of successful person-centered and environment-centered programs, their successful replication in other settings, and their relative potential to mobilize the levels of human and economic resources necessary to promote resilience in those children most at risk.

Influencing and transforming social environments is a most challenging and daunting endeavor. Although containing their own challenges, person-centered interventions are more consistent with extant theory, training, and practice in psychology and related human services fields. Nonetheless, consistent with the social ecological theme of this volume, our efforts to promote resilience in children, including those most at risk, depends substantially on our capacity to devote greater effort and to make sustained progress in the environmental transformation area. The current chapter contributes to that end by identifying multiple targets for such social transformation efforts, and indicating how they have, and can be, effectively addressed.

ACKNOWLEDGMENTS

This chapter is adapted from Maton, K. I. (2000), Making a difference: The social ecology of social transformation, *American Journal of Community Psychology, 28*, 25–57. The assistance of Tara Smith and helpful editorial feedback of Bonnie Leadbeater are both greatly appreciated.

REFERENCES

Black, M. M., & Krishnakumar, A. (1998). Children in low-income, urban settings: Interventions to promote mental health and well-being. *American Psychologist, 53,* 635–646.

Bloom, H. S., Ham, S., Melton, L., & O'Brien, J. (2001). *Evaluating the Accelerated Schools approach: A look at early implementation and impacts on student achievement in eight elementary schools.* New York: Manpower Development Research Center.

Bond, M. (1999). Gender, race and class in organizational contexts. *American Journal of Community Psychology, 27,* 327–356.

Booth, A., & Crouter, A. C. (Eds.). (2001). *Does it take a village? Community effects on children, adolescents, and families.* Mahway, NJ: Erlbaum.

Briggs, X. S. (2002). *The will and the way: Local partnerships, political strategy and the well-being of America's children and youth.* Cambridge, MA: Harvard University Press.

Brown, P., Butler, B., & Hamilton, R. (2001). *The Sandtown-Winchester Neighborhood Transformation Initiative: Lessons learned about community building and implementation.* Baltimore, MD: Annie E. Casey Foundation.

Caughy, M. O., O'Campo, P. O., & Brodsky, A. E. (1999). Neighborhoods, families, and children: Implications for policy and practice. *Journal of Community Psychology, 27,* 615–633.

Comer, J. P., Haynes, N. M, Joyner, E. T., & Ben-Avie, M. (Eds.). (1996). *Rallying the whole village: The Comer process for reforming education.* New York: Teachers College Press.

Connell, J. P., & Kubisch, A. C. (2001). Community approaches to improving outcomes for urban children, youth and families: Current trends and future directions. In A. Booth, & A. C. Crouter (Eds.) (2001). *Does it take a village? Community effects on children, adolescents and families* (pp. 177–202). Mahway, NJ: Erlbaum.

Dalton, J. H., Elias, M. J., & Wandersman, A. (2001). *Community psychology: Linking individuals and communities.* Belmont, CA: Wadsworth.

Elias, M. (1997). Reinterpreting dissemination of prevention programs as widespread implementation with effectiveness and fidelity. In R. P. Weissberg, T., Gullotta, R. L. Hampton, & B. A. Ryan (Eds.), *Healthy Children 2000: Establishing preventive services* (pp. 253–289). Thousand Oaks, CA: Sage.

Etzioni, A. (1993). *The spirit of community.* New York: Crown.

Felner, R. D., & Adan, A. M. (1988). The School Transitional Environment Project: An ecological intervention and evaluation. In R. H. Price, E. L. Cowen, R. P. Lorion, & J. Ramos-McKay (Eds.), *14 ounces of prevention: A casebook for practitioners* (pp. 111–122). Washington, DC: American Psychological Association.

Ferguson, R. F., & Stoutland, S. E. (1999). Reconceiving the community development field. In R. F. Ferguson & W. T. Dickens (Eds.), *Urban problems and community development* (pp. 33–76). Washington, DC: Brookings Institution Press.

Finnan, C., & Levin, H. M. (2000) Changing school cultures. In H. Altrichter & J. Elliot (Eds.), *Images of educational change* (pp. 87–98). Buckingham, England: Open University Press.

Fisher, C. S., Hout, M., Jankowski, M. S., Lucas, S. R., Swidler, A., & Voss, K. (1996). *Inequality by design: Cracking the bell curve myth.* Princeton, NJ: Princeton University Press.

French, W. L., & Bell, C. H. (1999). *Organizational development: Behavioral science interventions for organization improvement* (6th ed.). Upper Saddle River, NJ: Prentice-Hall.

Garbarino, J. (1995). *Raising children in a socially toxic environment.* San Francisco: Jossey-Bass.

Henderson, N., & Milstein, M. M. (1996). *Resiliency in schools: Making it happen for students and educators.* Thousand Oaks, CA: Corwin Press/Sage.

Jason, L. (1998). Tobacco, drug, and HIV prevention media interventions. *American Journal of Community Psychology, 26,* 151–188.

Kelly, J. G. (2000). Wellness as an ecological enterprise. In D. Cicchetti, J. Rappaport, I. Sandler, & R. P. Weissberg (Eds.), *The promotion of wellness in children and adolescents* (pp. 101–131). Washington, DC: CLWA Press.

Kubisch, A. C., Auspos, P., Brown, P., Chaskin, R., Fulbright-Anderson, K., & Hamilton, R. (2002). *Views from the field II: Reflections on comprehensive community change.* Washington, DC: Aspen Institute.

Kupersmidt, J. B., Coie, J. D., & Howell, J. (2004). Resilience in children exposed to negative peer influences. In K. I. Maton, C. J. Schellenbach, B. J. Leadbeater, & A. L. Solarz, (Eds.), *Investing in children, families and communities: Strengths-based research and policy* (pp. 251–268). Washington, DC: American Psychological Association.

Levine, M. (1998). Prevention and community. *American Journal of Community Psychology, 26,* 189–206.

Lotz, J. (1998). *The lichen factor: The quest for community development in Canada.* Sydney, Nova Scotia: UCCB Press.

Martin, J. (1992). *Cultures in organizations: Three perspectives.* New York: Oxford University Press.

Maton, K. I. (2000). Making a difference: The social ecology of social transformation. *American Journal of Community Psychology, 28,* 25–57.

Maton, K. I., Schellenbach, C. J., Leadbeater, B. J., & Solarz, A. L. (Eds.). (2004). *Investing in children, families and communities: Strengths-based research and policy.* Washington, DC: American Psychological Association.

McLloyd, V. C. (1998). Socioeconomic disadvantage and child development. *American Psychologist, 53,* 185–204.

Moos, R. H. (1996). Understanding environments: The key to improving social processes and program outcomes. *American Journal of Community Psychology, 24,* 193–201.

Olweus, D. (1994). Bullying at school: Basic facts and effects of a school-based intervention program. *Journal of Child Psychology and Psychiatry, 35,* 1171–1190.

Perkins, D. D., Crim, B., Silberman, P., & Brown, B. B. (2004). Community development as a response to community-level adversity: Ecological theory and research and strengths-based policy. In K. I. Maton, C. J. Schellenbach, B. J. Leadbeater, & A. L. Solarz (Eds.), *Investing in children, families and communities: Strengths-based research and policy* (pp. 321–340). Washington, DC: American Psychological Association.

Pilisuk, M., McAllister, J., & Rothman, J. (1996). Coming together for action: The challenge of contemporary grassroots community organizing. *Journal of Social Issues, 52,* 15–37.

Putnam, R. D. (1996). The strange disappearance of civic America. *American Prospect (Winter),* 34–48.

Rappaport, J. (1981). In praise of paradox: A social policy of empowerment over prevention. *American Journal of Community Psychology, 9,* 1–21.

Rossing, B., & Glowacki-Dudka, M. (2001). Inclusive community in a diverse world: Pursuing an elusive goal through narrative-based dialogue. *Journal of Community Psychology, 29,* 729–743.

Ryan, R. (1971). *Blaming the victim.* New York: Random House.

Saegert, S., Thompson, J. P., & Warren, M. R. (Eds.). (2001). *Social capital and poor communities.* New York: Russell Sage Foundation.

Sampson, R. J. (2002). Assessing neighborhood effects: Social processes and new directions in research. *Annual Review of Sociology, 28,* 443–465.

Sarason, S. B. (1971). *The culture of the school and the problem of change.* Boston: Allyn & Bacon.

Sarason, S. B. (1996). *Barometers of change: Individual, educational, and social transformation.* San Francisco: Jossey-Bass.

Schellenbach, C. J., & Trickett, P. K. (Eds.). (1998). *Violence against children in the family and the community.* Washington, DC: American Psychological Association.

Slavin, R. E., & Madden, N. A. (2001). *One million children: Success for All.* Thousand Oaks, CA: Corwin Press/Sage.

Solomon, D., Battistich, V., Watson, M., Schaps, E., & Lewis, C. (1996). A six-district study of educational change: Direct and mediated effects of the Child Development Project. *Social Psychology of Education, 4,* 3–51.

Taylor, S. E., Repetti, R., & Seeman, T. (1997). Health psychology: What is an unhealthy environment and how does it get under the skin? *Annual Review of Psychology, 48,* 411–447.

Thompson, B,. & Kline, S. (1990). Social change theory: Applications to community health. In N. Bracht (Ed.), *Health promotion at the community level* (pp. 45–65). Newbury Park, CA: Sage.

Wandersman, A., & Nation, M. (1998). Urban neighborhoods and mental health: Psychological contributions to understanding toxicity, resilience, and interventions. *American Psychologist, 53,* 647–656.

Weinstein, R. S. (2002). *Reaching higher: The power of expectations in schooling.* Cambridge, MA: Harvard University Press.

Wilson, W. J. (1987). *The truly disadvantaged: The inner city, the underclass, and public policy.* Chicago, IL: The University of Chicago Press.

Wolff, T. (Ed.). (2001). Community coalition building—Contemporary practice and research. Special Section, *American Journal of Community Psychology, 29,* 165–329.

CHAPTER 9

Promoting Resilience in the Inner City

Families as a Venue for Protection, Support, and Opportunity

DEBORAH GORMAN-SMITH, PATRICK TOLAN,
& DAVID HENRY

The conditions in the inner city create formidable impediments to healthy development. As a setting for children's development, the inner city offers scarce, and often unreliable, resources and frequent threats, many of which may be beyond a child's or family's control (Tolan, Sherrod, Gorman-Smith, & Henry, 2004). The multiplicity and frequency of threats can seriously harm many children and families. Children living in these environments are at increased risk for most social and psychological problems (Children's Defense Fund, 1991), and the cumulative effect is to seriously hamper healthy and safe development. Given this ecological risk, we explore how to promote healthy or resilient development of inner-city children. Based on the available research, we address a set of issues pertinent to understanding risk and resilience of inner-city youth, with a particular focus on the family as an important venue for promoting positive development among children.

Promoting positive development within the inner city rests on remarkably similar premises as those helpful for all children and families in society. Yet, at the same time, the unique strains, challenges, and impediments in the inner city require us to simultaneously consider important distinctions and variations in risk factors when formulating approaches to positive development.

We begin this chapter by outlining the unique developmental context of inner-city neighborhoods, followed by a review of the current literature on resilience among children living in the inner city. We then offer a developmental-ecological model to help guide research. We address differences in outcomes for children and youth living in inner-city neighborhoods, including the mechanisms through which more positive adaptation might occur and those that are promising focus areas for prevention. Finally, we outline our suggestions for future research and discuss the implications for intervention and prevention.

THE INNER CITY
AS A DEVELOPMENTAL CONTEXT

Recently, there has been resurgent interest in evaluating the effects on youth development of community characteristics, particularly the characteristics of poor urban communities (Brooks-Gunn, Duncan, Klebenov, & Sealand, 1993; Coulton, Korbin, Su, & Chow, 1995; Sampson, 1997). Much of the research has been spurred by the work of William Julius Wilson. In *The Truly Disadvantaged*, Wilson (1987) argued that the deindustrialization of the U.S. economy—the shift of jobs from cities to suburbs and the flight of the minority middle-class from the inner cities—led to increasingly concentrated poverty in urban areas. The number of neighborhoods with poverty rates that exceed 40 percent, a threshold definition of extreme poverty or underclass neighborhoods, rose precipitously over the intervening decades of the 1970s and 1980s. Wilson argued that as a result, people living in neighborhoods of concentrated poverty had become isolated from job networks, mainstream institutions, and role models and that this isolation could be linked to a number of problems, including school dropout and the proliferation of single-parent families. With this increased focus on the characteristics of inner-city life came interest in understanding what this context meant for children's development (e.g., see Brooks-Gunn, Duncan, & Aber, 1997).

There are obvious distinctions between urban, rural, and suburban contexts, with equally distinct implications for children's development. There is also variation *within* each of these broad types of settings that is important to consider. We focus on inner-city neighborhoods and distinguish these from other types of urban neighborhoods, particularly those occupied predominately by residents falling into the middle to upper socioeconomic status, but also from those that are more simply "poor" (Crane, 1991; Wilson, 1987). As noted by Wilson (1987), inner-city neighborhoods are characterized by high concentrations of families living in poverty (greater than 40%), high crime rates, low rates of owner-occupied housing, more public housing, and a higher proportion of single-headed households. Urban poor (but not inner-city) neighborhoods are also economically impoverished compared with most communities (e.g., 20% to 40% of the population lives below poverty) and have elevated levels of most social problems, but they are distinguished from inner-city neighborhoods by the range of income levels, the extent of owner-occupied housing, business investment levels, and greater access to resources for social and economic problems. Although both types of impoverished urban neighborhoods can be linked to increased risk for most developmental problems, researchers have contended that life in the inner city has more pronounced effects on development and other outcomes for children and families (Garbarino & Sherman, 1980; Garbarino, Dubrow, Kostelny, & Pardo, 1992; Wilson, 1987). Evidence is accumulating that supports this contention. For example, Tolan, Henry, Guerra, Huesmann, VanAcker, & Eron (2004) found that rates for all types of psychopathology among children living in inner-city neighborhoods were above national rates, while this was not the case for other urban poor neighborhoods. Aggression and delinquency rates, for example, were 2.5 and 2.8 times greater, respectively, than the national rate in the inner-city communities. Similarly, Crane (1991) reported a sharp increase in risk of school dropout and teen pregnancy for adolescents living in inner-city neighborhoods over that found in other urban communities. These findings suggest a particularly risky developmental ecology associated with inner-city residence.

Characteristics of inner-city communities linked to increased risk include exposure to high rates of community violence (Gorman-Smith & Tolan, 1996; Richters & Martinez, 1993), absence of economic and social resources (McLoyd, 1989; Sampson & Laub, 1994), family disruption (e.g., higher percentage of female-headed households), economic homogeneity (Brooks-Gunn et al., 1993), and lack of neighborhood support and involvement (Gorman-Smith, Tolan, & Henry, 2000; Sampson, Raudenbush, & Earls, 1997). Families living in inner-city neighborhoods are more likely to be headed by single-parents and to face underemployment, irregular employment, and economic stress. It is more likely that children living in these neighborhoods have adolescent parents, incarcerated family members, and a parent with alcohol or drug problems. In addition, families are more likely to live in substandard housing, and their children are more likely to attend inadequate schools (Brooks-Gunn et al., 1997).

In addition to the specific stressors associated with living in the inner city, families living in urban environments are at increased risk for other life stressors, such as the loss of a friend or family member, significant health problems in the family, or separation or loss of a parent. They are more likely to be burdened by chronic and serious health problems (Hernandez, 1993), with less access to and familiarity with health care services (Aday, 1993). Women in lower socioeconomic classes are more likely to experience the illness or death of children, the absence of husbands, and major losses in childhood that may make coping with new losses even more difficult (Belle, 1982; McLoyd, 1989). Even when income is controlled, families headed by single mothers are more likely than two-parent families to experience stressful life events, such as unemployment and changes in income, job, residence, and household composition (McLanahan, 1983; McLoyd, 1989). High levels of stress are associated with greater risk of anxiety, depression, and other health problems. The psychological distress associated with such stress can undermine the quality of parenting and family relationships (McLoyd, 1989; Patterson, Reid, & Dishion, 1992). The prevalence of risk factors and associated problems across residents in the neighborhood may exacerbate the impact of life events.

Children living in economically disadvantaged communities are also exposed to significantly more stressful life events than children living in other settings. In one study, children in inner-city communities experienced the same number of stressful events in 1 year as other children experience over their entire lifetime (Attar, Guerra, & Tolan, 1994). The greater number and types of stressors, combined with characteristics of urban environments, provide a particularly challenging set of circumstances under which families must manage the daily needs of their children.

The bleak portrayal suggests a life fraught with ever-present harm, impediments, and limited resources for successful development. However, many children in inner-city neighborhoods function at typical or "normal" levels for our society. Despite social and economic disconnection, many families protect, nurture, and support their children toward conventional success and integration into the larger society. What accounts for these differences in response to risk among families and what factors promote positive child development in these settings?

RESILIENCE AMONG CHILDREN LIVING IN THE INNER CITY

The focus of this book is on resilience, a term receiving more scrutiny in recent years (Luthar, Cicchetti, & Becker, 2000). For example,

Table 9-1 Percentage Reporting Exposure to Violence
and Victimization

Item	Last Year	Lifetime
Family member robbed or attacked	16.5	33.3
Other than family member robbed or attacked	23.5	33.2
Seen someone beaten up	54.0	67.7
Seen someone shot or killed	15.8	22.5
Witnessed other violent crime	5.6	12.6
Close friend killed	5.6	8.8
Victim of nonviolent crime	5.6	10.5
Victim of violent crime	6.5	10.5
Victim of sexual assault	0.4	1.1

Perry (1997) argues that simply because children may be malleable (able to adjust to changing circumstances) does not mean they are necessarily resilient (able to develop despite negative events or to recover readily). As the research on resilience develops, more are calling for incorporating concepts of development and successive developmental influences in efforts to understand children's resilience (Leadbeater, Schellenbach, Maton, & Dodgen, 2004; Masten & Coatsworth, 1998), such as recognizing that functioning at any given point may depend on prior experience; current support for healthy functioning; and the pattern of support, opportunity, and effective developmental training within the child's environment over time (Gorman-Smith & Tolan, 2003). We would add to this the importance of considering the setting within which a child develops and his or her social relationships as salient and ongoing influences on development and risk.

In considering development within the inner city, it is likely unrealistic to assume that children will be unaffected by exposure to chronic and pervasive stressors such as economic strain, overtaxed schools, and community violence (Bell, Flay, & Paikoff, 2002). For example, Table 9-1 lists violence exposure for our Chicago Youth Development Study sample of inner-city adolescents. It should be noted that this is a sample with overrepresentation of more aggressive youth by design. Nevertheless, the data are consistent with other inner-city samples (e.g., Attar et al., 1994), suggesting very high rates of serious violence exposure.

The chronic threats to healthy development and the requirements of adapting to conditions in the inner city may also create longer-term impediments to success as one moves toward adulthood (e.g., educational achievement and employment skills) (Tolan & Gorman-Smith, 1996). Therefore, it may be more informative in developmental research to expand the focus beyond current functioning to include a longer-term perspective, specifically as it relates to coping, resources, and opportunities that can promote positive adaptation and long-term functioning (Bell et al., 2002; Tolan et al., 2004). There has simply not been enough research to yet understand both the limits of positive adaptation and the extent to which positive outcomes along multiple dimensions are even possible (Garbarino, 2001).

DEVELOPMENTAL-ECOLOGICAL MODEL

Our work, and the work of many others in this area, is guided by a developmental-ecological model of risk and development (Bronfenbrenner, 1979). A central tenet of developmental-ecological theory is that individual development is influenced by the ongoing qualities of the social settings in which a child lives or participates and the extent and nature of the interaction between these settings (Bronfenbrenner, 1979, 1988). Family functioning, peer relationships, schools, communities, and larger societal influences (e.g., media) affect child development. Interactions among these settings and factors also affect risk and development. Thus, an important implication of developmental-ecological theory is that the impacts of major developmental influences, such as family functioning, are dependent, at least in some part, on the sociological characteristics of the communities in which youth and families reside. How families function or how they parent may differ depending on the neighborhood in which they live, and the same level of family functioning may carry different risks depending on neighborhood residence (Furstenberg, 1993; Gorman-Smith et al., 2000; Sampson, 1997).

A developmental-ecological model also views time as an important consideration, recognizing children's capacity for change over time. The same factor may have a different impact depending on the age of the child. Thus, risk and risk factors must be considered within the developmental trajectory.

We outline this perspective because in considering factors that promote resilience among inner-city children, it is important to recognize that each level of system is related to another. It is particularly important to consider how neighborhood characteristics and related social processes can frame family functioning and its impact on child development. In addition, we are suggesting a focus on family functioning that includes not only the traditional considerations of parenting practices and the quality of family relationships, but also family problem solving, coping, and management of developmental and ecological challenges. In Figure 9-1, we illustrate a conceptual model of how families cope with the stressors of inner-city life. This model has four components, each with multiple dimensions that may be important to consider. For

Figure 9-1 Conceptual model of family resilience promotion in the inner city.

example, stressors may be distinguished in form and likely impact as *chronic environmental stress*, such as poverty or community violence; *life events*, such as death of loved ones; *daily hassles*, such as difficulty getting to and from school or the grocery store; and *role strain*, such as conflict between expectations for behavior and attitudes locally and those at school or work settings. Also outlined are various coping resources used by families that relate to child (and parent) outcomes. This theorized process illustrates how the family's context and its management of typical challenges in a stressful ecology might help explain child functioning over time. The model also emphasizes the family as a central system among neighborhood effects and as a focus of interest in resilience among inner-city children. Readers are referred to Tolan and Gorman-Smith (1997) for a more detailed discussion.

THE INTERTWINED ROLE OF NEIGHBORHOOD SOCIAL PROCESSES AND COMMUNITY STRUCTURAL CHARACTERISTICS IN CHILD DEVELOPMENT

Recent work has suggested that it is not just community structural characteristics (such as poverty, economic investment, heterogeneity, or crime rates) that are important in understanding risk, but also the social processes or organization within the neighborhood (Leventhal &

Brooks-Gunn, 2000; Sampson et al., 1997). Social organization is reflected in felt social support and cohesion among neighbors, sense of belonging to the community, supervision and control of children and adolescents by other adults in the community, and participation in formal and voluntary organizations. Although the extent of the direct connection between neighborhood social organization and structural characteristics is unknown, researchers theorize that a community's structural barriers can impede neighborhood social organization, and minimal social organization, in turn, can increase various risks among youth (Elliott et al., 1996; Sampson et al., 1997).

This work suggests that a community's influence on development should be considered at two levels: the structure of the community (e.g., mobility, political economy, heterogeneity) and its social organization or network of relationships and organization. Perhaps the most influential study on this topic is the report by Sampson et al. (1997), who applied an elegant multilevel sampling procedure to evaluate these relations. They found that the relation of community structural characteristics to crime was mediated, in part, by neighborhood social processes. Sampson et al. (1997) labeled these processes "collective efficacy." Collective efficacy refers to the extent of social connection within the neighborhood combined with the degree of informal social control (the extent to which residents monitor the behavior of others with the goal of supervising and monitoring children and maintaining public order). This research suggests, by extension, that any attempt to understand protective processes should include neighborhood social processes. Tolan, Gorman-Smith, and Henry (2003a), for example, found that although community structural characteristics (e.g., poverty level, crime level, business investment) had some direct effects on youth risk for violence, these structural characteristics were mediated, in part, by neighborhood processes. Notably, the impact of these neighborhood processes on risk was primarily through family functioning.

Studies suggest that among communities with similar structural dimensions (e.g., poverty), there are significant differences in neighborhood social organization and networks that affect how families function and how parents manage their children (Furstenberg, 1993; Garbarino & Sherman, 1980; Sampson & Laub, 1994). For example, in a study of parenting among single mothers in poor, urban neighborhoods, Furstenberg (1993) found that those residing in the most dangerous neighborhood adapted by isolating themselves and their families from those around them. Although this served to increase the mother's sense of safety, it also cut her off from potential social supports. Similarly, Jarrett (1997) found that parents in poor neighborhoods often use "bounding" techniques that restrict children to their homes and limit access to neighborhood influences, particularly peers. Other research has pointed to the importance of "precision parenting" in poor, urban neighborhoods (Mason, Cauce, Gonzales, & Hiraga, 1996). That is, in some urban neighborhoods, the relation between parental monitoring and involvement is such that both too little and too much are associated with increased behavior problems among youth. This relation is not found in studies of families residing in other types of neighborhoods. This relation, dependent on neighborhood type, may reflect a variation by neighborhood in the relation between family functioning and risk.

In our Chicago Youth Development Study (Gorman-Smith et al., 2000), we found different relations between family patterns and types of delinquency in different types of neighborhoods. We found that youth from "task-oriented" families (i.e., families with relatively high levels of discipline consistency, parental monitoring, and structure in family roles, but low levels of emotional warmth and cohesion and beliefs about family importance) were at increased risk for serious and chronic (including violent) delinquency. However, this was only the case when the families lived in neighborhoods with low levels of social organization. These findings suggest that if emotional needs such as a sense of belonging and support are met by the neighborhood, the risk carried by the family is minimized. This may indicate an important ecological consideration for prevention: It may be as useful to help families connect to and build neighborhood support as it is to try to improve parenting skills (Sampson, 1997).

FAMILY AS FOCUS FOR RESILIENCE VENUE FOR INNER-CITY YOUTH

There is a considerable literature on how family-focused interventions can aid children and reduce risk (Kamon, Tolan, & Gorman-Smith, in press; Tolan, 2002), and many of these interventions are devoted to inner-city families, youth, and schools (Tolan & Gorman-Smith, 1996). In most cases, the interventions focus on promoting or mediating parenting skills and intra-familial problems. Few extend beyond parenting to helping a family manage excessive stress that challenges many inner-city families (Bell et al., 2002). We believe that efforts to increase resilience should focus on both effective parenting and building, sustaining, and using supports, protective processes, and opportunities for normal development (Bell et al., 2002).

Beyond the focus of intervention, however, lies a broader issue in the intervention research. Locating the source of risk in how well (or poorly) a family functions, and as such the sole target for intervention, may be largely misdirected and limit the effectiveness of the intervention (Gorman-Smith et al., 2000). It may be that the best approaches are those that support families in managing developmental and environmental challenges while also helping build or support strong parenting skills and good family relationships. In addition, aid and support for problem solving and promoting safety and opportunity for youth may need equal consideration (Tolan et al., 2004). We summarize here three areas of emphasis in our proposed approach: family functioning, family as a buffer to stress, and family coping.

Family Functioning

As indicated earlier, the evidence on family functioning and its relation to inner-city residence is still developing. Notably, there are many families within the inner city that are providing good parenting, have warm and effective communication, and have strong family problem-solving skills. There is also evidence that focusing on maintaining or improving parenting skills can reduce risk of inner-city children. For example, the Metropolitan Area Child Study, a preventive intervention for inner-city elementary aged school children, found that effects on aggression (reduced risk) were limited to those who had also been provided a family intervention that emphasized consistent parenting practices, positive parenting, and helped with family organization and problem-solving practices. A further analysis showed that the impact of the family intervention in promoting child cooperation and prosocial behavior, while reducing aggression, was linked to improved parenting skills (Tolan, Hanish, McKay, & Dickey, 2002). Similarly, in a more recent study of inner-city families with a child entering first grade, the SAFE Children preventive intervention (which focused on effective parenting skills among other areas) improved monitoring skills in high-risk families (those exhibiting poor parenting prior to entry). These examples suggest that supporting parenting practices, but with an expanded focus on problem-solving skills and strong and warm communication, is important in helping inner-city families to reduce child risk and to increase resilience.

Family as Buffer

Although families are affected by neighborhood and community characteristics, they can also act as a buffer to the effects of stress on youth (Compas, Worsham, & Ey, 1992). Important family characteristics that mitigate the stress of inner-city life for children are family resource-fulness, adaptability, and organization (McAdoo, 1982); the develop-ment of reliable and effective social ties (McAdoo, 1982); and protective parenting styles (Clark, 1983; Ogbu, 1985). For example, Staples (1978) notes that, historically, the African-American family has provided a sanctuary that buttresses against pervasive oppression and racism (Mason et al., 1996). Extended family and informal kin networks also create a buffer against stress (Massey, Scott, & Dornbusch, 1975). More recently, interest has turned to how family connections might help fam-ilies manage developmental and ecological risks (Gorman-Smith, Tolan, Henry, Quintana, & Lutovsky, in press).

Parenting practices have also been linked to the impact of stress on youth, although there have been few studies of any potential buffering effects among inner-city children. Research has shown that responsive, accepting, and stimulating parental care can promote resilience among low-birthweight, premature children living in poverty (Bradley et al., 1994). It has also been demonstrated that families that demonstrate good parenting skills, adequate problem-solving skills, and emotional cohe-sion create a protective effect in inner-city communities (Gorman-Smith et al., 2000). However, that protective effect depends on the extent of the family's sense of community involvement and ownership, including a social support network for parents. Again, these results suggest that focusing on skills and within-family relationships alone may be inad-equate. Instead, focusing on supporting or promoting parenting that is embedded in the community is critical in fostering the positive effect that good family functioning can have on development.

Family Coping

In addition to refuge from harm that families can provide, inner-city families may enhance the coping of children by teaching them strategies for survival and methods of mutual support, and by fighting negative myths of society (Massey et al., 1975). The effectiveness of a child's cop-ing skills also depends on family functioning, and the best approaches are those that are sanctioned by the family, modeled by others, and con-sistent with family beliefs and expectations (Tolan & Gorman-Smith, 1997). For example, Peters (1976) found that most African-American parents expected their children to encounter racism by age 6, but were uncertain how to prepare them or how to help them cope with it. Al-though it was clear that parents saw racism as an inevitable stressor, they also worried that it would have undue influence, making the child overly self-conscious about race and racism. Their primary strategy was to delay the encounter as long as possible. Thus, the effectiveness of coping can be compromised when the stress cannot be prevented or be adequately prepared for. Coping is directed toward minimizing actual and potential harm. As increasing evidence surfaces on the effectiveness for inner-city youth of incorporating a sociopolitical understanding of racism and economic inequities, more programs are needed that aid parents in determining how to navigate these and other difficult issues (Watts, Griffith, & Abdul-Adil, 1999; Zimmerman, Ramirez-Valles, & Maton, 1999).

PREVENTION TO HELP INNER-CITY FAMILIES ENHANCE CHILD RESILIENCE: AN EXAMPLE

Despite data pointing to the importance of family in buffering risk associated with inner-city residence, there are few empirically evaluated, family-focused interventions (Catalano, Berglund, Ryan, Lonczak, & Hawkins, 1998) that address this assumption. One example of a family-focused preventive intervention that has been empirically tested is the Schools and Families Educating Children (SAFE Children) (Gorman-Smith et al., in press; Tolan, Gorman-Smith, & Henry, 2003b). This intervention helps families with developmental and ecological challenges, and in doing so, helps them to garner support and resources. This project targeted families of first-grade children in inner-city neighborhoods in Chicago. The family-focused intervention is composed of 20 weekly multiple family group meetings (with four to six families per group) and addresses issues of parenting, family relations, parental involvement and investment in their child's schooling, peer relations, and neighborhood support. Embedded in the intervention is a focus of managing these within the context of inner-city life.

Analysis of outcomes 1 year after the intervention found general effects, with families assigned to the program maintaining initial levels of involvement in school, while controls who received no intervention decreased their involvement quickly and substantially. The intervention also improved reading achievement, with treatment children developing at a pace commensurate with national norms while controls dropped farther behind. Higher-risk families—those entering the program with limited parenting skills and lower family functioning—also saw significant gains in parental monitoring and decreases in child risk behavior (e.g., aggression, low concentration) and growing social competence in the children.

SEVEN OPPORTUNITIES TO SUPPORT
FAMILIES FOR RESILIENCY
IN THE INNER CITY

Effective interventions can be developed to address the ecological context and to help build opportunity and protect inner-city children and their families (Tolan et al., 2004). However, these efforts represent only a small portion of the avenues for building or supporting resilience among inner-city residents. Here we offer seven opportunities for supporting resilience. Each can be undertaken in many ways, but all can be focused through the family. None has been explored empirically to much extent, so they remain only promising or logically attractive rather than proven methods (Catalano et al., 1998).

1) *Support families to meet normal demands.* Much of parenting is providing clear and consistent rules and expectations that create an effective organizational atmosphere, and being involved in a way that supports the monitoring of a child's activities and friends. As in any context, parents vary in the extent of their ability to function well. Even in the inner city, most do function well (Gorman-Smith et al., 2000). However, these families may need additional support to maintain adequate levels of functioning. In addition, efforts to support positive child development may be more effective when combined with efforts to manage environmental challenges (Gorman-Smith & Tolan, 2003).

2) *Supporting access to and links between families, health care systems, and schools.* Because many families of the inner city are disengaged or alienated from health care and educational systems, they often do not make the best use of resources. In addition, many inner-city parents may feel intimidated by such systems, and as a result they may miss opportunities to advocate for their child. Concordantly, they may not understand methods of engaging these systems and those involved in administrating them. Creating access and links to these systems can build resilience in families by connecting them with other families, creating a network of support and aid in easing strains of parenting. It can also build resilience by connecting families to resources and information.

Beyond building links, families would benefit from efforts to maintain parental motivation in the face of environmental impediments. For example, one finding from our SAFE Children intervention was that it helped to maintain an initial level of enthusiasm for school involvement among parents; the involvement of those without the support and links dropped off precipitously during the first year of school (Tolan et al., 2003b). Such efforts can be extended to aiding parents in advocating effectively and engaging in collaborative efforts with health care, law enforcement, and educational professionals to build protection and opportunity for their children.

3) *Provide zones of safety, watchful adults, and community ownership.* In addition to bolstering parenting and helping parents engage in the systems that promote healthy development, families can increase their resilience through strong neighborhood social processes (Sampson et al., 1997). Informal social networks can help to increase resilience to various problem behaviors. In neighborhoods where adults report feeling connected to and responsible for the community, and are able to monitor children's behavior, children's risk for problem behaviors is lower, and particularly for those children living in higher-risk families (Gorman-Smith et al., 2000). In addition, providing safety zones—places where adults monitor the activities of children—allows for children to engage in normal recreational activities, or even in the more basic activity of getting to and from school.

4) *Embed parenting and families in the neighborhood.* Related strategies to the above are efforts to make parenting and family well-being a neighborhood value and concern. For example, early in the development of the Metropolitan Area Child Study, we conducted focus groups with parents about what they wanted from an intervention. One of the most common requests was to be able to develop networks with other families to make their parenting efforts more successful and to become a force in the community. Connecting families with similarly aged children and who are struggling to manage many of the same demands can provide sources of social support. Efforts to embed or re-embed parenting and family concerns in neighborhoods within the inner city seem likely to help build resilience (Catalano et al., 1998).

5) *Linking risk, problems, and impediments to civic and political issues.* Although often not considered in building resilience, efforts to help children and parents in the inner city to understand the political and civic processes that affect the concentration of poverty, the limited access to educational and child resources, and other issues might prove valuable. The focus may be on improving their ability or in increasing their confidence in their abilities to make use of resources (Watts, Abdul-Adil, & Pratt, 2002). For example, one effort uses rap music and other popular culture to address the economics of the drug trade and its relation to violence as a way of helping inner-city youth to develop constructive methods of attempting to address this scourge (Watts et al., 2002). A process study of that intervention suggested that, as political awareness increased, the tendency toward violence was replaced by focused interest in affecting the circumstances and political conditions of the drug trade and violence in their communities.

6) *Skills training and opportunity promotion.* It is evident that inner-city children face a more risky and less supportive developmental ecology than children elsewhere in this nation, and this in turn leads to lower academic performance and increasing disparities in preparedness for adult life (Leventhal & Brooks-Gunn, 2000). To counter this, skills training and increased opportunities to engage in roles and activities that will lead to success are important elements of resilience building (Bell et al., 2002). These may be specific programs to remediate relative deficits in reading or other academic skills, or opportunities to enroll in educational and vocational opportunities.

7) *Reconnecting the inner city to the political economy.* A major problem for inner-city communities is that they are not perceived as integral to the economy or political power bases of cities (Wilson, 1987). Thus, efforts to better connect the economic and social life of these communities to the rest of the city are likely to build protection and opportunity for youth residing there. Whether through increased business investment or greater access to and development of educational and health systems, reconnecting the inner city to the political economy of the city and region will benefit its children and families (Catalano et al., 1998; Tolan et al., 2004).

CONCLUSIONS

Our empirical understanding of the development of children residing in our country's inner cities is growing. What is emerging is a grim picture of the level and extent of risk faced by these children and their families. At the same time, there is evidence of strong family functioning that helps mitigate these risks. In addition, it appears that family functioning can be aided by neighborhood networks and growing opportunities and resources to manage normal child development. As we have noted, there are many opportunities for building resilience by building family strengths in these high-risk communities. However, few have explored the potential of these avenues and even fewer have conducted empirical tests of their impact.

ACKNOWLEDGMENTS

This work was supported by funding from the National Institute of Child Health and Human Development (R01 HD35415), Centers for Disease Control and Prevention (R49 CCR512739), and a Faculty Scholar Award from the William T. Grant Foundation to the first author.

REFERENCES

Aday, L. A. (1993). *At risk in America: The health and health care needs of vulnerable populations in the United States.* San Francisco: Jossey-Bass.

Attar, B. K., Guerra, N. G., & Tolan, P. H. (1994). Neighborhood disadvantage, stressful life events, and adjustment in urban elementary school children. *Journal of Consulting and Clinical Psychology, 23,* 391–400.

Bell, C. C., Flay, B., & Paikoff, R. L. (2002). Strategies for health behavior change. In J. Carrington (Ed.), *The health behavioral change imperative: Theory, education , and practice in diverse populations* (pp. 17–39). New York: Kluwer Academic/Plenum Publishers.

Belle, D. E. (1982). The impact of poverty on social networks and supports. *Marriage and Family Review, 5,* 89–103.

Bradley, R. H., Whiteside, L., Mundfrom, D. J., Casey, P. H., Kelleher, K. J., & Pope, S. K. (1994). Early indications of resilience and their relation to experiences in the home environments of low birthweight, premature children living in poverty. *Child Development, 65,* 346–360.

Bronfenbrenner, U. (1979). *The ecology of human development: Experiments by nature and design.* Cambridge, MA: Harvard University Press.

Bronfenbrenner, U. (1988). Interacting systems in human development. Research paradigms: Present and future. In N. Bolger, A. Caspi, G. Downey, & M. Moorehouse (Eds.), *Persons in context: Developmental processes* (pp. 25–49). New York: Cambridge University Press.

Brooks-Gunn, J., Duncan, G. J., Klebenov, P. K., & Sealand, N. S. (1993). Do neighborhoods influence child and adolescent development? *American Journal of Sociology, 99,* 353–395.

Brooks-Gunn, J., Duncan, G. J., & Aber, J. L. (Eds.). (1997). *Neighborhood poverty: Vol. 1. Context and consequences for children.* New York: Russell Sage Foundation.

Catalano, R. F., Berglund, M. L., Ryan, J. A., Lonczak, H. C., & Hawkins, J. D. (1998). *Positive youth development in the U.S.: Research findings of positive youth development programs.* Washington, DC: Department of Health & Human Services, National Institute of Child of Health and Human Development.

Children's Defense Fund. (1991). *The adolescent and young adult fact book.* Washington, DC: Author.

Clark, R. (1983). *Family life and school achievement: Why poor black children succeed or fail.* Chicago: University of Chicago Press.

Compas, B. E., Worsham, N. L., & Ey, S. (1992). Conceptual and developmental issues in children's coping with stress. In A. M. LaGreca, L. J. Siegel, J. L. Wallander, & C.E. Walker (Eds.), *Stress and coping in child health* (pp. 7–24). New York: Guilford Press.

Coulton, C. J., Korbin, J. E., Su, M., & Chow, J. (1995). Community level factors and child maltreatment rates. *Child Development, 66,* 1262–1276.

Crane, J. (1991). The epidemic theory of ghettos and neighborhood effects on dropping out and teenage childbearing. *American Journal of Sociology, 96,* 1226–1259.

Elliott, D., Wilson, W., Huizinga, D., Sampson, R., Elliot, A., & Ranking, D. (1996). The effects of neighborhood disadvantage on adolescent development. *Journal of Research in Crime and Delinquency, 33,* 389–426.

Furstenberg, F. (1993). How families manage risk and opportunity in dangerous neighborhoods. In W. J. Wilson (Ed.), *Sociology and the public agenda* (pp. 231–258). Newbury Park, CA: Sage.

Garbarino, J. (2001). An ecological perspective on the effects of violence on children. *Journal of Community Psychology, 29,* 361–378.

Garbarino, J., & Sherman, D. (1980). High-risk neighborhoods and high-risk families: The human ecology of maltreatment. *Child Development, 51*, 188–198.

Garbarino, J., Dubrow, N., Kostelny, K., & Pardo, C. (1992). *Children in anger.* San Francisco: Jossey-Bass.

Gorman-Smith, D., & Tolan, P. H. (1996). Prospects and possibilities: Next steps in sound understanding of youth violence: Response to McCord (1996), Henggeler (1996), Dakof (1996), and Kuppermince and Repucci (1996). *Journal of Family Psychology, 10*, 153–157.

Gorman-Smith, D., & Tolan, P. H. (2003). Positive adaptation among youth exposed to community violence. In S. Luthar (Ed.), *Resilience and vulnerability: Adaptation in the context of childhood adversities* (pp. 392–413). Cambridge, UK: Cambridge University Press.

Gorman-Smith, D., Tolan, P. H., & Henry, D. B. (2000). A developmental-ecological model of the relation of family functioning to patterns of delinquency. *Journal of Quantitative Criminology, 16*, 169–198.

Gorman-Smith, D., Tolan, P. H., Henry, D., Quintana, E., & Lutovsky, K. (in press). The SAFE Children Prevention Program. In P. Tolan, J. Szapocznik, & S. Sombrano (Eds.), *Developmental approaches to prevention of substance abuse and related problems.* Washington, DC: American Psychological Association.

Hernandez, D. (1993). *America's children: Resources from family, government, and the economy.* New York: Russell Sage Foundation.

Jarrett, R. L. (1997). Bringing families back in: Neighborhoods' effects on child development. In J. Brooks-Gunn, G. J. Duncan, & J. L. Aber (Eds.), *Neighborhood poverty: Vol. 2. Policy implications in studying neighborhoods* (pp. 48–64). New York: Russell Sage Foundation.

Kamon, J., Tolan, P. H., & Gorman-Smith, D. (in press). Interventions for adolescent psychopathology: Linking treatment and prevention. In D. Wolfe & E. Mash (Eds.), *Behavioral and emotional disorders in adolescents: Nature, assessment and treatment.* New York: Guilford Press.

Leadbeater, B., Schellenbach, C., Maton, K., & Dodgen, D. (2004). Research and policy for building strengths: Processes and contexts of individual, family, and community development. In K. I. Maton, C. J. Schellenbach, B. J. Leadbeater, & A. L. Solarz (Eds.), *Investing in children, youth, families and communities: Strengths-based research and policy* (pp. 13–30). Washington, DC: American Psychological Association.

Leventhal, T., & Brooks-Gunn, J. (2000). The neighborhoods they live in: The effects of neighborhood residence on child and adolescent outcomes. *Psychological Bulletin, 126*, 309–337.

Luthar, S. S., Cicchetti, D., & Becker, B. (2000). The construct of resilience: A critical evaluation and guidelines for future work. *Child Development, 71*, 543–562.

Mason, C. A., Cauce, A. M., Gonzales, N., & Hiraga, Y. (1996). Neither too sweet nor too sour: Problem peers, maternal control, and problem behavior in African American adolescents. *Child Development, 67*, 2115–2130.

Massey, G. C., Scott, M., & Dornbusch, S. M. (1975). Racism without racists: Institutional racism in urban schools. *The Black Scholar, 7*, 3.

Masten, A. S., & Coatsworth, J. D. (1998). The development of competence in favorable and unfavorable environments: Lessons from research on successful children. *American Psychologist, 53*, 205–220.

McAdoo, H. P. (1982). Stress absorbing systems in black families. *Family Relations, 31*, 479–488.

McLanahan, S. (1983). Family structure and stress: A longitudinal comparison of male and female-headed families. *Journal of Marriage and the Family 45*, 347–357.

McLoyd, V. C. (1989). Socialization and development in a changing economy: The effects of paternal job and income loss on children. *American Psychologist, 44*, 293–302.

Ogbu, J. U. (1985). A cultural ecology of competence among inner-city blacks. In M. Spencer, G. K. Brookins, & W.R. Allen (Eds.). *Beginnings: The social and affective development of black children* (pp. 45–66). Hillsdale, NJ: Erlbaum.

Patterson, G. R., Reid, J. B., & Dishion, T. J. (1992). *Antisocial boys: A social interactional approach.* Eugene, OR: Castalia.

Perry, B. D. (1997). Incubated in terror: Neurodevelopmental factors in the "Cycle of Violence." In J. D. Osofsky (Ed.), *Children in a violent society* (pp. 124–149). New York: Guilford Press.

Peters, M. F. (1976). *Nine black families: A study of household management and childrearing in Black families with working mothers.* Ann Arbor, MI: University Microfilms.

Richters, J. E., & Martinez, P. (1993). The NIMH community violence project: I. Children as victims of and witness to violence. *Psychiatry, 56*, 7–21.

Sampson, R. J. (1997). The embeddedness of child and adolescent development: A community-level perspective on urban violence. In J. McCord (Ed.), *Violence and childhood in the inner city* (pp. 31–77). Cambridge, UK: Cambridge University Press.

Sampson, R. J., & Laub, J. H. (1994). Urban poverty and the family context of delinquency: A new look at structure and process in a classic study. *Child Development, 65*, 523–539.

Sampson, R., Raudenbush, S., & Earls, F. (1997). Neighborhood and violent crime: A multilevel study of collective efficacy. *Science, 277*, 918–924.

Staples, R. (1978). *The black family: Essays and studies.* Belmont, CA: Wadsworth.

Tolan, P. H. (2002). Crime prevention: Focus on youth. In J. Q. Wilson & J. Petersilia (Eds.), *Crime* (pp. 109–128). Oakland, CA: Institute for Contemporary Studies Press.

Tolan, P. H., & Gorman-Smith, D. (1996). Families and the development of urban children. In O. Reyes, H. Walberg, & R. Weissberg (Eds.), *Interdisciplinary perspectives on children and youth* (pp. 67–91). Newbury Park, CA: Sage.

Tolan, P. H., & Gorman-Smith, D. (1997). Treatment of juvenile delinquency: Between punishment and therapy. In D. Stoff, J. Breiling, & J. Maser (Eds.), *Handbook of antisocial behavior* (pp. 405–415). New York: Wiley.

Tolan, P., Guerra, N., & Kendall, P. C. (1995). Introduction to special section: Prediction and prevention of antisocial behavior in children and adolescents. *Journal of Consulting and Clinical Psychology, 63*, 515–517.

Tolan, P. H., Hanish, L., McKay, M., & Dickey, M. (2002). Evaluating process in child and family interventions: Aggression prevention as an example. *Journal of Family Psychology, 16*, 220–236.

Tolan, P. H., Gorman-Smith, D., & Henry, D. (2003a). Developmental ecology of urban males' youth violence. *Developmental Psychology, 39*, 274–291.

Tolan, P. H., Gorman-Smith, D., & Henry, D. (2003b). *Supporting families in a high-risk setting: Proximal effects of the SAFE Children prevention program.* Unpublished manuscript, available from the first author.

Tolan, P. H., Sherrod, L., Gorman-Smith, D., & Henry, D. (2004). Building protection, support, and opportunity for inner-city children and youth and their families. In K. I. Maton, C. J. Schellenbach, B. J. Leadbeater, & A. L. Solarz (Eds.), *Investing in children, youth, and families: Strengths-based research and policy* (pp. 193–212). Washington, DC: American Psychological Association.

Watts, R., Abdul-Adil, J. K., & Pratt T. (2002). Enhancing critical consciousness in young African American men: A psychoeducational approach. *Psychology of Men and Masculinity, 3*, 41–50.

Watts, R. J., Griffith, D. M., & Abdul-Adil, J. K. (1999). Socio-political development as an antidote for oppression: Theory and action. *American Journal of Community Psychology, 27*, 255–272.

Wilson, W. J. (1987). *The truly disadvantaged: The inner city, the underclass, and public policy.* Chicago: The University of Chicago Press.

Zimmerman, M. A., Ramirez-Valles, J., & Maton, K. I. (1999). Resilience among urban African American male adolescents: A study of the protective effects of sociopolitical control on their mental health. *American Journal of Community Psychology, 27*, 733–751.

CHAPTER 10

A Community-Based Approach to Promoting Resilience in Young Children, Their Families, and Their Neighborhoods

RAY DeV. PETERS

Resilience, as defined in this volume and elsewhere, refers to positive human adaptation in the context of adversity (Roberts & Masten, Chapter 2; Werner, Chapter 1). Emmy Werner's pioneering studies on risk and protective factors affecting vulnerability and resilience in life span human development (e.g.,Werner & Smith, 1989, 2001), along with the work of Norman Garmezy (1971, 1991) and Michael Rutter (1979), have defined the field of resilience research for the past two decades.

The main focus of the present chapter is on intervention programs that attempt to promote resilience by fostering positive development in early childhood. The chapter begins with a review of the literature concerning early childhood development programs, and a discussion of several limitations of these programs. Virtually all the effective early childhood programs in the research literature that have demonstrated long-term positive adaptation have focused their interventions on high-risk children or young children with high-risk mothers. Several potential limitations of this individual risk approach are discussed in light of epidemiological measures of relative versus attributable risk. An alternative approach to resilience intervention is described; namely, a

universal intervention for all young children and their families living in
high-risk neighborhoods. An early childhood intervention project based
on this approach to resilience enhancement, the Better Beginnings, Better Futures Project, is described and the impacts on child, family and
neighborhood development are discussed.

EARLY CHILDHOOD DEVELOPMENT

Within the last 15 years, there has been increased interest in the
influence of the early years of life on children's subsequent health and
development, readiness to learn, and social-emotional well-being. This
interest in the importance of early childhood development appears to
have been spurred by several factors. One is a growing public awareness
of the importance of early experience on brain development and the
potential long-term value to children and society of promoting healthy
development during the period from birth to 6 years, especially among
the most vulnerable children living in impoverished and dysfunctional
families and communities (Cynader & Frost, 1999; McCain & Mustard,
1999; Shore, 1997).

Interest also has derived from longitudinal and epidemiological
studies of children's social, emotional and behavioral disorders, demon-
strating that: a) 15 to 20% of children between the ages of 4 and 16 suffer
from one or more serious adjustment difficulties (Bradenberg, Friedman,
& Silver, 1990; Costello, 1989; Offord et al., 1987); b) few of these children receive social and mental health services (Offord et al., 1987; Tuma,
1989); and c) children with early social and emotional problems, particularly those in low socioeconomic families, are at increased risk for
displaying a wide range of adolescent and adult dysfunctions, including school failure/dropout, unemployment, social welfare dependence,
and criminal behavior (e.g., Campbell, 1995; Loeber & Dishion, 1983;
Lynam, 1996; Moffitt, Caspi, Dickson, Silva, & Stanton, 1996; Reid,
1993). A recent review of the literature (Hertzman & Wiens, 1996) also
indicates the strong determining influence of early child development
on adult health and disease.

A third influence has been concern over high and increasing rates
of child and family poverty in the U.S. and Canada and the long-term
effects of low socioeconomic status on child development through adolescence into adulthood, with subsequent effects on socialization of the
next generation (Duncan & Brooks-Gunn, 1997; Willms, 2002).

This interest in early development has prompted renewed attention
to the effects of intervention programs designed to facilitate positive
development in children and their families, particularly those living in
high-risk, socioeconomically disadvantaged neighborhoods. Questions

concerning the long-term effects of these programs are of particular interest to government policy makers, specifically the degree to which investments in early childhood programs have later effects on academic, health, and social functioning in children and their families, resulting in decreased rates of unemployment, delinquency, welfare participation, and use of health services.

An indication of the importance of these questions is the large number of reviews of early childhood development programs that have been carried out recently, primarily focusing on the state of knowledge concerning long-term effects on young children at high risk and their families (e.g., Durlak & Wells, 1997; Hertzman & Wiens, 1996; Karoly et al., 1998; Mrazek & Brown, 2002; Ramey & Ramey, 1998; Webster-Stratton & Taylor, 2001).

Effective Early Childhood Development Programs

These reviews report that few early childhood development programs have been adequately designed, particularly for children younger than 7 or 8 years old. Most of the programs either have not been evaluated at all, or the evaluations have such serious flaws that no meaningful conclusions can be drawn from them (Mrazek & Brown, 2002).

Most demonstration studies that have shown effects have employed small samples. For example, the High-Scope Perry Preschool Project (Schweinhart, Barnes, & Weikart, 1993) involved 58 preschool children in the intervention, the Carolina Abecedarian Project (Ramey & Campbell, 1984) involved 57 very high-risk children, and the Elmira Nurse Home Visitation Program (Olds, 1997; Olds et al., 1997), found that all the positive long-term outcomes occurred in a small sub-sample of 37 high-risk mothers and their children. Attempts to expand such small-scale "efficacy" trials to multiple sites and to more children have been disappointing (see, for example, the Comprehensive Child Development Project; St. Pierre, Layzer, Goodson, & Bernstein, 1997).

Few studies have followed the children and parents after the program ended to determine long term outcome effects. Further, costs of implementing programs for young children are seldom collected or reported (Karoly et al., 1998). This failure to provide long-term follow-up and economic analyses makes it particularly difficult for policy makers to make informed decisions. Several notable exceptions are the three studies noted earlier (the Perry Preschool Project, the Carolina Abecedarian Project, and the Elmira Nurse Home Visitation Project), as well as the Chicago Child-Parent Centers (CPC) Project (Reynolds, Temple, Robertson, & Mann, 2003). All four of these early childhood intervention studies have now reported economic analyses based on follow-up data for children, and in some cases their parents, to the child's age of 15 (the Elmira project), 21 (Abecedarian and CPC Projects) and 35 (Perry Preschool project).

Another limitation is the narrow focus adopted by program models. In social policy discussions, there is much rhetoric about the potential importance of early childhood programs being comprehensive, holistic, ecological, community-based, and integrated. However, virtually no well-researched programs for young children have successfully incorporated these characteristics into the program model. In the few well-researched studies, focus has been predominately on children's cognitive and academic functioning, not on emotional and behavioral problems, social competence, or physical health. None of these projects has included activities designed to improve the quality of the local neighborhood for young children and their parents. Local community members have had little or no involvement in the development and implementation of the programs. Also, St. Pierre and Layzer (1998) report that few studies have examined the effects of prevention programs integrating with local service providing organizations.

The Risky Business of Risk in Early Childhood Programs

Virtually all of the well-researched early childhood development programs have adopted a targeted or high-risk approach. Studies have attempted to identify important risk factors or to implement targeted programs with children at high-risk for developmental problems (Karoly et al., 1998; Mrazek & Brown, 2002). A major issue facing programs targeted at high-risk children is the relative strength as well as the prevalence of the risk variables selected. Of interest here is the epidemiological concept of *population attributable risk.* The calculation of population attributable risk combines measures of relative risk and prevalence to indicate the maximum reduction in the incidence of a disease or disorder that could be expected if the effects of a causal risk factor could be eliminated (Rockhill, Newman, & Weinberg, 1998; Rothman & Greenland, 1998; Scott, Mason, & Chapman, 1999; Tu, 2003). For example, Offord, Boyle, and Racine (1989) identified five family risk factors and, based on an analysis of attributable risk, concluded that even if it were possible to eliminate these risk factors, the reduction in children's mental health problems would be only from 18% to 14%.

Also, Willms (2002) recently reported attributable risk analyses of the Canadian National Longitudinal Survey of Children and Youth (a large nationally representative sample of over 30,000 Canadian children and their families), begun in 1994 and following children from birth to their early 20's. Willms found that the five most important family risk factors associated with children's cognitive, emotional, and behavior problems were low maternal education, teenage motherhood, low family income; single parenthood, and low paternal occupational status. However, the total cumulative attributable risk for these five risk factors was 19.2 percent. According to Willms (2002), this finding "... indicates that even if we could eliminate all the risk factors associated with family background, we would reduce childhood vulnerability by less than twenty percent." (p.90)

These findings suggest that the major risk factors that have been identified for compromised early childhood development (e.g., family dysfunction, low income, one-parent family) appear to have a low population attributable risk, presenting serious challenges to targeted, high-risk prevention interventions. Even if it were possible to eliminate these risk factors from society, the overall reduction in children's vulnerability would not be great. These results also indicate that 80% of young children manifesting serious cognitive, emotional and behavioral problems do not come from "high-risk" families, but rather from two-parent families with adequate income and parental education. Thus, targeted programs for only high-risk children or families, even if highly effective, may have little impact on the community rates of early childhood difficulties.

Given the limitations of high-risk, targeted programs for early childhood development, there is an increased interest in *universal* programs for young children and their families (McCain & Mustard, 2002; Offord, 1996; Offord, Kraemer, Kazdin, Jensen, & Harrington, 1998; Peters, Petrunka, & Arnold, 2003; Willms, 2002). From a universal perspective, all children are considered to be at risk or potentially vulnerable for developmental problems and therefore should be eligible to participate in programs designed to prevent them. This is similar to the public health approach to preventing many diseases in young children, such as polio and rubella where vaccinations are considered important for all children, not just those considered to be at "high risk" for contracting the diseases.

Two types of universal programs have been identified: those that focus on particular neighborhoods, or on particular settings such as a school or a housing project, and those programs that are state, province, or countrywide (Offord, 1996). There has been little research to date on either type, especially with young children (Mrazek & Brown, 2002; Offord, 1996; Webster-Stratton &Taylor, 2001).

To summarize, much of the current knowledge about positive long-term effects of early childhood development programs rests on a few small-scale programs carried out with extremely disadvantaged, high-risk children or their mothers. These programs have focused primarily on the intellectual and cognitive development of young children or on improving the quality of life for their mothers. Few have reported cost data. There has been little reported attempt to integrate programs with other local services or organizations or to involve parents or other local residents in program planning or implementation. Finally, very few programs have been universal, e.g., focused on all children in a particular neighborhood. Rather, most projects have targeted very high-risk children and families employing risk variables that may have low population attributable risk with limited potential for reducing overall rates of childhood difficulties.

THE BETTER BEGINNINGS, BETTER FUTURES PROJECT

After reviewing these limitations of early childhood programs, the Ontario Government created a program called Better Beginnings, Better Futures (Government of Ontario, 1990), to discover effective ways of supporting the development of young children and strengthening family and community life in disadvantaged neighborhoods.

Project Description

Starting in 1991, funding was provided to eight disadvantaged neighborhoods in Ontario to develop and implement social, health, and educational programs for children from the prenatal period to age 4 in five *younger child* project sites and for children from ages 4 to 8 in three *older child* project sites.

These eight local communities were challenged to meet a combination of project goals: a) to improve the development and well-being of young children; b) to strengthen the abilities of parents to respond effectively to the needs of their children; c) to provide high-quality social, health, and educational programs for children and families that respond to the needs of the neighborhood; d) to develop the capacity of the local neighborhood to help itself by involving parents and other residents in the building of a local organization to deliver these programs; and e) to establish partnerships with other service organizations and coordinate programs to support young children and families in these neighborhoods.

Program Model

The Better Beginnings, Better Futures Project was designed to include the following characteristics in the program model:

Ecological. Programs are to recognize the many influences on the growing child, starting within the family, and expanding outwards to the local neighborhood and broader community;

Holistic. Programs should address all aspects of child development; that is, social, emotional, physical, and cognitive functioning;

Universal. All children in the age group living in the neighborhood and their families are eligible for program participation, not just those seen to be at highest risk;

Community-Based. The model allows the local eight sites considerable freedom and responsibility to tailor programs to local needs, within budget limitations and the overall mandate of the project;

Community-Led. Each site is to insure real and meaningful involvement by parents and other community residents in all aspects of local project development and implementation; and

Collaborative and Coordinated. This model program characteristic encourages partnerships among neighborhood and community organizations providing services for young children and families, and coordination among programs.

The Better Beginnings, Better Futures Project model, implemented in 1991, was unique in that it defined "high risk" by the characteristics of neighborhoods rather than by characteristics of children or their parents. The neighborhoods selected for project implementation were characterized by socioeconomic disadvantage, but all children in the designated age range living in the neighborhood and their families were eligible for program involvement. Thus, the Better Beginnings, Better Futures Project was designed as a universal intervention to foster resilience (i.e., improve developmental outcomes) in all children and their families living in a high-risk neighborhood environment.

Program Participants

Since the program model was universal, child- and family-focused programs were to be available to all children in the specified age range and their families living in the Better Beginnings neighborhoods. In the five younger child sites, the number of birth-to-4-year-old children averaged 600 per site, while in the three older child sites, the average number of 4-to-8 year olds was 500. This resulted in 4,500 children and families available for Better Beginnings programs across the eight project sites each year.

As mentioned previously, these eight neighborhoods were characterized by socioeconomic disadvantage. For example, 83% of the families in the younger child sites and 64% in the older child sites were below Statistics Canada's Low Income Cut Offs. On average, 37% of the families were headed by a lone parent.

Program Activities

The Better Beginnings project model required each community to develop and deliver high quality programs that could be expected to produce positive child, family, and neighborhood outcomes. High-quality programs were defined as paying careful attention to: a) staff recruitment, training, adequate compensation, and participation in decision-making; b) favorable child-staff ratios; c) curriculum development relating program activities to goals and objectives; and d) providing time for all staff to develop close relations with the families and communities in which they work.

The younger child sites, focusing on children from birth to age 4, were required by the Government funder at a minimum to provide home visiting programs, plus supports to increase the quality of local child care, for example, through additional staff and resources to existing day-care and preschool programs and organizing playgroup programs. The older child sites were required to provide in-classroom or in-school programs, plus supports to increase the quality of local child care, through, for example, before and after school and summer holiday art and recreation programs.

In addition, the sites provided a wide variety of other programs tailored to local needs, either by themselves or in partnership with other education and service providers. Examples include parent-child drop-in programs and toy-lending libraries, parent training and support groups, nutrition supports, neighborhood safety initiatives, cultural awareness activities, recreation, and mentoring programs. The younger child sites provided an average of 26 different programs, whereas the older child sites provided an average of 16 different programs for the children, their families and the local neighborhood.

Of the five younger child sites, three invested over half their base government funding in home visiting programs. One of these sites, however, was unique in putting almost all its programming efforts directly into home visiting, perinatal and postnatal support, and child care programming. A fourth younger child site distributed its resources more evenly among the program areas, with strong emphasis on local leadership development as a prevention vehicle. The fifth site is the only Better Beginnings, Better Futures Project located within a First Nation. Stressing values based on traditional culture, it put more than half its base budget into community development and community healing activities. It combined home visiting and playgroup activities with a pre-existing, high-quality child care center that was separately funded.

Of the three older child sites, two made substantial investments in school-based programming. Both of these sites funded classroom assistants who provided enriched support for children in Junior Kindergarten, starting at age 4, through Grade Two. The third site provided comparatively few in-school enrichment activities, concentrating more on before-and after-school and holiday arts and recreation programs, and emphasizing community and leadership development more than many of the other sites.

The Better Beginnings, Better Futures Project is neither a service nor a program. It is a project initiative for mobilizing disadvantaged neighborhoods to foster resilience; that is, promote positive functioning in young children, their families, and the neighborhood itself. According to ecological theory, young children, their families and the local neighborhood should be positively affected by the project through improved family and community environments and resources. In practice, some children and families were touched directly by these improved resources (e.g., home visitors, classroom programs, before and after school programs, parent training, play groups). Some attended programs on a regular basis, others on a very random or part-time basis. Some did not attend any programs but may have been touched indirectly; for example, by a neighbor who attended programs and offered advice/support, by safer streets and parks, or by increased community participation. Larry Schweinhart (personal communication, 2000), from the High-Scope Perry Preschool Project, has described the Better Beginnings, Better Futures Project as being not a program but a "meta-program" or general strategy for fostering resilience in children, families and communities.

Research Methods

A team of multidisciplinary researchers from seven Ontario universities and field researchers in each local site were responsible for the research design, and for data collection, analysis, and reporting. All research activities were coordinated by the Better Beginnings, Better Futures Research Unit with central offices at Queen's University in Kingston, Ontario.

Qualitative, Descriptive Research on Project Development and Organization. Local site researchers were trained to write descriptive reports on program development and implementation at each site using a common protocol. These local site reports were summarized in comprehensive cross-site reports covering a) how the Better Beginnings initiative was developed; b) how communities generated proposals for the original competition in 1990; c) how local residents were involved in project decision making; d) how local service providers and educators were involved in project decision making and resource provision; e) specific program activities and components, as well as staffing patterns; f) the formal and informal decision-making structures and values, committee structure, and management procedures in each project site; and g) personal stories from program participants, staff, and local residents concerning their experiences with the Better Beginnings Project.

Quantitative Outcome Research. Information about children, parents, families, and neighborhoods was collected in a variety of ways: annual 2-hour, in-home parent interviews carried out by local site researchers employed by the Research Coordination Unit; annual direct child measures also collected by Research Coordination Unit researchers; annual teacher reports; and federal and provincial databases (e.g., Statistics Canada Census data, Ontario Principals' Reports of Special Education Instruction).

Baseline information in the eight project neighborhoods was collected in 1992–93 before the Better Beginnings, Better Futures programs were fully operational. Extensive information was collected to determine how children at the upper age of the project window were developing before the programs were in place, as well as characteristics of their families and neighborhoods. This 1992–93 baseline measurement involved 350 *4-year-old children* and their families at the younger child sites, and 200 *8-year-olds* and their families in the older child sites. This baseline sample represented approximately 50% of the eligible children of that age living in the project site.

In 1992–93, three comparison sites were selected for the eight Better Beginnings project sites. These sites were selected, using Statistics Canada Census data, as being similar to the Better Beginnings sites in terms of average annual family income, single parent status, parent education and employment, and cultural identity.

In 1993–94, 1,400 children and their families in the eight project sites and in the three comparison neighborhoods agreed to participate in a longitudinal research group. At the younger child sites, these children were born in 1994. At the older sites, these children were 4 years old in 1993. Data on these longitudinal research groups of children and their families were gathered regularly over a 5-year period in the project and comparison sites. Outcome measures were gathered in the younger child sites when the children were 3, 18, 33, and 48 months of age, and in the older child sites every year from age 4 until the children turned 8 in 1997–98.

In 1997–98, the outcome measures collected from the longitudinal research groups were compared to the baseline information that had been collected in 1992–93. This allowed changes in the children, their families, and the local neighborhoods to be determined within each of the sites during the first 5 years of the project.

Information was gained from the parent interviews, direct measures of child development, annual teacher reports, and the use of neighborhood-level, provincial, and national databases.

Thus, two research designs were employed, resulting in two "views" of the impact of the project. The first (a within-site, before-after design) assessed what changes, if any, occurred between children and families in each of the eight neighborhoods after 5 years of Better Beginnings, Better Futures programming, compared to the baseline data. The second (a quasi-experimental control-group design) examined how changes in children and families in the longitudinal research group in the eight Better Beginnings neighborhoods over 5 years of programming differed from changes in those from the demographically similar comparison sites that were not receiving Better Beginnings, Better Futures funding.

Project Costs. Costs were collected using a common accounting system and software at each site. The cost data collected included both direct dollar expenditures and other costs of operating the programs, particularly volunteer time (so-called service-in-kind or opportunity costs). These latter costs typically have not been measured in projects of this sort.

RESULTS

The results presented in this section summarize the data collected from 1991 to 1998. For detailed reports of these data, see Peters et al. (2000), and Peters et al. (2003).

Child Outcomes

Child Emotional, Behavioral, and Social Functioning

A major reason for undertaking Better Beginnings, Better Futures was to prevent emotional and behavioral problems and promote adaptive social functioning in young children. The Ontario Child Health Study (Offord et al., 1987) had found that one in six children from age 4 to 16 suffered from an emotional or behavioral disorder and less than 20% were getting professional help for their problems.

From 1993 to 1998, Junior Kindergarten teachers reported a 27% decrease in emotional problems (anxiety and depression) in children at three of the five younger child sites. Home visiting and playgroups for children and their parents were particularly important programs offered in these sites.

Among these three sites, the largest decrease in children's anxiety and depression was found in the site that invested the greatest amount of program resources in home visiting and in child care by enriching local child care centers in the neighborhood and by providing many informal child care experiences. Junior Kindergarten teachers in this site also reported improvements in aggressive and hyperactive behaviors and school readiness in the children who lived in the Better Beginnings, Better Futures neighborhood. School readiness ratings reflected the child's cognitive, behavioral, and physical skills considered important for primary school success.

Ratings by Junior Kindergarten teachers were not available from one site because Junior Kindergarten was not provided by the local public Board of Education. The other site for younger children did not show improvements in children's emotional and behavioral problems at Junior Kindergarten.

Recent reviews of early childhood intervention studies described earlier found that few studies have reported improvements in social-emotional functioning of children before school entry. Two studies that did report positive effects (the Abecedarian Project, Ramey & Campbell, 1984; and the Infant Health and Development Project, McCarton et al., 1997) provided full-time, year-round, center-based child care for 3 to 5 years, and in both cases, the improvements faded after children entered school. Nor have studies of infant home visiting programs reported reduced social-emotional problems during the preschool years (Gomby, Culross, & Berman, 1999; Olds & Kitzman, 1993). This makes the results of the Better Beginnings, Better Futures project quite important, because healthy social and emotional development at kindergarten is a key indicator of future school success.

In the three older child sites, teachers reported a 7% decrease in children's anxiety, compared to a 45% increase in the comparison sites. Teachers also reported a 3% increase in children's self-control in the project sites, compared to a 9% decrease in self-control in the comparison neighborhoods. Parents reported improved cooperative behavior in their children. In the two sites that showed the greatest improvements in children's social and emotional behavior, educational assistants provided in-classroom individual and group support to children continuously from Junior Kindergarten to Grade 2.

Child Cognitive Development, Special Education, and School–Family Relations

In the younger child sites, there were no consistent cross-site improvements found in direct measures of cognitive or intellectual development on standardized tests. This finding should not be surprising. Other projects that have demonstrated intellectual improvements in preschoolers have provided intensive, center-based, educational programs to very high-risk young children (e.g., the Abecedarian, Perry Preschool, and CPC Projects described earlier).

In the older child sites, there were also no improvements found in cognitive development or school achievement. It is unlikely that the Better Beginnings, Better Futures in-school programs were intensive enough to improve children's scores on these measures, over and above the effects of regular classroom experiences.

However, in the older child sites, there was an interesting change in the area of special education where the number of students receiving special education services showed a significant decrease in schools in two of the three project sites, and an increase in schools in the comparison neighborhoods. The two Better Beginnings sites that showed improvements in special education provided programs in school classrooms while the major child-focused programs in the third site were outside the classroom and most were outside school hours.

Child Physical and Nutritional Health

Parents of children in the younger sites reported significantly more timely immunizations at 18 months, and also felt they had improved access to professionals, such as doctors, dentists, and social workers, for their children relative to parents in the comparison site

In the older child sites, there was a general improvement in children's nutritional intake in the first 2 years of the project. There were also improved parent ratings of their children's general health. In the baseline data in 1993, 42% of parents rated their 8-year-old children as having excellent health; 4 years later, 61% of parents said their 8-year-old children had excellent health.

Summary of Child Outcomes

These results indicate a positive impact of the Better Beginnings, Better Futures Project on children's social-emotional functioning and physical health. There was little indication of positive project impacts in the areas of cognition and academic performance except in the decreased special education rates in schools at two of the three older child Better Beginnings sites. The variation noted on positive outcomes across the project sites on child outcomes appears to be, at least in part, a result of the percentage of program resources that each local project dedicated to programs focused directly on children. More discussion of differential program effects appears later in the chapter.

Parent and Family Outcomes

At all of the project sites, there was reduced smoking by mothers. This finding is encouraging since smoking levels tend to be high in disadvantaged communities, and the long-term health effects of smoking are well known.

In the younger child sites, an average of 45% of the women interviewed smoked before the Better Beginnings, Better Futures Project began, compared to 28% of women of the same age across Ontario. After 5 years, the percentage of women smoking in the younger child Better Beginnings sites had dropped to 35%, much closer to the provincial average. The relative decrease was greatest among the heaviest smokers.

In the older child sites, 46% of the parents smoked before Better Beginnings, Better Futures programs began, and 26% smoked after 4 years of project implementation. The reduction in parent smoking rates in the Better Beginnings sites from 1993 to 1998 is impressive. National smoking rates for women of the same age only changed from 30% in 1994 to 27% in 1998. The change in smoking rates in Better Beginnings, Better Futures sites may be related to the fact that parents had increased opportunities to meet other parents, participate in support groups or committees, or to volunteer in community activities, especially if meetings and events were held in locations such as schools where smoking is restricted or discouraged.

There were no other consistent *cross-site* changes in measures of parent health and well-being. However, there were strong effects at one of the three older child sites where parents reported less tension juggling child care and other responsibilities, more social support, reduced alcohol consumption, increased exercise and reduced use of prescription drugs for pain. This combination of changes might be expected to reduce illness, particularly stress-related illness. Parents at this site also reported improved family relations as reflected in increased marital satisfaction, more consistent and less hostile-ineffective parenting, and increased parenting satisfaction.

It is difficult to specify the exact pathways through which the results in this site were achieved, but it is possible to point to a distinctive feature of the program that could have produced the difference between this site and others; namely, the consistent, ongoing attempts to involve parents in Better Beginnings programs and in school events. Project staff visited all the parents in the longitudinal research group regularly for 4 years, discussing how their children were coming along at school, issues in child-rearing, and questions about family living. Parents were encouraged by the staff to become involved in parenting programs and other activities at the school and informed about community resources that could help them. Overall, this group of parents and their children was the focus of more frequent, intensive, and wide-ranging attention from the Better Beginnings, Better Futures Project than those at any other site.

Neighborhood Outcomes

Neighborhood Quality of Life

In all of the younger child sites, parents reported increased safety when walking at night. Two of these five sites also perceived less neighborhood deviant activity (alcohol and drug abuse, violence and theft), and were more satisfied with the safety and general quality of their neighborhood.

In the three older child sites, parents reported greater satisfaction with the general quality of their neighborhood, and the condition of their housing. There was also a large increase in children using local playgrounds and recreational facilities in two of the sites. Thus, in all eight sites, there was some indication of parents perceiving an improvement in the quality of life in the neighborhood.

Local Project Development and Organization

An important goal of the Better Beginnings Project was to develop locally owned and operated Better Beginnings, Better Futures organizations. In all eight Better Beginnings Project sites across Ontario, low-income, highly stressed, and fractured neighborhoods have been able to build the organizations necessary to deliver locally appropriate programs for families and young children.

There were important findings from the qualitative research carried out during the project start-up phase from 1991 to 1993 concerning how the local projects developed their local organizations. The original plan in 1990 was that this demonstration initiative would last for 5 years. The start-up phase was only expected to take a year. That turned out to be quite unrealistic, given the complex challenges facing these communities, including: a) gaining the confidence and trust of parents and other residents who were distrustful of a government initiative; b) building local organizations with at least 50% resident participation in the governing structure; c) developing quality programs focused on children in the specific age groups (0–4 or 4–8 years), their families, and the neighborhood tailored to local needs; d) creating partnerships with other service organizations already operating in the community; and e) enhancing community capacity and developing local leadership.

Time and Support. Communities needed time to build trust and develop programs. Residents were initially wary of the initiative, and had little or no experience with a neighborhood-driven project like Better Beginnings, Better Futures. It took about 3 years before structures, procedures, and programs were stable. During this time, the sites received some assistance from the government funders with planning and organizational development.

Resident Involvement. The project's requirement that there be significant and meaningful local resident involvement was translated into the "50% rule," where every important planning and implementation committee was expected to include at least 50% local residents.

Local Control. It is ordinarily very difficult to achieve substantial resident involvement in high-risk neighborhoods. A major incentive for local participation was the high level of control given to the local organization. Residents participated in allocating budgets, deciding which programs to fund, writing job descriptions, and sitting on hiring committees.

Ground Rules. Although there was considerable flexibility in how the sites implemented programs locally, there were some requirements imposed by government funders. These included the requirement that all younger child sites implement home visiting and child care enrichment programs and all older child sites implement child care enrichment and school-based programs. However, it was not always clear as to what these requirements were and how they were to be implemented. It may have been more helpful to have been very clear from the start what the ground rules were, and what specific programs were required.

Program Focus. In this project, with its multiple goals and community control, local organizations had to choose where to put their prime program emphasis. In some sites, a stronger focus of programs on support for parents or community development may have diluted the focus of programs for children.

PLANS FOR LONGER-TERM RESEARCH

Supported by funding from the Ontario Ministry of Health and Long-term Care, the research team for Better Beginnings, Better Futures is continuing to follow the longitudinal research group of 1,900 children and their families from both the project and comparison sites to find out how well they are doing as the children develop into adolescence and early adulthood. This follow-up research will study the long-term costs and benefits of Better Beginnings, Better Futures for the research group of children, using measures of academic progress and secondary school graduation rates, use of health and special education services, employment, use of social assistance, and criminal justice system involvement.

This long-term research is also designed to answer important questions concerning the sustainability of the local projects over time, and their ability to maintain stable organizational structures with solid resident involvement, effective service system partnerships, and a range of child, family and neighborhood programs.

CONCLUSION

The hallmark of the Better Beginnings, Better Futures Project is the successful establishment of eight locally operated, community-based organizations. Faced with an extremely broad and complex mandate, high expectations, and relatively little explicit direction, each of the communities developed an organization characterized by significant and meaningful local resident involvement in all decisions. This alone represents a tremendous accomplishment in neighborhoods where 15 years ago, many local residents viewed government programs and social services with skepticism, suspicion, or hostility. In developing their local organizations, Better Beginnings projects have not only actively involved many local residents, but also played a major role in forming meaningful partnerships with other service organizations. They have developed a wide range of programs, many designed to respond to the locally identified needs of young children and their families, and others to the needs of the neighborhood and broader community. As they strengthened and stabilized over the 7-year demonstration period from 1991 to 1998, each Better Beginnings project increasingly gained the respect and support not only of local residents, service-providers, and community leaders, but also of the Provincial Government which, in 1997, transferred all projects from demonstration to annualized funding, thus recognizing them as *sustainable*.

The short-term findings from these projects reported in this chapter are encouraging, and provide a unique foundation for determining the extent to which a universal, comprehensive, community-based strategy can promote the longer-term resilience of young children, their families and their local neighborhoods.

ACKNOWLEDGMENTS

This research was funded under contract by the Ministries of Health and Long-Term Care, Education and Training, and Community, Family and Children's Services, Ontario, Canada.

This article reflects the views of the author and not necessarily those of the Ministries.

Requests for reprints should be sent to Ray DeV. Peters, Queen's University, 98 Barrie Street, Kingston, Ontario, Canada K7L 3N6. E-mail: petersrd@psyc.queensu.ca.

REFERENCES

Bradenberg, H. A., Friedman, R. M., & Silver, S. E. (1990). The epidemiology of childhood psychiatric disorders: Prevalence findings from different studies. *Journal of the American Academy of Child and Adolescent Psychiatry, 29,* 76–83.

Campbell, S. (1995). Behaviour problems in preschool children: A review of recent research. *Journal of Child Psychology and Psychiatry, 36,* 113–149.

Costello, E. J. (1989). Developments in child psychiatric epidemiology. *Journal of the American Academy of Child and Adolescent Psychiatry, 28,* 836–841.

Cynader, M. & Frost, B. J. (1999). Mechanisms of brain development: Neuronal sculpting by the physical and social environment. In D. Keating & C. Hertzman (Eds.), *Developmental health and the wealth of nations* (pp. 153–184). New York: Guilford Press.

Duncan, G. J., & Brooks-Gunn, J. (Eds.) (1997). *Consequences of growing up poor.* New York: Russell Sage Foundation.

Durlak, J. A., & Wells, A. M. (1997). Primary prevention mental health programs for children and adolescents: A meta-analytic review. *American Journal of Community Psychology, 25,* 115–152.

Garmezy, N. (1971). Vulnerability research and the issue of primary prevention. *American Journal of Orthopsychiatry, 41,* 101–116.

Garmezy, N. (1991). Resilience in children's adaptation to negative life events and stressed environments. *Pediatrics, 20,* 459–466.

Gomby, D. S., Culross, P. L., & Berman, R. E. (1999). Home visiting: Recent program evaluations—analysis and recommendations. *The Future of Children, 9,* 4–23.

Government of Ontario. (1990). *Better Beginnings, Better Futures: An integrated model of primary prevention of emotional and behavioural problems.* Toronto, Canada: Queen's Printer for Ontario.

Hertzman, C., & Wiens, M. (1996). Child development and long-term outcomes: A population health perspective and summary of successful interventions. *Social Science and Medicine, 43,* 1083–1095.

Karoly, L., Greenwood, P., Everingham, S., Houbé, J., Kilburn, M., Rydell, C., et al. (1998). *Investing in children: What we know and don't know about the costs and benefits of early childhood interventions.* Santa Monica, CA: RAND.

Loeber, R., & Dishion, T. (1983). Early predictors of male delinquency: A review. *Psychological Bulletin, 94,* 68–99.

Lynam, D. R. (1996). Early identification of chronic offenders: Who is the fledgling psychopath? *Psychological Bulletin, 120,* 209–234.

McCain, M. N., & Mustard, J. F. (1999). *Early Years Study: Reversing the real brain drain.* Toronto, Ontario: Ontario Children's Secretariat; www.childsec.gov.on.ca.

McCain, M. N., & Mustard, J. F. (2002). *The Early Years Study three years later. From early development to human development: Enabling communities.* Toronto, Ontario: Founders Network; www.founders.net

McCarton, C., Brooks-Gunn, J., Wallace, I., Bauer, C., Bennett, F., Bernbaum, J., et al. (1997). Results at age 8 years of early intervention for low-birth-weight premature infants: The Infant Health Development Program. *Journal of the American Medical Association, 277,* 126–132.

Moffitt, T., Caspi, A., Dickson, N., Silva, P., & Stanton, W. (1996). Childhood-onset versus adolescent-onset antisocial conduct problems in males: Natural history from ages 3 to 18. *Development and Psychopathology, 8,* 399–424.

Mrazek, P. J., & Brown, C. H. (2002). An evidenced-based literature review regarding outcomes in psychosocial prevention and early intervention in young children. In C. C. Russell (Ed.), *The state of knowledge about prevention/early intervention* (pp. 42–144). Toronto, Canada: Invest in Kids Foundation; www.investinkids.ca.

Offord, D. R. (1996). The state of prevention and early intervention. In R. DeV. Peters & R. J. McMahon (Eds.), *Preventing childhood disorders, substance abuse and delinquency* (pp. 329–344). Thousand Oaks, CA: Sage.

Offord, D. R., Boyle, M. H., Szatmari, P., Rae-Grant, N. I., Links, P. S., Cadman, D. T., et al. (1987). Ontario Child Health Study. II: Six month prevalence of disorder and rates of service utilization. *Archives of General Psychiatry, 44,* 832–836.

Offord, D. R., Boyle, M. H., & Racine, Y. A. (1989). *Children at risk.* Toronto, Canada: Ontario Ministry of Community and Social Services.

Offord, D. R., Kraemer, H. C., Kazdin, A. E., Jensen, P. S., & Harrington, R. (1998). Lowering the burden of suffering from child psychiatric disorder: Trade-offs among clinical, targeted and universal interventions. *Journal of the American Academy of Child and Adolescent Psychiatry, 37,* 686–694.

Olds, D. L. (1997). The Prenatal Early Infancy Project: Preventing child abuse in the context of promoting maternal and child health. In D. A. Wolfe, R. J. McMahon, & R. DeV. Peters (Eds.), *Child abuse: New directions in prevention and treatment across the lifespan* (pp. 130–156) Thousand Oaks, CA: Sage.

Olds, D. L., & Kitzman, H. (1993). Review of research on home visiting for pregnant women and parents of young children. *The Future of Children, 3,* 53–92.

Olds, D. L., Eckenrode, J., Henderson, C. R., Kitzman, H., Powers, J., Cole, R., et al. (1997). Long-term effects of home visitation on maternal life course, child abuse and neglect, and children's arrests: Fifteen year follow-up of a randomized trial. *Journal of the American Medical Association, 278,* 637–643.

Peters, R. DeV., Arnold, R., Petrunka, K., Angus, D., Brophy, K., Burke, S. et al. (2000). *Developing capacity and competence in the Better Beginnings, Better Futures communities: Short-term findings report.* Kingston, Canada: Better Beginnings, Better Futures Research Coordination Unit Technical Report; http://bbbf.queensu.ca.

Peters, R. DeV., Petrunka, K., & Arnold, R. (2003). The Better Beginnings, Better Futures Project: A universal comprehensive, community-based prevention approach for primary school children and their families. *Journal of Clinical Child and Adolescent Psychology, 32*, 215–227.

Ramey, C. T., & Campbell, F. A. (1984) Preventive education for high-risk children: Cognitive consequences of the Carolina Abecedarian Project. *American Journal on Mental Deficiency, 88*, 515–523.

Ramey, C. T., & Ramey, S. L. (1998). Early educational intervention and early experience. *American Psychologist, 53*, 109–120.

Reid, J. B. (1993). Prevention of conduct disorder before and after school entry: Relating interventions to developmental findings. *Development and Psychopathology, 5*, 243–262.

Reynolds, A. J., Temple, J. A., Robertson, D. L., & Mann, E. A. (2003). Age 21 cost-benefit analysis of the Title I Chicago child-parent centers. *Educational Evaluation and Policy Analysis, 24*, 267–303.

Rockhill, B., Newman, B., & Weinberg, C. (1998). Use and misuse of population attributable fractions. *American Journal of Public Health, 88*, 15–19.

Rothman, K. J., & Greenland, S. (Eds.). (1998). *Modern epidemiology.* New York: Lippincott, Williams, & Wilkins.

Rutter, M. (1979). Protective factors in children's responses to stress and disadvantage. In M. W. Kent & J. E. Rolf (Eds.), *Primary prevention in psychopathology: Social competence in children* (Vol. 8, pp. 49–74). Hanover, NH: University Press of New England.

Schweinhart, L. J., Barnes, H. V., & Weikart, D. P. (1993). *Significant benefits: The High-Scope Perry Preschool Study through Age 27.* Ypsilanti, MI: High/Scope Press.

Scott, K. G., Mason, C. A., & Chapman, D. A. (1999). The use of epidemiological methodology as a means of influencing public policy. *Child Development, 70*, 1263–1272.

Shore, R. (1997). *Rethinking the brain: New insights into early* development. New York: Families and Work Institute.

St. Pierre, R. G., & Layzer, J. I. (1998). Improving the life chances of children living in poverty: Assumptions and what we have learned. *Society for Research in Child Development Social Policy Report, 12*, 1–25.

St. Pierre, R. G., Layzer, J. I., Goodson, B. D., & Bernstein, L. S. (1997). *National impact evaluation of the Comprehensive Child Development Program: Final report.* Cambridge, MA: Abt Associates.

Tu, S. (2003). Developmental epidemiology: A review of three key measures of effect. *Journal of Clinical Child and Adolescent Psychology, 32*, 187–192.

Tuma, J. M. (1989). Mental health services for children: The state of the art. *American Psychologist, 44*, 188–199.

Webster-Stratton, C., & Taylor, T. (2001). Nipping early risk factors in the bud: Preventing substance abuse, delinquency, and violence in adolescence through interventions targeted at young children (0–8 years). *Prevention Science, 2*, 165–192.

Werner, E. E., & Smith, R. S. (1989). *Vulnerable but invincible: A longitudinal study of resilient children and youth.* New York: Adams, Bannister, Cox (originally published by McGraw Hill, 1982).

Werner, E. E., & Smith, R. S. (2001). *Journeys from childhood to midlife: Risk, resilience, and recovery.* Ithaca, NY: Cornell University Press.

Willms, J. D. (Ed.) (2002). *Vulnerable children.* Edmonton, Canada: The University of Alberta Press.

CHAPTER 11

Steps Toward Community-Level Resilience

Community Adoption of Science-Based Prevention Programming

MICHAEL W. ARTHUR, RENITA R. GLASER,
& J. DAVID HAWKINS

Prevention science provides a framework for community prevention planning that uses epidemiological data on empirically established predictors of health and behavior outcomes to identify specific short-term objectives for a community's prevention efforts, and to select effective preventive interventions that have been shown to address these specific risk factors and enhance community-level resilience. This approach offers promise for increasing the effectiveness of community prevention systems, yet a gap exists between the prevention science knowledge base and the actual practice of community-based prevention. This chapter reports findings from a study of the diffusion of science-based prevention planning in 41 communities across 7 U.S. states. Using telephone interviews with community leaders, the study assessed the adoption of science-based prevention planning by communities. Reliable and meaningful variation was found in adoption of science-based prevention planning across communities, though few communities had achieved widespread adoption of the approach. Diffusion processes related to greater adoption were identified. Training of community leaders in science-based prevention was found to predict greater adoption of science-based prevention programming.

The developing field of prevention science integrates epidemiological data on the prevalence of problem behaviors among adolescents with information on the predictors of these behaviors and information on effective prevention strategies derived from controlled intervention trials (Coie et al., 1993; Kellam, Koretz, & Moscicki, 1999; Kellam & Rebok, 1992). Longitudinal studies have identified risk factors that predict increased likelihood of adolescent problems behaviors, as well as protective factors that counteract the negative effects of risk exposure (Hawkins, Catalano, & Miller, 1992; Hawkins et al. 1998; Rutter, 1990; Werner & Smith, 1992). Interventions designed to reduce specific risk factors and bolster protective processes have been developed. Their efficacy has been demonstrated in experimental and quasi-experimental studies (Catalano, Arthur, Hawkins, Berglund, & Olson, 1998; Durlak, 1998; Hawkins, Arthur, & Catalano, 1995; Sloboda & David, 1997).

Armed with knowledge of the predictors of adolescent problem behaviors and efficacious prevention strategies, prevention planners can match tested prevention strategies to the specific needs of local populations (Arthur & Blitz, 2000; Hawkins, 1999; Hawkins, Catalano, & Arthur, 2002; Hawkins, Catalano, & Associates, 1992). Prevention planning systems like Communities That Care (CTC) (Hawkins & Catalano, 2002) assist communities to assess the epidemiology of risk and protective factors and adolescent problem behaviors to identify levels of need for specific prevention services. Communities using the CTC approach use these data to identify and prioritize elevated risk factors and depressed protective factors in a population in order to guide the selection of prevention actions. They select and implement empirically tested interventions that address the specific risk and protective factors they have prioritized. Following implementation of new preventive interventions, levels of risk and protective factors and behavioral outcomes can be monitored, and interventions can be adjusted or modified in a process of continuous quality improvement of the community's prevention system (Hawkins & Catalano, 2002; Hawkins, Catalano, & Associates, 1992).

In spite of progress in the development of strategies for using prevention science to guide prevention practice in communities, a gap remains between the prevention science knowledge base and prevention practice (Backer, 2000; Kaftarian & Wandersman, 2000). Despite efforts to disseminate information about science-based prevention principles and programs (e.g., Developmental Research and Programs, 1996, 2000; Drug Strategies, 1999; Elliott, 1997; Office of National Drug Control Policy, 2000; Sloboda & David, 1997; Substance Abuse and Mental

Health Services Administration, 1998; Western Regional Center for the Application of Prevention Technologies, 1999), many communities use prevention approaches with little or no evidence of effectiveness (Backer, 2000; Ennett, Tobler, Ringwalt, & Flewelling, 1994; Hallfors, Sporer, Pankratz, & Godette, 2000). An important challenge for the field of prevention is to translate advances in scientific knowledge into effective prevention programming on a broad scale (Biglan, 1995; Mitchell, Stevenson, & Florin, 1996).

One reason for the gap between prevention science and practice is that relatively little is known about the process of disseminating science-based prevention programming at the community level. Related research on community prevention coalitions (e.g., Arthur, Ayers, Graham, & Hawkins, 2003; Butterfoss, Goodman, & Wandersman, 1993; Florin, Mitchell, & Stevenson, 1993; Kumpfer, Turner, Hopkins, & Librett, 1993), diffusion of innovations (Rogers, 1995), and community readiness for prevention (e.g., Arthur et al., 1996; Edwards, Jumper-Thurman, Plested, Oetting, & Swanson, 2000; National Institute on Drug Abuse, 1997; Oetting et al., 1995) suggest several factors that may influence the rate of adoption of new prevention technologies. In particular, the relative advantages of the new technology (Lewin, 1951; Scrutchins & David, 1996), leadership supporting prevention (Beckhard & Harris, 1987; Fawcett, Paine, Francisco, & Vliet, 1993; Kumpfer et al., 1993), and interagency collaboration in implementing preventive interventions (Chavis, Florin, Rich, & Wandersman, 1987; Morrissey, Tausig, & Lindsey, 1985; Wickizer et al., 1993) are likely to influence community-wide adoption of science-based prevention programming. Studies of community prevention initiatives also indicate that implementation of science-based prevention activities can be promoted by providing community members with training and technical assistance in needs assessment and strategic prevention planning (Arthur et al., 2003; Feinberg, Greenberg, Osgood, Anderson, & Babinski, 2002; Greenberg, Osgood, Babinski, & Anderson, 1999).

The process of community adoption of a science-based prevention approach can be conceptualized as a process of diffusion of innovation. Diffusion theory posits that the process of innovation diffusion consists of a series of actions and choices individuals and organizations make to evaluate a new idea and decide whether or not to incorporate the new idea into ongoing practice (Rogers, 1995). Rogers suggests that organizations proceed through five stages when deciding to adopt and incorporate an innovation into organizational practice: (1) knowledge, (2) persuasion, (3) decision, (4) implementation, and (5) confirmation. The innovation diffusion process involves an organization's passage from initial awareness of the innovation to forming an attitude about

Table 11-1 Hypothesized Stages of Adoption of Science-Based Prevention Approach

Stage 0	Pre-awareness. Little or no awareness of science-based prevention. Lack of clear understanding of concepts of risk and protective factors or their relevance to strategic prevention planning.
Stage 1	Awareness of terminology and concepts of science-based prevention. Understands concepts of risk and protective factors and their basis in longitudinal research.
Stage 2	Adoption of the science-based prevention framework as the basis for strategic prevention planning.
Stage 3	Collection of epidemiological data on risk and protective factors as well as adolescent problem behaviors.
Stage 4	Use of epidemiological data for allocating prevention resources. Prioritization of specific populations and risk and protective factors for preventive action, and selection of evidence-based interventions that address prioritized risk and protective factors.
Stage 5	Repeated collection of epidemiological data over multiple years for program evaluation, monitoring, and administrative purposes. Feedback of monitoring data into the prevention planning cycle.

the innovation to a decision to adopt or reject the idea. If the idea is adopted, the fourth stage involves implementing the innovation and the fifth stage involves seeking confirmation or reinforcement for the decision to adopt the innovation. In this fifth stage, the decision to incorporate an idea or innovation into organizational practice can be reversed if the organization is exposed to information that disconfirms the value of the innovation.

Based on the prevention science framework for community prevention planning and Roger's (1995) stages of innovation diffusion, we hypothesize that communities can be characterized as falling into one of six distinct stages of adoption of the science-based prevention approach (see Table 11-1). The lowest stage, pre-awareness (Stage 0), is defined by a lack of awareness of prevention science among community leaders and prevention providers. Community leaders need to be aware of the concepts and postulates of science-based prevention before they can consider adopting the approach as their framework for prevention planning. Thus, awareness is Stage 1. If community leaders and prevention practitioners are aware of the approach and believe it provides an improvement over their current approach, they may decide to adopt science-based prevention as a planning framework; this defines Stage 2. At Stage 3, implementation of the new approach requires collecting epidemiological data on risk, protection, and behavioral outcomes among adolescents in order to guide prevention planning.

In the fourth stage, these data are used to allocate prevention resources. Populations experiencing high levels of risk and low levels of protection are identified, and specific elevated risk and depressed protective factors in those populations are prioritized. Tested and efficacious interventions that address the prioritized risk and protective factors are chosen and implemented. Finally, in the fifth stage, epidemiological data are re-collected periodically to monitor the community's progress in achieving its goals of reducing risk, increasing protection, and reducing the prevalence of problem behaviors. These stages are hypothesized to be ordinal, though not necessarily sequential in the order in which they first occur. For example, communities might collect data on adolescent drug use and related factors prior to awareness of prevention science and the decision to adopt a prevention science framework. However, Stage 3 can be attained only if leaders are aware of prevention science and have decided to adopt the framework in addition to collecting epidemiological data.

This chapter reports findings from a study investigating the adoption of the science-based prevention planning approach in 41 communities in seven states. Using the hypothesized six-stage model of adoption, two research questions are addressed: Can communities be characterized according to their stage of adoption of the science-based prevention approach? What factors are associated with community adoption of the science-based prevention planning approach?

METHOD

Sample

The 41 sample communities are part of a 5-year study of the natural history of adoption, implementation, and community-level effects of the science-based approach to prevention planning. This study, known as the Diffusion Project, is a collaborative effort of the state agencies responsible for alcohol and drug abuse prevention in Colorado, Kansas, Illinois, Maine, Oregon, Utah, and Washington; researchers in each state; and researchers at the Social Development Research Group at the University of Washington. The project is collecting data on the prevention systems and activities, as well as risk and protective factors and problem behaviors among adolescents in 41 communities across these seven states. The communities are small and medium-sized incorporated towns ranging in 2000 Census population from 1,578 to 106,221. Only 2 of the 41 communities have populations over 50,000, and the mean population is 17,589. The communities in each state were selected purposively to include both communities that had adopted the science-based approach to prevention planning as well as communities that were not using this approach.

Data for measuring community adoption of science-based prevention were obtained from telephone interviews conducted with community leaders. Approximately 15 key informants from each community were identified and interviewed. Of the 15 key informants, 10 were positional community leaders (e.g., mayors, chief law enforcement officers, school superintendents, senior public health officials), and 5 were identified by the positional leaders as experts in the community's drug abuse prevention activities using a snowball sampling technique (Kish, 1965). The five prevention leaders mentioned most frequently by the positional leaders in each community were interviewed. Due to variation across communities in response rates, the actual numbers of positional leaders interviewed in each community ranged from 8 to 12, while the actual numbers of referred prevention leaders ranged from 3 to 7.

Positional leaders were selected to represent a predetermined set of community leadership positions (e.g., mayor, superintendent of schools, police chief or sheriff, health agency or hospital director, business leader) to provide information about the knowledge and opinions of a comparable sample of those who control resources and shape opinion in each community. Prevention leaders were included to provide information from individuals thought to be the most knowledgeable about the community's prevention activities. The sample of referred prevention leaders was more varied across communities, but the majority were involved in some aspect of prevention service and included drug-free school coordinators, prevention coalition chairs, United Way directors, and school guidance counselors. Respondents identified in each community were contacted first by a letter informing them of the project, its goals and procedures, and requesting their participation in an interview focusing on current prevention activities in their community. Telephone interviews were conducted with both positional leaders and prevention leaders. Five hundred eighty-six interviews were conducted during the fall and winter of 1998–1999.

Measures

Trained interviewers conducted the key informant interviews using a semi-structured survey instrument programmed into a Computer-Assisted Interviewing (CATI) system. The interviews averaged about 1 hour in duration. The instrument was pretested with 10 community leaders and prevention providers from communities not participating in the study and revised prior to conducting the interviews for this study.

Closed-ended questions were developed specifically to assess the six stages of adoption of science-based prevention. For example, questions assessed the respondents' knowledge and attitudes toward the science-based approach to prevention planning, their perceptions of the community's adoption of the approach, and the use of data within the community to guide prevention strategy selection, resource allocation, and prevention program evaluation. Open-ended questions asked the respondent to describe the prevention planning approaches and activities undertaken by community organizations and agencies. The interview also included questions that assessed variables hypothesized to influence community adoption of science-based prevention.

Measures of Adoption Stage

A three-step process was used to code each respondent's rating of his or her community's stage of adoption. First, decision rules were created for scoring the closed-ended items. These rules were designed to categorize the community's stage of adoption by assessing whether or not the respondent's answers to specific questions met the criteria defining each stage. Based on the pattern of responses to the closed-ended items, each respondent was given an overall stage score representing the highest stage for which criteria were met.

Second, three open-ended questions asking about the community's prevention planning approach and activities were content coded for each respondent. Detailed coding rules were established, and a score of 1 (no evidence of attainment), 2 (some evidence of attainment), 3 (clear evidence of attainment), or 9 (missing because respondent did not talk about the criteria at a particular stage) was assigned to each respondent for each adoption stage based on the responses to the open-ended questions. Inter-rater reliability was assessed for the coding protocol by having two trained raters independently code the open-ended items for 50 respondents. Coefficient Kappa, which controls for chance agreement between raters (Fleiss, 1971) was computed for each stage score, resulting in satisfactory to excellent inter-rater reliability scores ranging from .46 to 1.0 across the six stages. A final open-ended stage score was assigned to each respondent reflecting the highest stage coded.

In the third step, the adoption scores derived from both the closed-ended and open-ended questions for each respondent were compared, and a final stage score reflecting the greater of the closed-ended and open-ended scores was assigned to the respondent. Thus, each respondent's rating of his or her community's adoption stage was the highest stage indicated by his or her responses to both the closed-ended and open-ended questions in the interview.

Using the final stage scores coded for each key informant, two aggregate measures of adoption of the science-based prevention approach were computed for each community. First, the scores of all the positional leader respondents in each community were averaged to create a Positional Leader Stage Score. As the average of all positional leader respondents within a community, this variable reflected the degree to which the science-based prevention model had spread throughout the community's leadership system to those individuals who controlled community resources that could support prevention. Second, the scores of all the referred prevention leader respondents in each community were averaged to create a Prevention Leader Stage Score. This measure reflected the degree to which a science-based approach had diffused among those individuals who were implementing the community's prevention efforts. These two measures were hypothesized to reflect two distinct levels of adoption of the science-based prevention planning framework within the communities.

Measures of Diffusion Processes

In addition, the interviews assessed several factors hypothesized to influence community adoption of a science-based prevention framework. The first factor was exposure to training in science-based prevention principles and/or practices. Respondents were asked whether or not they had been to a training to learn about science-based prevention and if they had seen a science-based prevention manual, training kit, or curriculum. For clarification, respondents who indicated that they had seen a prevention model manual, training kit, or curriculum were asked to name it. Depending on the respondent's answer, this variable was coded 3 for the Communities That Care training materials (a training kit specifically designed to help communities implement the science-based prevention model), 2 for any state or federally prepared training manuals, kits, or curricula in science-based prevention, 1 for any other training manuals, kits, or curricula, or 0 for none. This ordinal scale was created to reflect the degree to which the materials were likely to focus on the specific steps involved in implementing a science-based approach to prevention planning.

Respondents also were asked to rate on a 4-point scale how easy they thought the science-based prevention approach was to understand, and whether or not they supported this approach. These are factors identified by Rogers (1995) as influencing the likelihood an innovation will be adopted. Similarly, respondents were asked to rate on a 4-point scale the degree to which their adoption of the science-based prevention approach was influenced by the fact that it is supported by research, and were also asked to rate on a 4-point scale the degree to which adoption was influenced by a state mandate to use the approach. The extent of collaboration in the community was assessed with two questions asking about the degree to which community institutions, organizations, agencies, and individuals worked together to address community problems (Pearson's $r = .46$ for the two questions).

RESULTS

Stages of Adoption

The first question addressed was whether or not the 41 communities participating in the Diffusion Project could be characterized according to the hypothesized stages of adoption of a science-based prevention approach. To answer this question, properties of the two adoption measures were examined. First, the distributions of adoption stage score ratings were examined for the two categories of respondents (i.e., prevention leaders and positional leaders). The data in Table 11-2 show that a third of the prevention leaders (34%) and the majority of positional leaders (57%) were not aware of the science-based prevention approach.

Fewer than half of both the prevention and positional leaders rated their communities' adoption stage higher than Stage 1 (Awareness). Moreover, while 21% of prevention leaders reported their communities had implemented research-based prevention programs and were monitoring the impact of these programs, only 10% of positional leaders reported that their communities were doing these things. It is interesting to note that the distributions of adoption scores are U-shaped for both respondent categories, with relatively few respondents rating their communities at Stage 2 or Stage 3. This suggests that, once community leaders have made the decision to adopt the model, most believe that their

Table 11-2   Percent of Respondents at Each Stage of Adoption

	Positional Leaders ($n = 407$)	Prevention Leaders ($n = 278$)
Stage 0: Not aware of the framework	57.2%	34.2%
Stage 1: Aware of the framework	20.6%	25.2%
Stage 2: Adopted the framework	2.9%	2.9%
Stage 3: Collecting data to assess needs	2.5%	2.5%
Stage 4: Using research-based programs	7.1%	14.4%
Stage 5: Monitoring impact	9.6%	20.9%

communities have moved beyond data collection to begin using the data to select programs and, in some cases, to monitor the impact of these programs. Despite this similarity between the distributions, however, the ratings were significantly different across the two distinct groups of respondents ($\chi^2 = 43.38$, $p < .001$), indicating that the positional leaders rated their communities differently than the prevention leaders. Thus, the adoption scores were analyzed separately in subsequent analyses.

Before examining the community-level distributions of the two aggregate adoption stage scores, properties of the two aggregate measures were examined. Using the approach described by Sampson, Raudenbush, and Earls (1997), a two-level multi-level model was run for each measure of adoption using HLM 5.0 (hierarchical linear models version 5.0) (Raudenbush, Bryk, Cheong, & Congdon, 2000). The intraclass correlation (ICC) among the community leader ratings of adoption and the reliability of the community mean adoption scores were computed for each of the two measures of adoption.

In a two-level hierarchical model, the ICC is the ratio of the variability in the measure between level-two units (e.g., communities) to the total amount of variability in the measure (both within and between groups). Thus, in this study the ICC provides a measure of the agreement among key informants' adoption ratings within each community by estimating the proportion of the variance in the ratings that occurs between the communities. If there is perfect agreement among the raters within each community, then the ICC equals 1.0 and all the variability in the measure exists between communities. The results in Table 11-3 show that, for prevention leaders, 28% of the variability in adoption scores occurred between the 41 communities, while for position leaders, 23% of the variation occurred between communities. Thus, while individual respondents' perceptions of their community's adoption of science-based prevention varied, a substantial proportion of the variation in respondents' ratings of community adoption occurred between communities rather than between individuals. This finding indicates that the measures of community adoption stage reported here reflect meaningful differences between communities.

Table 11-3 HLM Reliabilities and Intraclass Correlations

	Positional Leaders	Prevention Leaders
Final stage score reliabilities	.749	.710
Intraclass correlations (ICCs)	.232	.275
Average cluster size	9.9	6.8
Cluster size range	8–12	3–7

The community-level reliability estimates reported in Table 11-3 represent the reliability of the aggregated community-level adoption scores for use in distinguishing among the communities. In the two-level models run for this study, the reliability of the adoption score is a function of the number of respondents within each community and the variability among respondents within and between communities; essentially, the reliability estimates presented are the averages of the reliabilities obtained from each of the 41 communities. The higher the reliability, the less error variation there is around the estimated parameters, in this case the mean community adoption scores. The reliability of the aggregated adoption scores for prevention leaders was .71, and the reliability of the scores for positional leaders was .75, suggesting that the aggregate community adoption scores obtained by averaging the positional leaders' and the prevention leaders' individual ratings were reasonably reliable. Thus, the analyses support the hypothesis that these communities did vary in their stage of adoption of a science-based prevention planning approach, and that such variation across communities can be measured through interviews with positional leaders and prevention leaders in those communities.

At the community level of analysis, most study communities were aware of the risk and protection-focused approach, regardless of respondent type. However, only 2% of the communities had progressed beyond stage 3 (collecting needs assessment data) according to the positional leader ratings, while fewer than 18% of communities had progressed beyond Stage 3 according to the prevention leaders' ratings (see Table 11-4). According to positional leaders, 24% of the communities had adopted the framework (summing across stages 2 and higher), and 14% were collecting data to assess youth prevention needs (summing across stages 3 and higher), but only 2% were using the data to select research-based programs and none had reached Stage 5. Using prevention leaders' ratings, 41% of the communities had adopted the

Table 11-4 Percent of Communities at Each Stage of Adoption
($N = 41$)

	Positional Leaders	Prevention Leaders
Stage 0: Not aware of the framework	24%	5%
Stage 1: Aware of the framework	51%	39%
Stage 2: Adopted the framework	10%	15%
Stage 3: Collecting data to assess needs	12%	24%
Stage 4: Using research-based programs	2%	15%
Stage 5: Monitoring impact	0	2%

framework and were collecting data to assess prevention needs (summing across stages 3 and higher), 17% were using the data to select research-based programs, and 2% of communities were monitoring the impact of their prevention programs on participants' exposure to risk and protective factors. Thus, while ratings differed significantly by respondent type $\chi^2 = 12.65$ $p < .001$), both sets of ratings suggested that the majority of leaders in most communities in the study were aware of the framework, while the majority of leaders in relatively few communities reported they were using the framework to guide selection and monitoring of research-based prevention strategies. These findings also show that prevention leaders tended to report that their communities were further along in adopting the science-based prevention approach than positional leaders.

Correlates of Adoption

Given the observed variation across the 41 communities in their degree of adoption of the science-based prevention approach, analyses were conducted to investigate factors expected to influence the adoption of the science-based prevention approach. Table 11-5 presents the correlations between community-level measures of these factors and the two aggregated community adoption scores. Correlations between both types of adoption scores and several factors were consistently positive and significant at the $p < .01$ level. The factors significantly correlated with adoption were the number of leaders in the community who: a) had attended a training in the approach; b) had seen a training manual, kit, or curriculum; c) were able to name the type of training manual, kit, or curriculum; d) supported the science-based prevention approach; and e) believed that the approach was supported by research, In contrast, community leaders' mean ratings that the approach was easy to understand and their ratings of the degree of collaboration in the community were not correlated significantly with community adoption scores, nor was a mandate from the state to adopt the science-based prevention approach significantly correlated with community adoption scores.

DISCUSSION

Positional leader and prevention leader ratings revealed reliable differences across communities in community adoption of science-based prevention. These findings indicate that communities can be characterized according to their stage of adoption of a science-based approach to prevention and enhancing resilience. Estimates of community adoption

Table 11-5 Correlations between Community Adoption Stage and Factors Hypothesized to Influence Adoption

Diffusion Factors	Positional Leaders ($N = 41$)	Prevention Leaders ($N = 41$)
Number of leaders attending training in the approach	.86**	.73**
Number of leaders who have seen a risk and protection-focused prevention training manual, kit, or curriculum	.75**	.73**
Number of leaders who can name the training manual, kit, or curriculum	.67**	.74**
Number of leaders who support science-based prevention	.92** ($N = 39$)	.67**
Number of leaders stating the science-based prevention approach was adopted because it is supported by research	.91** ($N = 30$)	.76** ($N = 37$)
Number of leaders stating that the approach was adopted because mandated by state agency	.24 ($N = 31$)	.19 ($N = 37$)
Rating: Science-based prevention is easy to understand	−.07 ($N = 38$)	−.04
Rating: Community groups collaborate	.15	.20

$^* p < / = .05$ $^{**} p < / = .01$

stages differed by type of respondent. Positional leaders who control resources and shape opinion generally rated their communities at a lower stage of adoption of science-based prevention than did leaders of prevention activities in the communities. These differences are not surprising. It is reasonable to expect that those people most involved in prevention work would be the first to learn of and adopt prevention science-based innovations available to guide prevention planning. These findings also indicate that, in 1998–1999, in most communities in this study, knowledge of prevention science had not yet diffused to the community leaders who control resources and whose leadership and support is likely to be needed for widespread community adoption of science-based prevention approaches and for reallocation of resources to support science-based prevention.

The findings document the "gap" between prevention research and practice at the community level (e.g., Kaftarian & Wandersman, 2000). Few respondents of any type reported that their communities had taken the science-based approach to prevention to full implementation, and less than 20% of communities were using needs assessment data to guide selection of tested prevention strategies. While increasing numbers of states and communities have begun to collect epidemiological data on risk and protective factors (e.g., Kansas Department of Social and Rehabilitation Services/Alcohol and Drug Abuse Services, 2001; Washington State Department of Social and Health Services, 2000), the findings reported here suggest that these data have not yet been used widely to guide prevention planning at the community level.

This study produced important findings regarding factors that influence community adoption of a science-based prevention framework. Training of community leaders in science-based prevention clearly was related to greater adoption. Across both respondent types, indicators of community leaders' participation in training in the science-based prevention approach were strongly and positively related to higher ratings of community adoption of the approach. Larger numbers of leaders within the community who reported having attended a training workshop in the approach; having seen a manual, kit, or curriculum describing the approach; and being able to name the manual, kit, or curriculum were all clearly related to greater adoption of the approach.

In addition, communities reached higher stages of adoption when more leaders reported that they supported a science-based approach to prevention or that the community adopted such an approach because it was supported by research. However, respondents' ratings of ease of understanding of the approach were not related to community levels of adoption. Interestingly, while community leaders' reports of the level of collaboration in the community were positively correlated with stage of adoption, these correlations were weak and non-significant. Importantly, the present data indicate that mandates from state funding agencies to use science-based prevention approaches are insufficient, by themselves, to increase adoption of science-based prevention actions in communities.

Limitations of this study should be noted. The communities included in the sample were not randomly sampled. Rather, they were purposely sampled to maximize variability in the degree of adoption of a science-based approach to prevention. Thus, the findings cannot be interpreted as representing the true distribution of community adoption of science-based prevention planning. If anything, it is likely that communities at higher levels of adoption of this approach are over-represented in this sample due to the intentional inclusion of such communities.

This study is a step in bridging the gap between prevention science and effective community level prevention. The study has shown that communities can be characterized according to their level of adoption of an approach to prevention grounded in prevention science and has identified factors related to higher levels of adoption of science-based

prevention. Results emphasize the need for quality training to disseminate research-based prevention approaches, and the importance of the
research foundation of the approach in influencing community leaders'
decisions to adopt it.

ACKNOWLEDGMENTS

Work on this chapter was supported by research grants 1 R01
DA10768-01A1 from the National Institute on Drug Abuse, a grant from
the US. Department of Education, and collaborative funding from the
Center for Substance Abuse Prevention, DHHS, and the Office of Juvenile Justice and Delinquency Prevention, DOJ.

REFERENCES

Arthur, M. W., & Blitz, C. (2000). Bridging the gap between science and practice in drug
    abuse prevention through needs assessment and strategic community planning. *Journal of Community Psychology, 28,* 241–255.
Arthur, M. W., Brewer, D., Graham, K. A., Shavel, D., Hawkins, J. D., & Hansen, C. (1996).
    Assessing state and community readiness for prevention. Rockville, MD: Center for
    Substance Abuse Prevention, National Center for the Advancement of Prevention.
Arthur, M. W., Ayers, C. D., Graham, K. A., & Hawkins, J. D. (2003). Mobilizing communities to reduce risks for drug abuse: A comparison of two strategies. In W. J. Bukoski &
    Z. Sloboda (Eds.), *Handbook of drug abuse prevention: Theory, science and practice*
    (pp. 129–144). New York: Kluwer Academic/Plenum Publishers.
Backer, T. E. (2000). The failure of success: Challenges of disseminating effective substance
    abuse prevention programs. *Journal of Community Psychology, 28,* 363–373.
Beckhard, R., & Harris, R. (1987). *Organizational transitions: Managing complex change.*
    Reading, MA: Addison-Wesley.
Biglan, A. (1995). Translating what we know about the context of antisocial behavior
    into a lower prevalence of such behavior. *Journal of Applied Behavior Analysis, 28,*
    479–492.
Butterfoss, F. D., Goodman, R. M., & Wandersman, A. (1993). Community coalitions for
    prevention and health promotion. *Health Education Research, 8,* 315–330.
Catalano, R. F., Arthur, M. W., Hawkins, J. D., Berglund, L., & Olson, J. J. (1998). Comprehensive community and school based interventions to prevent antisocial behavior.
    In R. Loeber & D. P. Farrington (Eds.), *Serious and violent juvenile offenders: Risk
    factors and successful interventions* (pp. 248–283). Thousand Oaks, CA: Sage.
Chavis, D., Florin, P., Rich, R., & Wandersman, A. (1987). *The role of block associations in
    crime control and community development: The Block Booster Project.* Final report
    to the Ford Foundation.
Coie, J. D., Watt, N. F., West, S. G., Hawkins, J. D., Asarnow, J. R., Markman, H. J., et al.
    (1993). The science of prevention. A conceptual framework and some directions for
    a national research program. *American Psychologist, 48,* 1013–1022.
Developmental Research and Programs. (1996). *Promising approaches to prevent adolescent problem behaviors.* Seattle, WA: Author.

Developmental Research and Programs. (2000). *Communities That Care: A comprehensive prevention program*. Seattle, WA: Author.

Drug Strategies. (1999). *Making the grade: A guide to school drug prevention curricula*. Washington DC: Author.

Durlak, J. A. (1998). Common risk and protective factors in successful prevention programs. *American Journal of Orthopsychiatry, 68*, 512–520.

Edwards, R. W., Jumper-Thurman, P., Plested, B. A., Oetting, E. R., & Swanson, L. (2000). Community readiness: Research to practice. *Journal of Community Psychology, 28*, 291–307.

Elliott, D. S. (Ed.). (1997). *Blueprints for violence prevention*. Denver, CO: C&M Press.

Ennett, S. T., Tobler, N. S., Ringwalt, C. L., & Flewelling, R. L. (1994). How effective is drug abuse resistance education? A meta-analysis of Project DARE outcome evaluations. *American Journal of Public Health, 84*, 1394–1401.

Fawcett, S. B., Paine, A. L., Francisco, V. T., & Vliet, M. (1993). Promoting health through community development. In D. S. Glenwick & L. A. Jason (Eds.), *Promoting health and mental health in children, youth and families* (pp. 233–255). Binghamton, NY: Springer.

Feinberg, M. E., Greenberg, M. T., Osgood, D. W., Anderson, A., & Babinski, L. (2002). The effects of training community leaders in prevention science: Communities That Care in Pennsylvania. *Evaluation & Program Planning, 25*, 245–259.

Fleiss, J. L. (1971). Measuring nominal scale agreement among many raters. *Psychological Bulletin, 76*, 378–382.

Florin, P., Mitchell, R., & Stevenson, J. (1993). Identifying training and technical assistance needs in community coalitions: A developmental approach. *Health Education Research, 8*, 417–432.

Greenberg, M. T., Osgood, D. W., Babinski, L., & Anderson, A. (1999, June). *Developing community readiness for prevention: Initial evaluation of the Pennsylvania Communities That Care Initiative*. Paper presented at the Society for Prevention Research, New Orleans, LA.

Hallfors, D., Sporer, A., Pankratz, M., & Godette, D. (2000). *Drug free schools survey: Report of results*. Chapel Hill, NC: School of Public Health, The University of North Carolina.

Hawkins, J. D. (1999). Preventing crime and violence through Communities That Care. *European Journal on Criminal Policy and Research, 7*, 443–458.

Hawkins, J. D., Arthur, M. W., & Catalano, R. F. (1995). Preventing substance abuse. In M. Tonry & D. Farrington (Eds.), *Crime and justice: Vol. 19. Building a safer society: Strategic approaches to crime prevention* (pp. 343–427). Chicago: University of Chicago Press.

Hawkins, J. D., & Catalano, R. F. (2002). *Investing in your community's youth: An introduction to the Communities That Care system*. South Deerfield, MA: Channing Bete Company.

Hawkins, J. D., Catalano, R. F., & Arthur, M. W. (2002). Promoting science-based prevention in communities. *Addictive Behaviors, 27*, 951–976.

Hawkins, J. D., Catalano, R. F., & Associates. (1992). *Communities That Care: Action for drug abuse prevention*. San Francisco: Jossey-Bass.

Hawkins, J. D., Catalano, R. F., & Miller, J. Y. (1992). Risk and protective factors for alcohol and other drug problems in adolescence and early adulthood: Implications for substance abuse prevention. *Psychological Bulletin, 112*, 64–105.

Hawkins, J. D., Herrenkohl, T., Farrington, D. P., Brewer, D., Catalano, R. F., & Harachi, T. W. (1998). A review of predictors of youth violence. In R. Loeber & D. P. Farrington (Eds.), *Serious and violent juvenile offenders: Risk factors and successful interventions* (pp. 106–146). Thousand Oaks, CA: Sage.

Kaftarian, S. J., & Wandersman, A. (2000). Bridging the gap between research and practice in community-based substance abuse prevention. *Journal of Community Psychology, 28*, 237–240.

Kansas Department of Social and Rehabilitation Services/Alcohol and Drug Abuse Services. (2001). *Connect Kansas regional planning report.* Topeka, KS: Author.

Kellam, S. G., Koretz, D., & Moscicki, E. K. (1999). Core elements of developmental epidemiologically based prevention research. *American Journal of Community Psychology, 27*, 463–482.

Kellam, S. G., & Rebok, G. W. (1992). Building developmental and etiological theory through epidemiologically based preventive intervention trials. In J. McCord & R. E. Tremblay (Eds.), *Preventing antisocial behavior: Interventions from birth through adolescence* (pp. 162–195). New York: Guilford Press.

Kish, L. (1965). *Survey sampling.* New York: Wiley.

Kumpfer, K. C., Turner, C., Hopkins, R., & Librett, J. (1993). Leadership and team effectiveness in community coalitions for the prevention of alcohol and other drug abuse. *Health Education and Research, 8*, 359–374.

Lewin, K. (1951). *Field theory in social science.* New York: Harper and Row.

Mitchell, R. E., Stevenson, J. F., & Florin, P. (1996). A typology of prevention activities: Applications to community coalitions. *Journal of Primary Prevention, 16*, 413–436.

Morrissey, J. P., Tausig, M., & Lindsey, M. L. (1985). Community mental health delivery systems: A network perspective. *American Behavioral Scientist, 28*, 704–720.

National Institute on Drug Abuse. (1997). *Community readiness for drug abuse prevention: Issues, tips and tools.* Rockville, MD: U.S. Dept. of Health & Human Services, National Institutes of Health.

Oetting, E. R., Donnermayer, J. F., Plested, B. A., Edwards, R. W., Kelly, K., & Beauvais, F. (1995). Assessing community readiness for prevention. *The International Journal of the Addictions, 30*, 659–683.

Office of National Drug Control Policy. (2000). *National Drug Control Strategy: 2000 annual report.* Washington, DC: U.S. Government Printing Office.

Raudenbush, S. W., Bryk, A. S., Cheong, Y. F., & Congdon, R. T. (2000). *HLM 5: Hierarchical linear and nonlinear modeling* (Version 5). Lincolnwood, IL: Scientific Software International.

Rogers, E. (1995). *Diffusion of innovation* (4th ed.). New York: The Free Press.

Rutter, M. (1990). Psychosocial resilience and protective mechanisms. In J. E. Rolf, A. S. Masten, D. Cicchette, K. Neuchterlein, & S. Weintraub (Eds.), *Risk and protective factors in the development of psychopathology* (pp. 181–214). New York: Cambridge University Press.

Sampson, R. J., Raudenbush, S. W., & Earls, F. (1997). Neighborhoods and violent crime: A multilevel study of collective efficacy. *Science, 277*, 918–924.

Scrutchins, Z., & David, S. L. (1996, May). *Celebrating difference, overcoming challenges, fighting youth tobacco wars in hard to reach communities.* Paper presented at the Communities for Tobacco Free Kids: Drawing the Line conference, Chicago, IL.

Sloboda, Z., & David, S. L. (1997). *Preventing drug use among children and adolescents: A research-based guide.* Rockville, MD: National Institute on Drug Abuse.

Substance Abuse and Mental Health Services Administration. (1998). *Science-based practices in substance abuse prevention: A guide (working draft).* Rockville, MD: Department of Health and Human Services.

Washington State Department of Social and Health Services. (2000). *Washington State Incentive Grant. A guide to the community substance abuse prevention projects.* Olympia WA: Author.

Werner, E. E., & Smith, R. S. (1992). *Overcoming the odds: High risk children from birth to adulthood.* Ithaca, NY: Cornell University Press.

Western Regional Center for the Application of Prevention Technologies. (1999). *Best practices and promising practices. Guide to building a successful prevention program.* University of Nevada, Reno: Author.

Wickizer, T. M., Von Korff, M., Cheadle, A., Maeser, J., Wagner, E. H., Pearson, D., et al. (1993). Activating communities for health promotion: A process evaluation method. *American Journal of Public Health, 83,* 561–567.

Index

Made in the USA
Middletown, DE
08 August 2017